Constantine and the Divine Mind

CONSTANTINE
—— AND THE ——
DIVINE MIND

The Imperial Quest for Primitive Monotheism

Kegan A. Chandler

FOREWORD BY
Dale Tuggy

WIPF & STOCK · Eugene, Oregon

CONSTANTINE AND THE DIVINE MIND
The Imperial Quest for Primitive Monotheism

Copyright © 2019 Kegan A. Chandler. All rights reserved. Except for brief quotations in critical publications or reviews, no part of this book may be reproduced in any manner without prior written permission from the publisher. Write: Permissions, Wipf and Stock Publishers, 199 W. 8th Ave., Suite 3, Eugene, OR 97401.

Wipf & Stock
An Imprint of Wipf and Stock Publishers
199 W. 8th Ave., Suite 3
Eugene, OR 97401

www.wipfandstock.com

PAPERBACK ISBN: 978-1-5326-8992-5
HARDCOVER ISBN: 978-1-5326-8993-2
EBOOK ISBN: 978-1-5326-8994-9

Unless otherwise noted, Scripture quotations taken from the New American Standard Bible® (NASB), Copyright © 1960, 1962, 1963, 1968, 1971, 1972, 1973, 1975, 1977, 1995 by The Lockman Foundation. Used by permission. www.Lockman.org

Manufactured in the U.S.A.   12/02/19

This book is dedicated to my wife,
without whom I would be lost in life.

*Among all nations, through the darkest polytheism
glimmer some faint sparks of monotheism.*

—Immanuel Kant, 1781

Contents

Foreword by Dale Tuggy | ix
Preface | xi

Introduction: Constantine Scholarship and the Quest for Monotheism | 1
    Conflicting Portraits of Constantine · 2
    Our Premise · 6
    Models of Religious Conversion · 7

1 The Challenge of Monotheism | 12
    Biblical Monotheism · 14
    Pagan Monotheism · 15
    Distinctions in Pagan Monotheism · 17
    Monotheism and Pluralism · 19

2 Solar Monotheism in the Late Roman Empire | 22
    The Rise of Roman Solar Monotheism · 23
    Imperial Monotheism · 24
    Aurelian's God · 30

3 An Empire in Turmoil | 35
    Diocletian's Reforms · 36
    The God of Constantius Chlorus · 38
    Constantine in Diocletian's Court · 39
    Constantine and Lactantius · 43

4 A History of Religion: The Decline of Monotheism | 46
    Euhemerism · 48
    The Narrative in Lactantius · 49

CONTENTS

5 Constantine as Divine Agent | 58
   The Narrative in Constantine · 58
   Coins and Monuments · 61

6 The Divine Mind and Pagan Monotheism | 64
   The Language of Mind and Monotheism · 64
   The Divine Mind in Constantine's Early Propaganda · 72

7 Constantine's Dream | 83
   Practical Concerns · 84
   Christians as a New Race · 88
   The Dream Is Threatened · 92

8 Nicaea and *Homoousios* | 99
   The Word *Homoousios* before Nicaea · 100
   Homoousios: Not a Matter of Debate · 104
   The Bishops and *Homoousios* · 106
   Constantine and *Homoousios* · 107
   The Divine Mind and the Valley of the Kings · 109
   Constantine's Christology at Nicaea · 111
   Aftermath · 119

9 Constantine's Program | 123
   A Policy of Intolerance or Concord? · 124
   Prohibition of Pagan Ritual? · 125
   Evidence of Persecution? · 129

10 Constantine the Christian | 137
    The Contemporary Paradigm in the Fourth Century · 138
    Transition · 140
    Baptism · 147
    Two Conversions · 150

11 Death of a Dream | 154
    The Emperor's Tomb · 154
    Pagan Monotheism after Constantine · 159
    A Final Plea for Pluralism · 163
    Conclusion · 166

Selected Bibliography | 169
Index | 181

Foreword

THE MOTIVATIONS UNDERLYING THE emperor Constantine's religious actions have long been in dispute. The famous church historian Eusebius praised Constantine as "outstanding in every virtue godliness confers,"[1] a great Christian emperor who, in imitation of the divine Word, "having purged his earthly dominion from every stain of impious error, invites each holy and pious worshiper within his imperial mansions, earnestly desiring to save with all its crew that mighty vessel of which he is the appointed pilot."[2] Not many historians have been so generous in their estimation of Constantine, though many have imitated Eusebius's extremity and one-sidedness. Following cues from some modern historians, popular literature and recent conspiracy theories paint Constantine as a cynical, power-mad tyrant, eager to exploit religion and religious disputes to enhance his own power. But many thoughtful inquirers have likewise puzzled over his post-conversion interest in the sun god, and some have questioned whether he truly converted to Christianity at all. Still others have determined to counteract modern cynicism about the emperor's motives, restoring his reputation as a faithful defender and promoter of catholic orthodoxy. Was Constantine a politically mighty imitator of Jesus? A Stalin in saint's clothing? Or is the mark he left on history doomed to be a Rorschach blotch, the interpretation of which only reveals something about the interpreter?

In this important and illuminating new study, Kegan Chandler aims to paint a clearer picture of Constantine's religion by engaging the mystery of his conversion in light of trends in late Roman paganism. He treats Constantine as an educated man of his time who adopted a sophisticated

---

1. Eusebius, *The Church History*, 10.9, tr. Paul Maier (Grand Rapids: Kregal Publications, 1999), 370.

2. Eusebius, *Oration in Praise of Constantine*, 2, tr. Arthur C. McGiffert in *Nicene and Post Nicene Fathers*, Vol. 1 (Oxford: Parker and Company, 1890), 583.

outlook on religious diversity and understood Christianity in light of this general framework. Chandler builds on some recent studies which take seriously Constantine's pagan background and the views of his adviser (and possible teacher) the apologist Lactantius. This emperor had what we can loosely call a Messiah complex, but this was grounded in a coherent worldview. This distinctive religious outlook, so different from the ones at work in our day, explains Constantine's initially puzzling mix of pro-Christian and pro-pagan actions. It explains how this emperor could both involve himself in the formulation of orthodox Christian theology and also depict himself on coins and statuary in the garb of the sun god. Chandler employs recent scholarly advances on pagan monotheism, late Roman religion, Roman archeology, the Hermetic writings, religious conversion, the history of Christian theology, and alternate conceptions of godhood and of religious pluralism to shine an invincible sun onto the complexities of religious thought in Constantine's pagan-Christian context.

The light of this multifaceted evidence reflects from the stage to illuminate the actor. We get a nuanced and sympathetic account of a genuinely religious Constantine pursuing what Chandler calls his "dream." It's a page-turning story of considerable human, historical, theological, and philosophical interest, and it should supersede the many simpler, fictitious, and ideologically-driven versions of what Constantine was up to.

Dale Tuggy
White House, Tennessee
2019

Preface

As I write these words I am visiting the Eternal City in the wake of her first snowfall in six years. Her white-capped monuments have now thawed; her snowy streets have warmed in the swell of early spring—only the cold air remains. This morning it occurred to me that the glory of Rome has also melted away, and long ago, leaving only memories. And yet her genius, now a departed spirit, has by no means lost its power to intrigue and inspire. These memories and monuments still have much to tell us, it turns out, not only about the history of Western civilization, but about our modern religious world.

The Arch of Constantine, still standing proudly in Colosseum valley and covered in its famous patchwork of pagan imagery, perhaps marks a turning point in Western religious history more poignantly than any other. It commemorates Constantine's victory over his rival Maxentius—a victory without which the Christian religion might never have ascended in the West. Indeed, Constantine is remembered as Rome's first Christian emperor, and as the man whose reign permanently legalized the faith. The inscription on Constantine's arch tells us that he had been a man *divinely inspired*—but by which god? The Christian God? On the arch's eastern frieze we see the pagan sun deity Sol Invictus driving his solar chariot across the universe. But this monument was completed several years after Constantine reportedly converted to Christianity. What are we to make of all this?

Constantine's turn to the Christian faith—why it took place and whether it took place at all—has regularly challenged historians. Indeed, the importance of this topic is only surpassed by its difficulty. I nevertheless believe that a clearer picture can be drawn of Constantine's conversion, and his mysterious reasons for it, than what has heretofore been achieved. While most books on Constantine have been more biographical or have emphasized his military career, political rivalries, or familial relationships, this study is dedicated to making sense of Constantine as a theologian, and to exploring the theological motivations behind both his conversion and his reign. Many have gone before me, of course, and I admit to only standing on giants' shoulders and looking behind us at the patterns forming in the trail. And while I trust that I have several things to add to the ongoing discussion about Constantine's religion, my sincere hope is that my modest contribution be only a useful spark stimulating further illumination.

I would be remiss not to mention the range of debts I've incurred while producing this book. Special thanks are owed to Dr. Joseph Early for his support of the project; to Dr. John Hurtgen of Campbellsville University for his grace and encouragement during my studies; to Dr. Pier Franco Beatrice of the University of Padua for his inspiring scholarship and the helpful article he sent my way; to Dr. Elizabeth Digeser of the University of California for her invaluable work on Lactantius, to Sir Anthony Buzzard, Seth Ross, Atlanta Bible College, and Jeff Grant for their generous sponsorship of my research; to Dr. Dale Tuggy for his many helpful recommendations and his important article on monotheism; to Menashe Israel, Brandon Duke, and Andrew Davis for their diligent reviews of the manuscript; and above all, to my wife Lauren, to whom this book is dedicated, for her good spirit, strength, and eternal support. My love is with you all.

Kegan A. Chandler
Rome, Italy
2019

Introduction

Constantine Scholarship and the Quest for Monotheism

ON AN ANXIOUS OCTOBER evening in 312 CE, just before a battle against his brother-in-law that would decide the course of Western civilization, the emperor Constantine "considered which god he could rely upon for protection and help." After reflecting on the sad fate of all the polytheistic emperors before him, however, and following a dramatic celestial vision, he changed course and became a Christian monotheist. So says Eusebius in his *Life of Constantine*.[1] But how accurate is this portrait?

Constantine's storied conversion to the Christian religion—precisely when it took place, why it took place, and whether it took place at all—has been regularly debated by scholars since at least the middle of the nineteenth century. The emperor's evident shift towards the advancement of Christianity after 312 CE, and his subsequent efforts to resolve the Donatist and Arian controversies, have been conversely interpreted as either purely "political" actions, or, concurring with Eusebius, as the theologically-driven efforts of a sincere and orthodox Christian.[2] Still other historians have located in Constantine both a politically and religiously agile magistrate working to bridge the gap between paganism and Christianity in his empire.[3] But what is the modern student to make of this disconcerting range of interpretation? And what hope can we have that yet another book on Constantine might help to clear the air after a century-and-a-half of animated debate?

---

1. Eusebius, *Vit. Const.* 27.

2. For the former opinion see the famous study of Burckhardt, *Age of Constantine the Great*; for the latter, see Leithart, *Defending Constantine*.

3. See Drake, *Constantine and the Bishops*.

I am by no means ignorant of the difficulties at hand, and am especially conscious of the challenge posed by both the scarcity of the historical sources and their politically-charged nature. Nevertheless, this book represents a new attempt at better identifying the religion of Constantine, and it does so by focusing on the process by which Constantine embraced Christianity, and how the original reasons for that embrace continued to manifest in his religious policies. In the coming chapters I will argue that a clearer picture of Constantine's conversion and its sociopolitical consequences can be acquired by concentrating on the overarching theological meta-narrative which I believe forms the essential backdrop of the Constantinian drama—a meta-narrative about monotheism. As I hope to demonstrate, it is precisely this narratival framework which fills Constantine's actions with their elusive meaning and links them together in a more coherent interpretive schema than I believe has heretofore been achieved. But the place of this book and its contribution to the ongoing dialogue about one of Christianity's most famous (and arguably most important) converts must be considered in light of those diverse studies which have undeniably paved its way.

Conflicting Portraits of Constantine

The challenging lines of evidence marking out Constantine's religious policies have allowed at least three general portraits of the man to emerge. Before we can begin exploring the history of monotheism as a hermeneutical tool, these three perspectives must be briefly sketched.

The first portrait has framed Constantine as a man whose turn to Christianity was motivated solely by an interest in political power. This view was most famously advanced by Swiss historian Jacob Burckhardt, whose biography (1853, revised in 1880) presented a scheming Constantine manipulating the Christian masses for political gain. According to Burckhardt, attempts to penetrate the emperor's religious consciousness and to chart any changes in his theological convictions are "futile," since Constantine was "an essentially unreligious person, one entirely consumed by his ambition and lust for power" and "in matters of religion not only inconsistent but 'intentionally illogical.'"[4]

It is now clear to many historians that Burckhardt's analysis ultimately rested on an artificial dichotomy between politics and religion, a

---

4. See Burckhardt quoted in Pohlsander, *Emperor Constantine*, 2.

paradigm inspired largely by post-Enlightenment distinctions between public policy and personal ethics.⁵ Indeed, we should no longer speak of Constantine's conversion as an irreligious and purely political affair. After all, a hallmark of modern Western government has been the (essential) separation of church and state, but in the Rome of late antiquity that division did not so clearly exist. Proper piety was thought to be the guarantor of civil prosperity. As we will see, assuming Constantine was irreligious will prove insufficient for reconciling the available data.

The second portrait has painted Constantine as "the first Christian emperor," boldly driving the Christianization of his empire, and as a crusader taking an openly belligerent stance against paganism. This vision of Constantine aligns closely with the Eusebian picture of the emperor as both a genuine convert and an anti-pagan.⁶ This portrait remains the official story for many Christians, like those in the Eastern Orthodox churches, who every year celebrate the feast of "Saint Constantine."⁷ Critics of this image have often gestured at the emperor's ostensibly less-than-Christian behavior, such as his continued use of pagan imagery, and his regular slaughter of his own family members, including several brothers-in-law, his father-in-law, his nephew, his own wife Fausta, and favorite son Crispus.⁸ Paul Keresztes's 1981 study is emblematic of attempts to reconcile the Eusebian portrait with these more unsightly elements of Constantine's legacy, concluding that while "Constantine was not a perfect Christian in his life," and "was not always well informed in matters of doctrine," he was nevertheless

---

5. As has been observed, a spirit of *privatization* took hold of post-Enlightenment religion in Western culture—in essence a propensity to keep religion, progressively cast as a system of individual ethics, out of the sphere of public affairs. The reasons for this have been sharply debated. See the influential study of Wilson, *Religion in Secular Society*; see also the work of Martin, *On Secularization*.

6. See Eusebius's panegyrical *Life of Constantine* (339 CE).

7. Saint Constantine's feast day is May 21, which he shares with his mother Saint Helena. In Orthodox liturgy, he continues to be remembered as ἰσαπόστολος (equal to the apostles), which, as Thompson points out, effectively ranks him above many other fathers and doctors of the church; see Thompson, "From Sinner to Saint," 20.

8. Constantine's continued use of pagan imagery will occupy a large space in this study. While the killings of his in-laws (the emperors Maxentius, Maximian, and Licinius) occurred in the context of political rivalry and civil war, the circumstances surrounding the deaths of Fausta and Crispus remain murky. For a brief introduction to the subject, and the effect which these killings may have had on Constantine's decision to send his mother Helena on her famous pilgrimage to Jerusalem, see Carroll, *Constantine's Sword*, 202–3. As has been said, "Even if all of these executions were justifiable, as some of them certainly were, it is an appalling list" (Coleman, *Constantine the Great*, 92).

"a sincere Christian, a truly great Christian Emperor and a genuine Apostle of the Christian Church."[9] With such passionate defenses of Constantine's orthodoxy, Keresztes and others may have only revealed what critics have called "a passionate need to defend Catholicism."[10] But not all defenses of the Eusebian portrait have rung with such partisanship. Prominent classicist Timothy Barnes, for example, has agreed that Constantine was not only a genuine convert, but a fierce anti-pagan.[11] Since the early 1980s, Barnes has vigorously argued that Constantine took an aggressively anti-pagan stance and even outlawed traditional cults. While most modern scholars have believed that Constantine ultimately made no major changes in the traditional form of worship in the empire,[12] in 2011 Barnes summoned new evidence from the pagan epigrammatist Palladas, first discovered by historian Kevin Wilkinson, to support his view.[13]

Barnes's conclusion that Constantine became an anti-pagan who outlawed paganism during his reign will need to be qualified. As we will see, Constantine indeed shifted in his attitude towards traditional worship during his career, but this does not necessarily mean that he had closed himself off from the pagan world, or that his was a pure and untouched Christianity. It does not even demonstrate that Constantine had truly "converted" to Christianity as early and as neatly as Barnes and others believe it does. From a methodological standpoint, Barnes has argued that the early Constantinian propaganda ("coins, inscriptions, and monuments") should take second place to the testimony of Eusebius and Lactantius about Constantine's conversion.[14] But can we afford such a lopsided approach? It seems clear that we should strive to give equal weight to both streams of evidence, one pagan and the other Christian, and to embrace their respective power to flesh out a more accurate image of Constantine.

---

9. Keresztes, *Constantine*, 8. Other more recent studies, such as that of Leithart, have similarly sought to rehabilitate the emperor's image, hoping to repeal the negative legacy attributed to him by scholars like Anabaptist theologian John Howard Yoder; see Leithart, *Defending Constantine*.

10. See Kee's assessment of Keresztes's 1981 study: Kee, *Constantine Versus Christ*, 12.

11. Barnes, *Constantine and Eusebius*; Barnes, *Constantine*.

12. Barnes, *Constantine*, 6, 10–11.

13. Barnes, *Constantine*, x–xi. See Wilkinson, "Palladas and the Age of Constantine," 36–60.

14. Barnes, *Constantine*, 16–17. Barnes suggests, and with good reason, that Constantine's propaganda is full of lies about himself. See Barnes, *Constantine*, 2–6, 54. But is the Eusebian propaganda to which Barnes gives priority free of lies about Constantine?

It may be, however, that such an approach will only reveal an image of a man very much standing between two worlds.

Following this approach, the third portrait of the emperor offered by historians has been that of a both religiously and politically astute leader who earnestly sought to bridge the chasm between Roman pagans and Christians. Harold Drake and Elizabeth Digeser are representative of unique perspectives within this general approach.[15] What Digeser's study achieved was a proper consideration of Constantine's pagan background, namely his association with pagan monotheism and Hermeticism. She revealed not only the influence of Constantine's advisor Lactantius on the emperor's religious policies, but also Lactantius's exposure of Constantine to Hermeticism.[16] Pier Franco Beatrice, in a powerful and revolutionary study, considered Constantine's reported authorship of the word *homoousios* at Nicaea in the context of this Hermetic background.[17] What Digeser and Beatrice accomplished was a new window to the pagan aspects of Constantine's theology, and a vision of an emperor who believed that Christianity could be expressed through the conceptual and terminological forms of paganism and Gnosticism.

Interestingly, though Beatrice and Digeser's conclusions in regard to Constantine's Hermetic background have been well-regarded, the virtual silence on the topic of Hermeticism in recent Constantine monographs is deafening.[18] Not only did Barnes ignore this evidence, none of the following

---

15. Drake, *Constantine and the Bishops*; Digeser, *Making of a Christian Empire*. Digeser's work has emphasized Constantine's pagan background and his relationship with his advisor Lactantius, while Drake's monograph focused largely on Constantine's nuanced relationship with the world of Christian bishops.

16. Digeser has released a host of important studies working in this same direction: Digeser, "Lactantius and Constantine's Letter," and most recently "Platonism in the Palace," 49–62.

17. Beatrice, "Word 'Homoousios,'" 243–72.

18. For agreement with Beatrice's conclusion that Constantine's gnostic-Hermetic background likely played a role in the establishment of the *homoousian* of Nicaea, see Mitchell, *Church, Gospel, and Empire*, 51–52. See also the agreement with Grillmeier, *From the Apostolic Age*, 109. See also Digeser, "Platonism in the Palace," 53. Attempting to challenge Beatrice, M. Edwards argued, and with far less force, that Alexander sanctioned and even championed the use of *homoousios* before Nicaea, and that Alexander was among Constantine's anti-Arian Christian mentors and introduced it upon their advice. See Edwards, "Alexander of Alexandria," 482–502. Digeser, however, has rightly pointed out that we should not follow Edwards in favoring Ambrose's testimony, who was not there and whose account arrives over half a century after the events. Digeser has drawn attention to the fact that even Athanasius, no friend of Eusebius, ostensibly

monographs have adequately investigated Constantine's relationship with the Hermetic corpus: Odahl, Pohlsander, Veyne, Stephenson, Van Dam, Harries, and Lenski.[19] The following investigations pursued briefly the pagan background of the "Divine Mind" language in Constantine's propaganda, which occupies space in the present study, but they did not consider its Hermetic background: Drake, Bardill, and Potter.[20] The new door opened towards Constantine's pagan background by Beatrice and Digeser has been a threshold too few have been willing to cross. Nevertheless, if we hope to recover the nature of Constantine's conversion, it is precisely within the emperor's pagan soil that we must dig.

Our Premise

As the range of perspectives in Constantine scholarship has been extraordinary, it will be helpful to know upfront where this book falls on the spectrum. I confess that in the present study the portrait of Constantine espoused by Burckhardt—that of an essentially unreligious person—will be treated as inadequate.[21] The second portrait, that of a sincere Christian and anti-pagan, most forcefully promoted by Barnes, will be challenged on several points. The third portrait—essentially that of a religious syncretist—will be explored, clarified, and ultimately enhanced. Indeed, it is this latter portrait which I believe provides the best substrate on which to build, though further enrichment is needed, and, I think, possible through a reconsideration of the reasons for Constantine's conversion.

This short book admittedly circumvents the ever-popular question about whether or not Constantine's involvement with the church was ultimately detrimental to the Christian faith. Peter Leithart's *Defending Constantine* attempted to challenge the long-held assumption that Constantine's conversion (or more precisely his marriage of church and state) marked a "Constantinian

---

accepts the Eusebian testimony (Digeser, "Platonism in the Palace," 51). More on Constantine and the use of *homoousios* of Nicaea will be said in the forthcoming chapters.

19. Odahl, *Constantine and the Christian Empire*, 123; Pohlsander, *Emperor Constantine*; Veyne, *When Our World Became Christian*; Stephenson, *Constantine*; Van Dam, *Remember Constantine at the Milvian Bridge*; Harries, *Imperial Rome AD 284 to 363*; Lenski, *Constantine and the Cities*.

20. Drake, *Constantine and the Bishops*; Bardill, *Constantine*; Potter, *Constantine the Emperor*.

21. See Barnes, *Constantine*, 10–11; see also Edwards, "Pagan and Christian Monotheism," 224, no. 20; see also Drake, *Constantine and the Bishops*, 11–14.

shift" in a negative direction.[22] Leithart's proposal has received a barrage of full-force rebuttals in recent years, and it is not my aim to recapitulate these arguments. Because this is a book about Constantine's conversion, and one concerned with history and not necessarily with the theological import of that history, it will deliberately withhold comment on whether Constantine's conversion was ultimately good or bad for Christianity. Doubtless the present study lends ammunition to that important debate, though to which side I leave to the conclusions of the reader.

How does this book hope to achieve its aim to recover the nature of Constantine's conversion? While much light has already been shed in recent decades by the diligent studies of several nimble historians (candles by which I admittedly and gratefully read), I believe yet further clarity can be achieved through a reconsideration of the Constantinian sources (coins, monuments, speeches, and biographies) in light of pagan and Christian historiography, Constantine's self-image in the context of that history, Constantine's relationship with his advisor Lactantius, the Hermetic writings, and trends in "pagan" monotheism. The picture of Constantine which will ultimately emerge is one of a deeply religious man, and a man who eventually found himself on a grand quest to revive a primordial monotheism in the Roman empire. In the coming chapters I will argue that Constantine believed this ancient monotheism was once the original religion of all mankind, and that to him it was still a potential source of civil stability and prosperity for the empire. I will furthermore argue that Constantine understood himself to be the chief agent of the Supreme God, divinely elected to retrieve true religion and thus God's favor on the human race. Constantine was inspired to this grand narrative, as we will see, by both Christian and pagan teaching, and it is this overarching story which provides the necessary context for the emperor's challenging religious policies.

Models of Religious Conversion

The central question of this book is a simple one: *Why did Constantine embrace Christianity?* In 2011, Timothy Barnes claimed that the psychological process which led to Constantine's conversion is now both undiscoverable and unimportant, and perhaps was even unclear to Constantine himself.[23] Yet I suggest that the reasons for Constantine's turn to the Christian religion

---

22. Leithart, *Defending Constantine*.
23. Barnes, *Constantine*, 80.

are not only recoverable, but vital for properly framing his wider career and Christianity's incredible change in status during his reign.

But where do we begin in a reassessment of Constantine's conversion? We must first ask what religious conversion is. The great A. D. Nock, in his influential study of religious conversion in late antiquity, once defined conversion as "the reorientation of the soul of an individual, his deliberate turning from indifference or from an earlier form of piety to another, a turning which implies a consciousness that the old was wrong and the new is right."[24] In this light, it is not enough to simply add new beliefs onto one's own without giving anything up; the mark of conversion appears to be the real exchange of one set of principles for another. But "conversion" seems to invoke much more than a simple intellectual transaction. At least in the context of Christianity, we often conjure notions of sin and guilt; conversion is something which happens on the heels of some moral or emotional turbulence.

In the history of Constantine scholarship, I suggest that one of the reasons why Constantine's conversion has been so difficult to chart is due to certain assumptions we have had about what religious conversion looks like. Generations of reflection on the experiences of other famous Christian converts, like the Apostle Paul (d. ca. 64 CE) and Augustine of Hippo (d. 430 CE), have perhaps unduly shaped our expectations. Indeed, Paul's visionary encounter with Jesus on the road to Damascus has remained a steady waypoint for religious conversion in Western consciousness.[25] To this day, a "road to Damascus moment" idiomatically refers to any point of sudden reversal in someone's life when a serious change of beliefs takes place. The relationship between the Eusebian report of Constantine's conversion in 312 and Paul's experience is obvious: both not only feature sudden revelations and visions of Jesus, but both stories condense their subject's conversions to a single time and place. For many Christians, Eusebius's story about the emperor reflects precisely the kind of Christian conversion experience which Paul's story in the New Testament has conditioned them to look for. On the other hand, Augustine's emotionally traumatic turn to Christianity in 386 CE, recounted in his *Confessions*, seems to have encouraged the additional notions of sin and guilt which we have come to expect. Some Constantine scholars have been so convinced

---

24. Nock, *Conversion*, 7. See also the influential study of James, *Varieties of Religious Experience*.

25. Acts 9:1–22.

that emotional trauma plays a vital role in genuine conversion, that on the basis of the fact that Constantine's experience looks more like a rational calculation than an "emotional crisis," they conclude that he cannot possibly have ever become a Christian.[26] Alistair Kee, for example, contrasted the experience of Augustine with the emperor: the former had struggled with questions of morality, was convicted of sin, and had "great tumult" in his "inner dwelling place."[27] The day Augustine was baptized was the day this religious and emotional crisis was resolved, and, according to Kee, this resolution is called conversion. There is no indication, he says, "that Constantine underwent an experience even remotely resembling that of Augustine."[28] But do the examples of Paul and Augustine, as archetypes for religious conversion, satisfy the range of possible experiences?

Kee's expectations, founded precisely on these archetypes, represent an outdated and unhelpful approach. The above model, which searches for a singular and sudden experience, a 180-degree change in thinking or behavior, and perhaps some moral or emotional trauma, fits comfortably into what modern psychologists have identified as the "older paradigm" in the psychology of religious conversion. In this psychological framework, conversion has often been cast as both "a sudden 180-degree turn in religious outlook" and as an emotionally-driven process reflective of a "stern theology of sin and guilt."[29] Reading the evidence through this older paradigm, many scholars have been prepared to identify a single turning point in Constantine's faith, a moment of conversion, and most have settled on the emperor's famous vision of the cross (or perhaps of some other Christian symbol), which Eusebius reports Constantine saw in the sky before his famous battle. It is thus not surprising that many studies of Constantine have had difficulty dealing satisfactorily with the emperor's continued use of pagan symbolism long after his purported "conversion" in 312.[30]

Other models for interpreting Constantine's experience are available to us. In our contemporary paradigm of religious conversion, conversion is regularly understood to be an intellectual and gradual process.[31] Indeed,

---

26. See Kee, *Constantine Versus Christ*, 16–17.

27. Augustine, *Confessions* 7.8.

28. Kee, *Constantine Versus Christ*, 13.

29. Keri and Sleiman, "Religious Conversion to Christianity," 3; Drake, *Constantine and the Bishops*, 187.

30. See Drake, *Constantine and the Bishops*, 188.

31. See M. P. Strickland's influential work contrasting the classic paradigm of sudden

since the 1960s, social psychologists have focused more on "gradual conversions" in which the subject is treated not as passive and emotionally-driven, but as an intentional and evaluating being.[32] In this paradigm the emphasis is on the subject's conscious striving towards a goal, and conversion ultimately comes about by way of active searching and study.[33] This process may involve a series of religious awakenings throughout the subject's life, resulting in major changes in personal beliefs. One of the primary characteristics of this conversion paradigm, according to modern specialists, is the subject's "search for meaning in the aspect of '*quest*.'"[34]

Following this psychological model, I will argue that Constantine's conversion to Christianity was not the result of a sudden, impactful experience (like a heavenly vision), but was in fact the result of an intellectual and gradual process, and one achieved by Constantine's own conscious religious searching. Defining "conversion" as a sudden and emotionally-driven 180-degree turn from former beliefs will ultimately prove inadequate for describing Constantine's experience. It is likewise misguided to assume that because Constantine's turn to the Christian god appears to lack a preceding "emotional crisis" akin to Augustine's, that his conversion was not genuine. It will be more appropriate, in light of the forthcoming evidence, to identify Constantine's religious journey as precisely that: a *journey*, and one with several important stops along the way which we will need to carefully trace in order to map out precisely where Constantine has come from and where he has ultimately gone.

While Barnes argued that what was really important was the simple fact that Constantine had become a Christian, Digeser rightly clarified that "the problem is not whether Constantine became a Christian, but it is to understand what kind of Christian he became. The Hermetic frame in which Constantine articulated his Christianity presents a very different portrait of the emperor than that which Eusebius paints in his *Life of Constantine*."[35] The emperor clearly approached Christianity from the vantage point of the pagan world, and his expedition out of that world will prove to have been much more gradual and intellectually motivated than

---

conversion to model of gradual conversion, *Psychology of Religious Experience*.

32. Stout and Dein, "Religious Conversion and Self Transformation," 30.
33. Hood et al., *Psychology of Religion*, 215.
34. Stout and Dein, "Religious Conversion and Self Transformation," 30.
35. Digeser, "Platonism in the Palace," 55.

many previous studies have allowed. It may even be that he never fully transitioned out of that world at all.

But merely identifying Constantine's conversion as a gradual process does not solve the problem of how that process began. If the starting point is not to be found in a sudden visionary experience in 312, but in an intellectual searching, we must uncover the impetus and the nature of that quest. In pursuing Constantine's quest we will ultimately discover at least the outline of the psychological process behind his conversion which Barnes claimed was undiscoverable, unimportant, and even unknown to Constantine himself. What we find will illuminate not only the personal religious journey of the most famous and controversial emperor of the fourth century, but also the rise of orthodox Christianity, which inarguably owes Constantine for its matchless place in the tapestry of Western civilization.

1

The Challenge of Monotheism

CONSTANTINE IS TRADITIONALLY SAID to have made his dramatic turn towards the Christian deity in 312 CE. As Harold Drake concluded in his grand 2000 study, however, prior to the year 312, the pagan Constantine already "seems to have been a monotheist."[1] But what is *pagan* monotheism? How were Christian expressions of monotheism in late antiquity similar or different?

There is no question that most of the present confusion about monotheism rests on a terminological muddle: what, exactly, do we mean when we describe a religion as "monotheistic?"[2] Many students of history and religion often assume a modern definition of monotheism in which only one deity exists. But this is an unhelpful guide. As John McKenzie once noted, even in the ancient monotheism described in the Hebrew Bible, "the question was not whether there is only one *elohim*, but whether there is any *elohim* like Yahweh."[3] Likewise Michael Heiser has demonstrated that the ancient Israelite monotheism, and the succeeding Judaism in the Roman era under investigation, allowed for a *plurality of deities* beneath the one God.[4] But were these *real* deities? Our final definition of monotheism seems to depend a great deal on what we mean when we describe an entity as a "god," a "deity," or a "divine being." In this light, it is easy to see how the remarkable nuance required in this conversation, and the charged nature of the subject, continue to invite misunderstanding.

Heiser was mostly right when he concluded that our modern terminology (monotheism, monolatry, henotheism, polytheism), thanks to changing

---

1. Drake, *Constantine and the Bishops*, 189.
2. For a review of these issues, see Heiser, "Monotheism," 1–30.
3. McKenzie, "Aspects of Old Testament Thought," 1287.
4. Heiser, "Monotheism," 1–30.

definitions, has proven inadequate, and that we should instead simply describe what certain ancient peoples believed about God.[5] A noble task, to be sure, but often an impractical one. Both the wider public and the scholarly world are not yet ready to give up on the word "monotheism."

In order to salvage the term "monotheism," however, we may need to sacrifice another word: *polytheism*. Dale Tuggy, in his important article, suggests a replacement of the long-standing (and "confused and confusing") trichotomy *monotheism-polytheism-atheism*, with a new trichotomy of *monotheism*-polydeism-*atheism*.[6] Tuggy ultimately argues that since the word "god" is ambiguous, we must differentiate between a *god*, a *deity*, and an *ultimate reality*. For example, the personal Yahweh figure of the Bible would qualify as a *god*; the biblical angels and demons, being supernatural personalities subordinate to Yahweh, would qualify as *deities*; and the highest principle of Platonic philosophy, being impersonal and thus neither a god nor a deity, would be an *ultimate reality*. "While *godhood* implies *deity*," says Tuggy, "*deity* doesn't imply *godhood*, though . . . *deity* is compatible with *godhood*."[7] In other words, all gods are deities but not all deities are gods.[8] The difference between a *god* and a mere deity is that a god is an ultimate being, a source of all things, an uncreated creator; there is nothing higher than a god. A deity, on the other hand, may or may not have other beings above him. Thus, the Yahweh of the Bible would be a god—there is nothing higher than him, nor could there ever be. In contrast, Zeus had a father (Cronos), and currently sits on top of the Greek pantheon only because he forced other deities out. Paula Fredriksen has summarized monotheism as "one High God on top."[9] But we must take care with such encapsulations: it is only monotheism if this High God is an ultimate being, and not merely a deity who has for some reason gained supremacy over other deities.

In light of Tuggy's distinctions, we are able to speak more clearly about what people believe. Someone who believes in the existence of only one deity would be a monotheist (or a monodeist); a pagan who believes only in a host of deities would be a polydeist; a Christian who believes in Yahweh as well as a host of angels and demons would be a monotheist, but he would also be a polydeist—someone who believes in the existence of more than

5. Heiser, "Monotheism," 27.
6. Tuggy, "On Counting Gods," 188–213.
7. Tuggy, "On Counting Gods," 194.
8. Tuggy, "On Counting Gods," 197.
9. Fredriksen, Review of *Lord Jesus Christ*, 539.

one deity. The Christian would best be described, according to Tuggy, as a monotheistic polydeist.[10]

While Heiser may be content with abandoning "monotheism" altogether, in light of Tuggy's helpful distinctions I will continue to use "monotheism" as an umbrella term which describes both theologies in which a Supreme God is the only deity that exists (*monodeism*) as well as theologies which posit both a Supreme God and a host of lesser deities (*monotheistic polydeism*).[11] In late antiquity, this broader monotheism was certainly entertained by various groups, each bringing to it their own nuance. Through this lens we can begin to recognize in the late Roman empire a family of "monotheisms" beneath the umbrella term "monotheism."

Biblical Monotheism

One distinguishing feature of the brand of monotheism widely entertained by Jews and Christians, which we might label *biblical monotheism*, was its prohibition of the cultic worship of other deities without necessarily denying their existence. This prohibition was enacted on account of the inherent inferiority of these deities to the Supreme God, being actually created by him, as well as biblical commandments from the Supreme God to avoid their worship. These lesser deities, according to many Jews and Christians, were actually masquerading demons. These demons might have something to do with the entities worshiped by the pagans (unaware of their true, demonic nature, of course). But in essence, the pagan deities, as the pagans saw them, did not exist. Nevertheless, in biblical monotheism, some form of lesser deities did exist beneath the one God, and a positive belief in such beings is asserted repeatedly by the early Christian apologists.[12]

Armed with this clarity, we may embark upon what monotheism meant to the pagans of the late empire. Again, ideas like "monotheistic polydeism" will still be helpful here. But monotheism, as we will soon

---

10. Tuggy, "On Counting Gods," 205, 210.

11. I see this as a return to monotheism's original meaning. Indeed, the seventeenth-century word "monotheism" was not, as has been observed, created to be an antonym to "polytheism," but rather to "atheism"—a monotheist was someone who affirmed the existence of God, not someone who affirmed that only one entity could ever be called "god." See MacDonald, *Deuteronomy and the Meaning of "Monotheism,"* 1–21. See also Heiser, "Monotheism," 27.

12. See for example Justin Martyr, *1 Apol.*, 5–6.

discover, tended to be expressed by pagans in ways radically divergent from the Judeo-Christian system.

Pagan Monotheism

A brief survey of the modern debate over the existence of "pagan monotheism" is in order. Michael Frede, in a now-famous book edited with Polymnia Athanassiadi in 1999, argued that monotheism had been widespread among pagans in antiquity.[13] He appealed primarily to a spirit of monotheism he detected in Greek philosophy, and ultimately found it difficult to distinguish between the positions of Plato, Aristotle, Zeno, and Christians.[14] He suggested, rather daringly, that Platonists especially were "monotheistic in precisely the sense the Christians were."[15] Frede's position was ultimately that the Jewish and Christian monotheists who acknowledged a host of lesser deities, namely demons and angels, were akin to the "majority" of philosophers, who likewise allowed for the existence of lesser deities beneath the highest principle, or "god."

Some scholars reacted strongly to Frede's blurring of the lines between the personal god of the biblical faiths and the ultimate realities of the philosophers. Frede's lack of nuance was famously attacked by Mark Edwards, who argued that Frede had misunderstood the doctrines of the philosophers, who had never made their highest principle an object of cultic worship like the personal God of Jews and Christians. Plotinus, for example, never made the principle of the One a truly personal being, and for Edwards, since monotheism requires taking a religious attitude toward a *god*, Plotinus's One was too abstract to qualify.

In 2010, Frede responded to this criticism by arguing that it simply does not follow "that a philosopher, just because as a matter of theory he believes in a certain principle, cannot take the appropriate attitude towards this principle, namely in the case of God a religious attitude."[16] In his eyes, Plotinus clearly expresses a religious attitude towards the One.[17] If this is

13. Frede, "Monotheism," 41–67.
14. Frede, "Monotheism," 41.
15. Frede, "Monotheism," 67.
16. Frede, "Case for Pagan Monotheism," 67.
17. "One can see this, for instance, by looking at Plotinus' Enneads 6.8, in which Plotinus among other things tries to disabuse us of a blasphemous view about the One or God, namely that God does what he does of necessity, given his nature" (Frede, "Case

correct, and if religious attitude is the marker of monotheism, how much does it matter if one worshiper thinks of this god as more or less abstract or more or less personal than the other?

In one sense, I see that Edwards's concerns were valid: there must be a line drawn somewhere regarding what does and does not count as monotheism. But Edward's final conclusion, that "pagan monotheism" simply never existed, was clearly an overreaction.[18] How can we satisfy both those scholars who cannot recognize someone like Plotinus as a monotheist, and those who continue to insist on the historical reality of "pagan monotheism"? It may be helpful to forge a middle ground between the positions of Edwards and Frede, narrowing our definition of "monotheism" to exclude those systems which posit an impersonal ultimate reality, but including those systems which believe in a personal Supreme being.

In this light, we can easily identify the presence of such a monotheism among the pagans of late antiquity, *pace* Edwards. For example, John Whittaker and Frederick Brenk have argued, and convincingly, that Plutarch (d. 120 CE), though a Platonist, was not merely an ultimist, but a monotheist akin to the Jewish Philo (d. 50 CE).[19] The oft-discussed cult of Theos Hypsistos, analyzed most notably by Stephen Mitchell, likely provides another example of monotheism in the pagan world.[20] Later in

for Pagan Monotheism," 68).

18. See Edwards, "Pagan and Christian Monotheism in the Age of Constantine," 211-235. Frede responded to Edwards in 2010, arguing against a definition of monotheism which allowed for only Jewish and Christian expressions. See Frede, "Case for Pagan Monotheism," 53-81. Frede's analysis reveals how important Tuggy's distinctions between a "god" and "deity" are to us; the monotheism of Greek philosophers like Chrysippus, for example, would be more obvious to more scholars if only these ancients "had another term to mark the difference between these divine beings and human beings" (Frede, "Case for Pagan Monotheism," 74). Also supportive of Frede was Timothy Barnes in his "Monotheists All," 142-53. Alongside Frede, Van Nuffelen also presented "pagan monotheism" as a wider term for monotheistic Graeco-Roman tendencies. See Van Nuffelen, "Pagan Monotheism as a Religious Phenomenon," 13-33.

19. Whittaker, "Ammonius on the Delphic E," 185-92; Brenk, "Philo and Plutarch," 79-92.

20. Mitchell, "Cult of Theos Hypsistos," 81-148. The debate over the existence of this cult was revitalized in 1987 with the publication of inscriptions from Aphrodisias referring to persons as θεοσέβής (god-worshipers); for an introduction, see Koch, "God-fearers between Facts and Fiction," 62-90. Mitchell has argued that the "god-fearers," or "god-worshippers" (φοβούμενος τον Θεόν or θεοσέβής), mentioned in the book of Acts (13:16, 26) are members of the Hypsistos cult, though in 2010 he revised his assessment to ends that the god-fearers are only "very closely related" to the *Hypsistarii*; see Mitchell, "Further Thoughts on the Cult," 196. Much has been made about the LXX translation of

this study we will investigate in detail both the Roman solar cult of Sol Invictus and the Hermetic tradition of Graeco-Egyptian religious philosophy, traditions with which Constantine was familiar, and which also stand squarely in the realm of personal monotheism.

Distinctions in Pagan Monotheism

I have identified at least three types of monotheism current in monotheistic pagan circles in the Roman empire from the second to the fourth centuries CE.[21] Each of these pagan monotheisms assumed that there is one personal Supreme Being, who has no father and is unoriginated, but they each differed in how they interpreted the traditional deities of the world's religions.

The first type of monotheism understood the various deities to be distinct and subordinate entities beneath the Supreme God. These entities were created or fathered by the Supreme God, and are often thought of as his agents or servants. From about the second century CE onward, Roman commentators can be found referring to a "common opinion" among people throughout the empire that the traditional deities were all "produced" by a Supreme God and are related to him as his "sons."[22] These lesser deities, who owe the one god for their existence, would correspond to angels in biblical traditions.

The second type of monotheism treated the many deities as simply different names for the same one god. This has sometimes been described as "pluriform" or "polymorphous" monotheism: the various deities are

---

the Hebrew "El Elyon" (Most High God) as θεὸς ὕψιστος. Some have seen this as a turn towards a more universal (pagan) monotheism; to others this has seemed only a "negotiation" at the borders of Jewish and Hellenistic communities; see Lanckau, "Hypsistos," 847–75: "the cult of Hypsistos was not uniform, but rather shaped by diverse forces and marked differently from situation to situation . . . The Jewish use of Hypsistos attempted to translate exclusive notions of YHWH into *this* environment."

21. Peter Van Nuffelen observes that the rise of monotheism among pagans "was not a uniform or sudden process: change was gradual and took many different forms and tendencies, which we can group under the heading of 'pagan monotheism.' Whereas the evidence for the first century seems predominantly literary and philosophical, from the second century epigraphical texts seem to testify to a wider acceptance of such ideas. There seems to be a continuous spread of pagan monotheism up to the end of paganism. Indeed, at the end of the fourth century a correspondent of St Augustine can claim that any serious person believes in a single god" (Van Nuffelen, "Pagan Monotheism as a Religious Phenomenon," 33).

22. MacMullen, *Paganism in the Roman Empire*, 86–88.

different manifestations of the same unitary entity. While each manifestation may appear to be a distinct deity, they are in fact only "modes" of the same one being. This interpretation effectively collapses all deities into a single deity (monodeism). As we will see, the Roman deity Sol Invictus was indeed treated by many Romans as "the one universal Godhead . . . recognized under a thousand names."[23]

The third type of monotheism, similar to the second, was a variation of pluriform monotheism which I call "monotheistic emanationism." This interpretation identified the many deities as various spiritual *emanations* of the Supreme God. Pagan solar monotheism in the late Roman empire, as will be properly introduced in the coming sections, was interpreted by many Neoplatonists along these lines: the traditional deities do exist in some sense, but they are emanations of an underlying principle which unites them all as one. We know that by at least the fourth century, solar monotheists were applying the philosophy of emanationism to the sun god and portraying the various deities as the many rays of the sun, emanating out of one grand, celestial source.[24] Each of these rays could be numerically distinguished from the sun, but they were nevertheless connected to it, and shared the same properties. This scheme thus straddled the line between first and second interpretations of monotheism: the different deities were not mere modes of a unitary entity, but each simultaneously existed in some sense, and remained ontologically connected to the one god. The result was a Supreme God who could truly receive worship through the veneration of his many colorful emanations.

Of course, as we will see, not all Roman pagans interested in monotheism were careful about making the above distinctions. The common Roman may not have given much thought to precisely how it was that all gods were one, while monotheists interested in philosophy might have thought about it a great deal, and found it necessary to apply emanationism to justify the traditional worship of the Roman pantheon. Regardless, it is clear by the time of Constantine that not only had many Romans already been interested in monotheism for centuries, but the relationship between the Supreme God and the rest of the deities had remained a topic of conversation.

What is important to note is that regardless of whether a pagan viewed the traditional deities as emanations of the Supreme God, or as distinct and subordinate deities to him, or even as different names for the

---

23. J. N. D. Kelly, cited in Carroll, *Constantine's Sword*, 180–81.
24. See Liebeschuetz, "Speech of Praetextatus," 197.

same unitary entity, the traditional deities ultimately remained worthy of worship. And herein lies the most penetrating disagreement between pagan and biblical monotheists: for the former, worshiping the traditional deities was an appropriate and often even necessary element of monotheism; for the latter, worshiping these deities was *sin*. For this reason, it has been fair to describe biblical monotheism as typically monolatrous, and pagan monotheism as typically polyolatrous. The biblical monotheist would see the pagan's worship of the lesser deities as base, ignorant, and an affront to God.[25] Pagan monotheists, on the other hand, would see the refusal of Jews and Christians to honor the traditional deities as likewise an affront to the divine, and at the very least as dangerously disrespectful to the traditions of the elders.

Monotheism and Pluralism

In modern discussions of religious diversity, Judaism, Christianity, and Islam are regularly grouped together on the basis of monotheism and contrasted with those faiths which assert many gods and goddesses, or even no gods at all. The sharp differences between these Abrahamic faiths, however, and their exclusivist truth-claims have regularly overwhelmed any optimism about potential unity between them on this point. Mutual agreement on monotheism has not been enough to overwhelm their massive differences in other areas.

Other modern religions have arguably been more open to justifying pluralism on the basis of monotheism: for example, some forms of Hinduism are openly monotheistic, and in these traditions, the one Brahman is said to manifest as a plurality of divinities like Vishnu, Krishna, and Shiva, and even as the figures of the Abrahamic faiths. Modern Hindu theologians have employed terms like *polymorphic monotheism* to describe some forms of Hinduism which envision "a single unitary deity who takes many forms and manifests at different levels of reality."[26] Here the one God, being the ul-

---

25. At the very least, Jews and Christians would think it wrong for them to associate with the lesser deities, but it remains possible that some biblical monotheists might think that members of the other nations have been consigned to the care of those deities by the Supreme God.

26. Rosen, *Essential Hinduism*, 25. In Vaishnavism, for example, "polymorphic monotheism is perhaps the best description of divinity, though lesser deities are acknowledged as well" (Rosen, *Essential Hinduism*, 235). See also Schweig, "Krishna, the Intimate Deity," 18–19.

timate Truth beyond all limitations, has unlimited forms (*ananta-rupa*), each worthy of worship.[27] Indeed, the oldest of the Vedas states that "Truth is one, the wise call it by various names."[28] Here we immediately detect an affinity with the pluriform solar monotheism of the late Roman empire and its one Supreme God recognized under a thousand names.

Considering the challenge of monotheism in late antiquity in light of our modern religious diversity may prove helpful. Like the modern adherents of the Abrahamic faiths, many modern Hindus, like Vaishnavites, would consider themselves monotheists[29]—but could modern Vaishnavite theologians ever convince Jews, Christians, and Muslims that their polymorphic or pluriform monotheism was compatible with biblically-informed monotheism? Could they convince them that they all worshiped the same Supreme God? If this seems like a difficult task then we may have glimpsed the sort of challenge which those interested in religious harmony would have faced in the late Roman Empire, when modernity and the spirit of tolerance had yet to prevail upon the West. But solar monotheism in the late third and early fourth century, supported by Neoplatonic philosophy, had at least offered a powerful metaphysical substrate on which to construct a theological unity. Any such unity between modern Abrahamics, Hindus, and other monotheisms will not have the support of that unifying agent. Nevertheless, in our own time, monotheism may still prove attractive to philosophers looking to meet the challenge of religious diversity: just as monotheism offered the late Roman Empire a path towards resolving religious tension, some have begun to discern a similar answer to the diversity of our modern religious world.[30]

Reacting to problems within John Hick's famous arguments for pluralism,[31] Swedish philosopher Mikael Stenmark presented (but did not endorse) what he describes as a "some-are-equally-right" model.[32] Previous-

---

27. Schweig, "Krishna, the Intimate Deity," 26.

28. *Rigveda* 1.164.46; Dutta and Robinson, *Rabindranath Tagore*, 245.

29. Salem and Foskett, "Religion and Religious Experiences," 240.

30. For a modern defense of the great monotheistic religions' relationship with religious tolerance, see Erlewine, *Monotheism and Tolerance*.

31. "Religious pluralism" almost always refers to a theory which looks to resolve religious diversity by affirming positive value in each of the world's religions; in other words, for a pluralist, all religions are the same in some valuable respects. See Tuggy, "Theories of Religious Diversity."

32. Stenmark, "Religious Pluralism," 21–35. Many thanks to Dale Tuggy for his recommendation of this work.

ly Hick had proposed that *many* of the world's great religions were equally true, being only different responses to the same transcendent Reality.[33] But according to Stenmark, because the Real is experienced by even the great religions in tremendously different ways, this creates a "problem of emptiness" for the pluralist view, in which the Real is ultimately deprived of content and logical connection to good human life.[34] Stenmark's proposed alternative is an assertion that only some religions are equally true, and only in some respects. For example, the monotheistic religions, or at least the Abrahamic monotheisms, could be seen as equally right about core religious truths. As Stenmark puts it, Christians, Jews, and Muslims who adhered to the some-are-equally-right model could "agree that there is a God and that this God is mighty but [is] also just and compassionate . . . [while] on those issues where Christianity and Islam contradict each other, it is reasonable to believe that sometimes neither of the religions is right, sometimes it is one of them and sometimes it is the other one, but generally speaking they are equally successful in tracking the truth."[35] On the other hand, to the extent that other world religions claim that God is not one, or not a person, or evil, they would maintain that those religions are wrong.[36] Tuggy thus characterizes Stenmark's model as a form of "core pluralism," in which unity is discovered on the basis of agreement on core truths about "the one God and our need for relationship with God."[37]

I will ultimately argue that Constantine was motivated by a similar outlook, and that the emperor eventually came to believe that certain monotheistic religions in the empire were equally true in their core beliefs about God, and that sometimes one or the other was right in certain areas where they disagreed. At the same time, Constantine was able to reject other religions in the empire to the extent that they contravened with the core truths agreed upon by the monotheistic religions. It will be important to keep this "some-are-equally-right" model in mind as we move to investigate the nature of monotheism in the late Roman Empire, Constantine's religion, and his religious policies.

---

33. Hick, "Religious Pluralism."
34. Stenmark, "Religious Pluralism," 33.
35. Stenmark, "Religious Pluralism," 33.
36. Stenmark, "Religious Pluralism," 33.
37. Tuggy, "Theories of Religious Diversity."

2

Solar Monotheism in the Late Roman Empire

THE IDEA THAT A single sun deity might dominate all other deities was by no means new or uniquely Roman. The ancient Egyptians, whose religion would later enthrall the Graeco-Roman world, offer the good examples of the sun gods Amun-Ra and Aten. Egyptologists still struggle to understand how and why solar monotheism first appeared in Egypt, and the mysterious case of the pharaoh Akhenaten (d. 1334 BCE), whose monotheism emerged more than a millennium and a half before the rise of Constantine, occupies all scholarly surveys of the subject. On the pylons at Karnak we read that in Akhenaten's Egypt, all of the other deities had "ceased," but there was one god who had not ceased: Aten, the great Sun-disc. Precisely what this "cessation" meant for the lesser deities is not clear.[1] Nevertheless, the text does say that this Aten, being utterly unique and all-powerful, "gave birth to himself, and . . . he [go]es where he pleases and they know not [his] g[oing]."[2] This is clearly an uncreated being, an ultimate personality towering over the Egyptian pantheon. As one column at Karnak says of him, "How matchless is [Akhenaten's] god!"[3] Precisely how Aten achieved this status in the mind of Akhenaten remains a mystery. Donald Redford, the foremost authority on Akhenaten's monotheism, points out that the inscriptions on columns 8–11 also stress the pharaoh's close personal relationship with the Supreme God: Aten is "his father," and the pharaoh is the "fair child of the Sun-disc."

---

1. "We would love to know what exactly is implied by the verb in *3bw* (translated above as "ceased") when it is applied to the gods and their statuary. Does it mean, for instance, that the Sun-disc has thrown over all the other gods in the Egyptian pantheon? Or does it mean that these gods were the creation of the Sun-disc in the first place? Or is Akhenaten suggesting that the other gods never really existed at all?" (Redford, "Monotheism of Akhenaten," 24).

2. Quoted in Redford, "Monotheism of Akhenaten," 23.

3. Quoted in Redford, "Monotheism of Akhenaten," 24.

In the official imagery, "rays of light from the Sun-disc end in human-like hands that fondle and protect the beloved son, Akhenaten, and his wife, Nefertity."[4] Later, the idea that the Supreme God has a unique, father-son relationship with a human king will make a return in the national monotheism of Israel.[5] Similar themes will continue to prove important in the much later days of the Roman Empire, and especially in the monotheistic propaganda of the sun-worshiper Constantine.

We know that after Akhenaten died, the Egyptians reversed his religious decrees, tore down his monuments, and went back to worshiping their family deities as if Egypt's affair with monotheism had never happened. Standing on this side of history, we also know that where Akhenaten's revolution failed, Constantine's monotheism had unimaginable success. To this day, Christian monotheists constitute nearly one third of the world's population, each of them owing some degree of thanks, consciously or not, to Constantine's program. But the road to Constantine's monotheism was, as we will see, a difficult and even tragic one.

The Rise of Roman Solar Monotheism

Centuries prior to Constantine's ascension, Roman paganism had been in the throes of evolution. By the end of the first century CE, the intimacy with a deity promised by early Gnosticism and the mystery cults had attracted Romans dissatisfied by the cold remoteness of the traditional pantheon and Greek philosophy. By at least the third century CE, the syncretistic energy boiling in the wake of Middle Platonism, no doubt fueled by the unifying tendencies progressing in philosophy, had given rise to a powerful monotheistic inclination among the empire's religionists. For reasons ultimately both religious and political, the late pagan world had begun to find increasingly useful a Supreme Deity who could subsume the worship of the many traditional deities.

---

4. Redford, "Monotheism of Akhenaten," 24.

5. About the Israelite King Solomon the Supreme God promises: "I will be a father to him and he will be a son to me... my lovingkindness shall not depart from him" (2 Sam 7:14a, 15a). The theme remained central to the messianic Judaism of the first century CE, as demonstrated in the Christian Gospels: "Nathanael answered him, 'Rabbi, you are the son of God! You are the King of Israel!'" (John 1:49). For a helpful investigation into how this divine sonship language interacted with Roman paradigms during the first to fourth centuries CE, see Peppard, *Son of God in the Roman World*.

The long-standing worship of the sun offered the most expedient religious substrate. Not only were sun gods among the oldest and most universally appealing deities, Platonism, with its comparison of the highest principle of the Good with the sun, had already provided the necessary intellectual foundation for a solar monotheism that could be both understood and justified philosophically.[6] Even before the Severan dynasty (193–235 CE), the old sun gods had begun to take on new life: the titanic Helios, once standing over the ancient Greeks as the Colossus of Rhodes, came to tower over the entire Roman pantheon, standing on the intellectual triumph of Roman Platonism. Zeus, of course, had long ruled the Olympians, but eventually Apollo, dragging his solar chariot through the heavens, rode a new wave of syncretism which catapulted him to the highest levels of divinity.[7]

In the two centuries preceding Constantine, we can summarize the development of Roman sun-worship by identifying the progress of a lateral syncretism which identified the various sun gods, as well as an increasing tendency to view all other deities as manifestations of this one Supreme Deity. As discussed in the previous chapter, Roman solar monotheism eventually produced a "pluriform" monotheism in which the many traditional deities were seen as emanations or manifestations of the One God.

Imperial Monotheism

The deity Sol Invictus, the Invincible Sun, provides the most significant example of this emerging pluriform solar monotheism. The mapping of Sol's origins and precise evolutionary trajectory has remained a topic of debate.[8] It has long been thought that the cult of Sol Invictus was originally a Syrian religion, and one haphazardly forced on the Roman Empire by the irreverent

---

6. Plato, *Republic* 6.508–9, 7.516–17. See Liebeschuetz, "Speech of Praetextatus," 187.

7. Zeus had experienced some identification with the sun himself, thanks to the use of his name in Stoicism, and to his association with other supreme (solar) deities in various parts of the world. Sources describing Apollo as a sun god can be located in the fifth century BCE; by the third century CE, the identification was widely known. See Liebeschuetz, "Speech of Praetextatus," 193. See also Parkes, *Oracles of Apollo*, 98, 162.

8. Florin Curta observed that the Roman adoption of Sol Invictus "coincides with the first known attempt to place one god above the others" in the empire (Curta, "First Dedication to Sol Invictus," 182). One of the earliest Roman inscriptions, dating to 158 CE, is a dedication by a soldier named Amandus who has thankfully constructed an altar to the deity for enabling his election for an important mission.

young emperor Elagabalus (203–22 CE). Barely fifteen at the time of his ascension, Elagabalus had been the hereditary high priest of the sun god in Emesa and had taken his name, Elagabal, for himself. Capitalizing on the sun worship which had been steadily rising in the empire since the reign of Septimus Severus,[9] Elagabalus identified his god as Sol Invictus, and introduced him to the city of Rome with raucous spectacle. He pulled behind him in his golden chariot the cult object of his god, a black conical stone, nearly two thousand miles from Emesa and had it set up in a lavish temple on Palatine Hill. This was only the beginning of his tactless and ill-fated revolution. The *Augustan History* records that Elagabalus proclaimed "that all gods were the servants of his own god, while terming some its chamberlains, others, its slaves, others, its servants of various sorts."[10] He ordered the holy objects of all other cults, "all that the Romans held sacred," to be transferred to his temple, and sought to "extinguish Roman rites," purposing "that no god might be worshipped at Rome" save his own.[11] Consolidating the various religions with a heavy hand, he declared that the "rites of the Jews and Samaritans and Christian sorcery" should be conducted in his new temple,[12] and ordered the worship of the sun, not in the Roman way, but "in the manner of Emesa."[13] To make matters worse, he married his indelicate doctrine with ceremonies of the most distasteful and barbaric cruelty, even shocking the Romans, no strangers to blood and sex.

Historians of Roman religion have usually concluded that the worship of Sol Invictus was initially met with resistance as an Eastern incursion.[14] However, over the past decade scholars have

> convincingly challenged the long-held popular notion that Sol Invictus was a distinct, late imperial sun god whose cult was imported from Syria. It has become quite clear that Romans themselves venerated the sun as a god continuously, in the city of Rome,

---

9. Halsberghe, *Cult of Sol Invictus*, 36.

10. Quoted in MacMullen, *Paganism in the Roman Empire*, 86.

11. *Augustan History*, 2.6.1; Magie, *Historia Augusta*, 117.

12. Quoted in Moralee, *Rome's Holy Mountain*, 126. The authenticity of some of the stories of Elagabalus's practices in this history have been questioned; see Syme, *Emperors and Biography*, 218, 263.

13. Winn, *Eusebius of Emesa*, 43.

14. For an introduction to the debate on the origins of Sol Invictus (Roman vs. Syrian) see Curta, "First Dedication to Sol Invictus," 182–83. Hijmans sees Elagabalas's cult as a short-lived movement, not to be confused with the standard Roman worship of Sol, an ancestral Roman deity. See Hijmans, "Temples and Priests of Sol," 382.

from at least the mid-Republic (and probably much earlier) until the end of the fourth century AD.[15]

In this light, Romans had not taken issue with Sol, but with how Elagabalus had derisively forced their traditional protectors into submission and their own customs into irrelevance. Elagabalus's strange rituals and legendary debauchery did not help his arguments with his subjects about the proper form of piety. Indeed, in matters of religion, men may be compelled by a tyrant (for a time), but they can only be persuaded by one they believe to be a righteous man. Elagabalus was clearly not the latter. The young emperor, ruling only four years, was assassinated by his own guards in 222 CE.

It is no surprise that the cult of Sol Invictus experienced a period of hibernation during the reign of Elagabalus's cousin and successor Alexander Severus (ruled 222–35 CE). Alexander had the symbol of Sol Invictus, the great conical stone, sent back to Emesa, effectively halting the deity's official worship in Rome.[16] However, "what Alexander removed from Rome, was merely the symbol of the cult, rejected by many prominent Romans because its peculiar liturgy demanded more from them than they were prepared to give."[17] Nevertheless, "the deeper meaning of the cult continued to exert a spiritual influence" on the Roman empire.[18] Religion in Rome had not only been pushed towards syncretism, "the general religious trend was towards monotheism, not only locally but universally."[19] Despite Elagabalus's failures, the *monotheistic* worship of Sol—worship that assumed Sol was a god, not a mere deity—would rise sharply in prominence by the last quadrant of the third century CE.[20]

Alexander Severus, while weakening the peculiar cult of his cousin, would nevertheless also be representative of early efforts to synchronize pagan and Christian monotheism. Friendly to both Jews and Christians, Alexander is reported to have filled his own oratory with a private pantheon of statues, each of whom he believed to be pointing the way to the Supreme

---

15. Hijmans, "Temples and Priests of Sol," 381.
16. Halsberghe, *Cult of Sol Invictus*, 138.
17. Halsberghe, *Cult of Sol Invictus*, 106.
18. Halsberghe, *Cult of Sol Invictus*, 138.
19. Halsberghe, *Cult of Sol Invictus*, 149. See also Lenski, *Constantine and the Cities*, 74.
20. Halsberghe, *Cult of Sol Invictus*, ix. See also Hijmans, "Temples and Priests of Sol," 381. See also Sommer's discussion in the context of traditional Roman conceptions of divinity: Sommer, "Challenge of Aniconism," 588.

God.²¹ An image of Jesus Christ was among them.²² His mother, Julia Mamea, was likewise interested in Christianity, and Eusebius reports that she once summoned the great Origen (d. 254 CE) to her court to hear his Christian teaching.²³ For the moment, Rome enjoyed a gasp of religious latitude and a spirit of exploration. The preceding Elagabalus, addled by his own excesses and delusions, had forced his cult on Rome, disrespected her traditional protectors, and married the good message of monotheism with the unfortunate theatrics for which Rome eventually killed him. Alexander, however, restored religious balance, and on his own pursued the Supreme God, not in the streets with fanfare and wine, not dragging a foreign cult-object into the Eternal City, but with dignity and esteem for Rome's great traditions. As Durant characterized his reign, "Under Alexander Severus peace seemed established among all the rival faiths."²⁴ In such a space, *Roman* monotheism had room to breathe and grow.

During the five-year reign of Marcus Julius Phillipus (d. 249 CE), also known as Philip the Arab, Roman Christians enjoyed a final moment of calm before the third century erupted in imperial persecution. Eusebius of Caesarea (d. 339 CE), who would later become Constantine's biographer, wrote more than sixty years after Philip's death that Philip had provided such latitude because he himself had been a convert to Christianity.²⁵ This report was echoed by a host of later Christian writers happy to assign Philip the title of "first Christian emperor," though none of their records seem independent of Eusebius's testimony.²⁶ While agreeing that he was acquainted to some degree with Christian theology and practice, modern scholars tend to doubt that he was personally committed in any meaningful sense to the Christian religion. Historians often

---

21. Cohen, *Beginnings of Jewishness*, 143.

22. Also in his collection was a figure of Abraham. Due to either Jewish gratitude for Alexander's favorable relationship with Judaism, or because a Torah scroll given by Alexander was housed there, a synagogue in Rome was named the Synagogue of Severus. For skepticism of the synagogue's existence see Leon, *Jews of Ancient Rome*, 162–63.

23. Eusebius, *Hist. eccl.* 6.21.3.

24. Durant, *Caesar and Christ*, 650.

25. Louth has argued for an original publication date of 313 CE for Eusebius's *Hist. eccl.*; see Louth, "Historia Ecclesiastica," 111–23.

26. Pohlsander has located this report in a host of writers from the fourth century and beyond, including Jerome, Orosius, the Anonymus Valesianus, Prosper Tiro, Polemius Silvius, Cassiodorus, Jordanes, Isidore the Younger, and Bede. As Pholsander concluded, and rightly so, all of these reports depend on the Eusebian passage; see Pohlsander, "Philip the Arab," 463.

point to the fact that not only are pagan sources silent on Philip's alleged Christianity, but his behavior hardly aligns with Christian standards of the third century. Philip publicly deified his own father Julius Marinus (d. ca. 244 CE), allegedly arranged the murder of his nineteen-year-old predecessor Gordian III (d. 244 CE), slaughtered countless exotic animals in religious rituals, and offered one thousand pairs of gladiators at the Secular Games in 248 CE. Such a legacy, peppered with so many activities widely condemned by third-century Christian leaders, has made it difficult for modern analysts to recognize in Philip the Christian convert presented by Eusebius.[27] Still, other records indicate that Philip seems to have gone beyond simply tolerating Christianity in his empire. Fourth-century traditions connected to a bishop named Babylas of Antioch (who would become a martyr in 253 during the persecutions which immediately followed Philip's reign) report that Philip had once desired to enter a Christian church in order to join a worship service, but Babylas refused him entry due to the emperor's hands being stained with Gordian's blood.[28] While some historians have been quick to write off such stories as apocryphal, we should not forget that myth very often has its genesis in fact. Such rumors may have been the product of the emperor's sincere interest in Christianity. In light of trends in Roman monotheism, the fact that the emperor facilitated the traditional games of the empire, signaling his commitment to Roman religion, may not preclude a genuine interest in the Christian god. It seems reasonable that Philip, as a Roman pagan and *pontifex maximus*, could have been interested in the Christian religion in a similar way that Alexander Severus had been. We know from Eusebius that Origen did write letters to Philip and to Philip's mother Severa, reminding us of the earlier contact between Origen and Alexander's mother Julia.[29] Of course, Christian theologians were known to write to unsympathetic or indifferent emperors as well.[30] Both the scarcity of the sources and the clouds gathered by later Christian writers ultimately make Philip's real doctrines impossible to know. At the very least he did not persecute Christians and was friendly enough towards them that

---

27. See Pohlsander, "Philip the Arab," 465–67.
28. See Pohlsander, "Philip the Arab," 466.
29. Eusebius, *Hist. eccl.* 6.36.3.
30. A tradition seen as early as Justin Martyr's *First Apology*, written to Antoninus Pius, ca. 155–57 CE.

their later historians would judge his reign as "more kindly" than that of his tyrannical successor Decius (d. 251 CE).[31]

Regardless of Philip's true feelings about Christianity, and despite the waves of oppression initiated by Roman emperors after Philip's death in 249, the third quadrant of the third century CE continued to host the rise of Roman monotheism. The progressive association of Christian and pagan monotheism during this period was certainly made easier by Christianity's striking similarities to Roman sun cults like that of Mithras.[32] Both Christianity and Mithraism featured a revealed doctrine, an initiated brotherhood, a communal meal, and a promise of intimacy with the Supreme God. Christian churches were typically built to face the rising sun, and Christians worshiped on the day of the sun (Sunday).[33] Thanks to these similarities and others, some scholars have been prepared to conclude that Roman pagans must have seen Christianity as yet another manifestation of solar monotheism.[34] Evidently, some Christians were likewise happy to cast their religion in the solar imagery of pagan monotheism, as evidenced by a famous Christian mosaic produced sometime in the mid-to-late third century depicting Christ as the Sun, driving the solar quadriga typically piloted by Sol Invictus.[35] The blurring of the lines between the supreme deities of Christian and pagan monotheism, while certainly in its early stages during the Severan dynasty, would become, as we will see, a preoccupation of Constantine's early reign. But a quarter century before Constantine took up the purple, pagan monotheism, in the form of a reinvigorated Sol Invictus cult, would rise to prominence during the rule of Aurelian (270–75 CE).

---

31. See Eusebius, *Hist. eccl.* 6.41.9.

32. Mithras was, according to Liebeschuetz, "not originally a sun god, but quite early in the history of the cult the god came to be identified with the sun, and to be known as Sol Invictus Mithras" (Liebeschuetz, "Speech of Praetextatus," 189).

33. Liebeschuetz, "Speech of Praetextatus," 190.

34. White, *Emergence of Christianity*, 79. As has been observed, and as Cumont once concluded, "The propagation of the Oriental [sun] cults levelled the roads for Christianity and heralded its triumph" (Cumont, *Oriental Religions in Roman Paganism*, 134).

35. The mosaic is housed under St. Peter's Basilica on the ceiling of the Mausoleum of the Julii, and despite its use of pagan imagery is probably Christian. For an introduction to this artwork and its significance, see Bardill, *Constantine*, 326–30.

Aurelian's God

The emperor Aurelian revealed to his subjects that it had been the divine favor of Sol Invictus, the Supreme God, which had delivered his victory at the battle of Emesa.[36] By 274, Aurelian had reformed Elagabalus's cult and had constructed an elaborate temple in Rome, proclaiming Sol Invictus "Master of the Roman Empire,"[37] and making him "the one universal Godhead... recognized under a thousand names."[38] Not only were the sun gods Helios, Apollo, and to some mysterious degree Mithras, essentially dissolved into Sol Invictus, all other deities came to be seen as manifestations or emanations (indeed, in a Neoplatonic sense) of the Invincible Sun.[39]

From this point onward, Sol appears to have become the champion of Aurelian's vision of Roman unity—a harmony desperately needed in light of the civil wars of the third century. Sol's success as a national deity owed directly to his ability to interface with the other Roman cults: pagans could keep their traditional deities while progressives interested in a purer monotheistic ideal might move quietly away from them. In this

---

36. See Potter, *Constantine the Emperor*, 79–80; see also Liebeschuetz, "Speech of Praetextatus," 189.

37. MacMullen, *Paganism in the Roman Empire*, 86.

38. So the famous description of J. N. D. Kelly, cited in Carroll, *Constantine's Sword*, 180–81. Supporting this cult, Aurelian established a new college of priests for Sol, the *pontifices solis*, akin to the old order of *pontifices*. See Liebeschuetz, "Speech of Praetextatus," 189.

39. By the time of the Sol Invictus cult's complete establishment, Halsberghe believes Mithraism to have been "already on the wane" (Halsberghe, *Cult of Sol Invictus*, x). It has been pointed out, however, that after Aurelian's reforms, Mithras's influence was revived, and this is demonstrated at least by the Mithraic inscriptions on the altar built by Diocletian and his co-emperors in 308. It is possible that the altar represents an imperial effort to placate the military, ever strong with the love of Mithras, who may have also seen Aurelian's overshadowing of Mithras with Sol Invictus as an *overreach*. See István Tóth's review of *Cult of Sol Invictus*, 448. Kirsch thinks that at least by the time of Julian's rule (361–63 CE) the cult of Mithra was "fully conflated" with that of Sol Invictus; see Kirsch, *God Against the Gods*, 221. However, Liebeschuetz sees that Aurelian's "state cult of Sol remained quite distinct from that of other sun deities, for instance the ancient Roman cult of Sol Indiges or the private mystery cult of Mithras. In terms of ritual the Sol Invictus of Aurelian and Sol Invictus Mithras were quite separate, even though it was understood that both deities represented the sun, and though both had their festival on the 25 December, the day of the winter solstice—Christmas Day" (Liebeschuetz, "Speech of Praetextatus," 189). Burckhardt was probably right when he said that "We can probably never know how far Mithras was merged with this sun-god" (Burckhardt, *Age of Constantine the Great*, 180).

way, Sol Invictus had the potential to unite the disparate religionists of Aurelian's empire, while even the intellectual community could find here something worthy of reflection.[40]

Alaric Watson, in his 2003 book, sought to distance Aurelian's solar cult from monotheism, casting Aurelian as a mere polydeist and reducing his god to only one deity among many in the traditional pantheon.[41] Watson argued that the persistence of other traditional cults alongside Aurelian's cult is evidence that Aurelian had not tried to subsume them into his. Watson pointed also to the presence of Mars and Hercules on coinage alongside Sol Invictus, which proves, according to Watson, that Aurelian was not a solar monotheist who believed all deities were manifestations of Sol. But all of this dramatically misunderstands the nature of imperial solar monotheism in the late third century. Aurelian, in his embrace of solar monotheism, was certainly not looking to subvert the traditional deities, or to completely replace their cults with that of Sol—indeed, the great strength of Aurelian's monotheism, and of pagan monotheism in general, was that it allowed these deities to exist in some sense, and could even encourage their worship. We must not make the mistake of assuming that if Aurelian truly were a solar monotheist he would not have allowed Mars and Hercules to be depicted alongside Sol on official coinage—that he would have depicted Sol standing alone. A comparison with Hindu pluriform monotheism may once again prove helpful. Those Hindu monotheists who believe Krishna to be the Supreme Lord, for example, have no problem depicting him alongside his various manifestations in their art. That Aurelian was capable of something similar is not unreasonable.

The traditional view that Aurelian's solar religion was monotheistic indeed still has its merits, and is supported by trends in Roman solar religion found in the literature of the periods both before and after Aurelian's rule. Ramsay MacMullen, in the 1980s, already recognized the strong monotheistic spirit present in Roman solar religion in the second, third,

---

40. The cult's role in public life was perhaps not as prominent as past scholarship has believed. The fact that the cult's leadership eventually became reserved for Rome's elite does not indicate that it effectively elevated itself beyond the cults of other Roman deities on a grand scale. See Hijmans, "Temples and Priests of Sol," 381–420. As MacMullen notes, "The schools still taught, as they had taught for many centuries, that all the gods were but the applications of the one, or that they drew their strength only from One. So rarefied a doctrine left the gods in fact quite undisturbed and independent entities, so far as ordinary worship was concerned" (MacMullen, *Paganism in the Roman Empire*, 89).

41. Watson, *Aurelian and the Third Century*, 196–98.

and fourth centuries.⁴² For example, in Plutarch (d. 120 CE), Apollo is already referred to as "the Sun, or the Lord of the Sun and Father, and of all else beyond our seeing."⁴³ Likewise Maternus, living during the reign of Constantine (306–37 CE), describes "the Sun, Best and Greatest," which MacMullen pointed out are Jupiter's usual epithets, "who holds the center of the heavens, the mind of the world, the moderator, chief of all and prince."⁴⁴ And Dio Chrysostom (d. 120 CE) reveals that already in the second century pagans were preaching a pluriform monotheism: "Some people," he writes, "say Apollos, Helios and Dionysus are all one . . . and many people combine into one strength and power absolutely all the gods, so that there is no difference in honoring one or the other."⁴⁵ Chrysostom describes an ostensibly widespread belief that the various traditional deities "were engendered by the first god—as is also the common opinion . . . And to some, god seems to be one and the same, and unites in himself the power of a number of gods, as they say Helios and Apollo are the same . . . For not all gods are recognized among all, but some by one people, some by another."⁴⁶ Maximus of Tyre (fl. late second century CE) is similarly found writing that despite the visible contests between mankind's religions, "you will see throughout the world one uniform rule and doctrine, that there is one god, king and father of all things, and many gods, sons of god and his coregents. The Greek says so, likewise the non-Greek."⁴⁷ This data, combined with the histories of Elagabalus and Alexander Severus, demonstrate that monotheism, in one form or another, had long been appreciated by Romans before Aurelian instituted his cult, and that sun deities like Apollo, Helios, and Sol Invictus had played a leading role. While there is admittedly more research needed on Aurelian's religion, it still seems reasonable to include Aurelian's Sol Invictus in the wider Roman tradition of solar syncretism, a tradition which had already learned to express itself through a pluriform monotheistic spirit. Indeed, Aurelian had images of other deities, for example the Greek Helios and the Eastern Baal, set up in Sol Invictus's temple in Rome.⁴⁸ Surely this was because of monotheism, not in spite of it.

42. MacMullen, *Paganism in the Roman Empire*, 83–88.
43. MacMullen, *Paganism in the Roman Empire*, 86.
44. MacMullen, *Paganism in the Roman Empire*, 86.
45. MacMullen, *Paganism in the Roman Empire*, 86.
46. MacMullen, *Paganism in the Roman Empire*, 88.
47. MacMullen, *Paganism in the Roman Empire*, 88.
48. Halsberghe, *Cult of Sol Invictus*, 142. The ancient Baal, or at least certain local

Aurelian's acknowledgement of traditional deities, and his failure to subvert or subsume their cults, in no way demonstrates that he was not a monotheist. On the contrary, his behavior is precisely what one would expect from an imperial solar monotheist in the third century.

It is true that Aurelian set himself up as a moral and religious reformer, as opposed to an innovator (as Elagabalus had evidently appeared). As has been pointed out, the evidence does not suggest that Aurelian introduced an entirely new sun cult to the empire, and his ultimate achievement was clearly a cult which was recognized as "Roman religion for the Romans," and one which formed, deliberately or not, a seawall around Roman religion, stemming the rising tide of the Christian cult.[49] Nevertheless, Aurelian's embrace of Sol seems to have enhanced to some degree monotheism's appeal in Rome, and ultimately "while Aurelian did not intend to innovate, his concentration on Sol Invictus, with its associated ideas of light, victory and celestial supremacy, would influence the early religious ideals of Constantine, and with them the nature of imperial Christianity."[50]

In the late third and early fourth centuries, and just before Constantine's rise, solar monotheism continued to be appreciated by philosophers. For example, Porphyry (234–305 CE) evidently explained solar syncretism philosophically, and through a Neoplatonic prism which doubtless recognized the many deities of the empire as emanations from the sun. Sadly, Porphyry's treatise on sun worship is now lost to us, thanks probably to Constantine's pronouncement, made sometime after the Council of Nicaea (325 CE), that all of Porphyry's anti-Christian material should be destroyed.[51] But we know that Porphyry, as antagonistic as he was towards

---

versions of the deity, was often identified with the sun, and the Romans knew this. At Baalbek, the Romans appear to have built their temple complex on the remains of preexisting religious structures, and called the city "Heliopolis," or "City of the Sun." This likely referred to the solar cult of Baal and probably to the Egyptian city of the same name built in honor of the Egyptian sun god Re, who was thought to correspond to Baal. For a history of Canaanite religion at Baalbek, see Steiner, "On the Rise and Fall." For the relationship between the Roman imperium and the Syrian sun cults of Baal, see Winn, *Eusebius of Emesa*, 43–44.

49. Halsberghe, *Cult of Sol Invictus*, 137. See also Hijmans, who observes a spirit of conservatism in Aurelian; Hijmans, "Temples and Priests of Sol," 381. Koen Demarsin writes that Sol's cult, "as a provider of religious unity," was "a direct rival to Christianity" (Demarsin, "Paganism in Late Antiquity," 16). See also Dmitriev, "Traditions and Innovations," 568–78.

50. Harries, *Imperial Rome AD 284 to 363*, 20–21.

51. See Socrates, *Hist. eccl.* 1.9.30; Digeser, *Making of a Christian Empire*, 93.

the Christians, nevertheless is representative of pagan efforts to reconcile Christian and pagan worship at the beginning of the fourth century. He ultimately had no problem with the Christian worship of a Supreme God, or even with their love of the man Jesus—so long as such worship was carried out properly and in a way that did not eliminate the traditional cults. Porphyry, as has been observed, "not only assigned Jesus a place in the divine hierarchy; he also argued that the temple cults were one means by which to worship the one Supreme God, since 'God being One fills all things with various powers, and pervades all . . . in an incorporeal and invisible manner.' These divine powers could be worshipped by sacrificing in front of the gods' statues."[52]

It may well be, as Mark Roberts put it, that "monotheism was nothing new, but by the end of the Third Century, with the influence of the Neoplatonists, the new religious age seemed to be one of growing dissatisfaction with the old religion . . . Philosophy satisfied the urges of many, for others it was Sol, but both of these creeds seemed ultimately to point in the same general direction, as did the religion of the Jews and of the Christians—world domination by one deity."[53] Indeed, in the period before the rise of Constantine, we are probably safe in assuming that not only monotheism but monotheism's potential to unify the Roman religious world was a topic of conversation in both pagan and Christian circles.

After five years of rule, the treacherous and senseless murder of Aurelian in 275 CE shocked the empire, and ostensibly diminished the flame of any religious unity he had kindled. No doubt Aurelian's sudden death fueled the rise of the economic and political calamities which progressively marshaled Rome towards failure. After a tragic flurry of five emperors in the nine years that followed, it is not surprising that Diocletian, taking up the purple in 284 CE, was compelled to drastic measures in order to retrieve his empire from the threshold of collapse. In Diocletian's eyes, and in the eyes of many pagans, the various troubles of the empire were obvious signs that the traditional protectors of Rome were displeased. Something had obviously interfered with their worship, and the recent trajectory of Roman religion was easy to discern. It would thus be Diocletian's responsibility to recall and preserve Rome's oldest religious traditions, for the good of the realm and its people. The recent advance towards monotheism would need to be stalled.

52. Digeser, *Making of a Christian Empire*, 31.
53. Roberts, "Origins of Christmas and Epiphany," 71–72.

3

An Empire in Turmoil

AURELIAN'S SOL INVICTUS HAD been acceptable, and even helpful for an empire as religiously diverse as Rome, precisely because it did not look to extinguish the honor of the traditional deities. If a pagan wished, the myriad divinities of Rome could still be worshiped as deities existing beneath the Supreme Sun, and from the standpoint of pluriform monotheism, they were manifestations or emanations of the one God himself and likewise remained valid objects of veneration. However, the biblical form of monotheism entertained by the rising Christian cult openly undermined the old deities. The Christians even went as far as claiming that these figures did not exist, at least not in the sense that the pagans believed, and that regardless honoring them was both ignorant and sinful. This exclusivist Christian monotheism, antithetical as it was to both pluriform monotheism and to the traditional cults, was seen by many Romans as a threat to national stability. Christianity was labeled a form of "atheism" by its critics due to its alleged denial of the reality of other deities. Some Christians welcomed such charges that they had emptied the heavens of divinities, while other apologists combatted this claim as best they could, unpersuasively citing their own Christian belief in legions of demons and angels.[1] But the essential Christian claim that the traditional deities were at the very least not who

---

1. This was a tactic already employed in previous eras of persecution. Justin Martyr (d. 165 CE), for example, wrote that ancient pagans, "not knowing that these [gods] were demons, they called them gods . . . we not only deny that they who did such things as these are gods, but assert that they are wicked and impious demons . . . Hence we are called atheists. And we confess that we are atheists, so far as gods of this sort are concerned, but not with respect to the most true God, the Father of righteousness . . . But we worship and adore both him, and the Son who came forth from him and taught us these things, and the host of the other good angels who follow and are made like to him, and the prophetic Spirit" (Justin Martyr, *1 Apol.* 5–6; Roberts and Donaldson, *Justin Martyr and Athenagoras*, 11).

the Romans thought they were, and were ultimately unworthy of worship, proved increasingly intolerable. If Christianity's denial of Rome's traditional protectors represented the final consequences of the trend towards monotheism, then in the eyes of some late-third-century pagans, monotheism may have looked like yet another novel sociopolitical development which must be leading the empire down a disastrous road.

Diocletian's Reforms

Diocletian and the co-emperors of his tetrarchy (the "rule of four"), being ostensibly of this mind, established themselves as the champions of the traditional pantheon, of "vast numbers" of deities, and of a distinctly Roman way of life.[2] Thanks to their publicists, they were portrayed as reviving a lost golden age of paganism which had lately disappeared under the influx of foreign creeds.[3] These emperors still acknowledged the sun god, evidently in the form of Sol Invictus-Mithras (*Deo Soli Invicto Mithrae*), whom they still called a defender of the empire (*fautor imperii sui*).[4] Their worship of him did not, however, pace beyond that of the other deities. The imagery of the sun remained prevalent, but without its recent attachment to overt imperial favor.[5] From roughly the years 300–305 CE, the unique imperial honor once enjoyed by Sol Invictus was siphoned away to the rest of the pantheon, whom Diocletian and his fellow restorationists sought to elevate in the social consciousness. Retrieving the proper honor of the traditional divinities of Rome would, they believed, provide the empire with the stability and security it had so tragically lacked in the previous century.[6] And it was precisely this anticipated stability that the continued rise of Christian

---

2. Barnes, *Constantine*, 56.

3. Fox, *Pagans and Christians*, 593.

4. Diocletian appears to have contributed to the renovation of the principal Mithraeum at Carnuntum, as well as a statue of the sun god at Sirmium; see Grant, *Augustus to Constantine*, 232. A. L. Frothingham went so far as to suggest that Diocletian held Mithras to be the Supreme God; see Frothingham, "Diocletian and Mithra," 146–55. Fox is confident, however, that the inscription at CIL 3.4413 is of "no general significance" (Fox, *Pagans and Christians*, 593).

5. "The sun god Sol Invictus, who had become popular under the Severans and was lionized by Aurelian in the 270s," was "then assigned a secondary role in the religious propaganda of the tetrarchs" (Lenski, *Constantine and the Cities*, 49).

6. White, *Emergence of Christianity*, 82.

monotheism endangered.[7] The forty-three years of unofficial tolerance enjoyed by Christians in the empire would need to come to an end.

The immediate reasons for Diocletian's "Great Persecution" of the Christians in 303 CE are still debated.[8] Lactantius famously reports that Diocletian was moved to persecution by his junior emperor Galerius, who urged him to act against the Christians after soothsayers identified Christian disdain for traditional cult as the cause of bad omens. Such omens had meant that Rome's traditional protectors were angry, and their anger could only mean disaster for the empire. Beyond pagan anxiety over portentous cyphers, however, Christians were being identified by some intellectuals as a source of civic unrest by their rejection of established Roman thinking and customs. Porphyry, writing in support of Diocletian's reforms, identified Christians as a group who deserved no tolerance, since they had forsaken "the things of their fathers,"[9] and the ideals of "emperors, lawgivers, and philosophers."[10] The Christians were ultimately, at least in the eyes of some powerful pagans, representative of a dangerous spirit of innovation which threatened to upend the hard-won stability recently earned by the tetrarchy. Such a spirit would need to be exorcised, at all hazard, before it was too late.

The high drama of Diocletian's pagan revival was intensified by his self-portrayal as the agent of Jupiter on earth. His co-ruler, Maximian, was likewise made the representative of Hercules. More than claiming special favor with a god, Diocletian took up the Jovian appellations, portrayed himself wearing Jupiter's clothing in his propaganda, and made himself both *dominus et deus* (lord and god), forcing his subjects to approach him on their knees. Some of Diocletian's panegyrists seemed to portray Diocletian as in some sense a mystical manifestation of Jupiter; one panegyric declared, in 291, that Diocletian was "a visible and present Jupiter, near at

---

7. Jews had received special permission from the emperors to worship in their own way, and to be excused from participation in traditional cult. This special status may have been earned thanks to Jewish cooperation in placating Palestine during the great revolts. See Digeser, *The Making of a Christian Empire*, 1.

8. See Lactantius, *On the Deaths of the Persecutors*, 10.

9. Porphyry, *Philosophy from Oracles*, cited in Eusebius, *Preparation for the Gospel*, 1.2.

10. See Digeser, *The Making of a Christian Empire*, x. "Porphyry did believe that many paths led to heaven: those of the philosophers, those of the traditional cults, and even the one that Jesus himself walked . . . And this sort of position is often associated with religious toleration . . . But . . . [in Porphyry's mind] there may well be many paths to heaven, but not all paths lead there . . . people who deviated from traditional worship should be 'justly' (*endikos*) punished" (Digeser, *The Making of a Christian Empire*, 108).

hand."[11] Diocletian was not officially Jupiter himself, but was son of Jupiter, and both he and Maximian "were the chosen instruments of Jupiter and Hercules, their deputies on earth and under their special protection."[12] By so grandiosely portraying themselves as the earthly agents of these powers, Diocletian and Maximian reinforced their message that the old deities were personally involved in the restoration of their worship. Indeed, "Diocletian and Maximian were claiming to be the means by which Jupiter and Hercules acted in the world."[13] This model, in which the emperor acts as a deity's living agent of revival, will be helpful to have in mind when we consider the subsequent behavior of Constantine.[14]

In 305 CE, Diocletian abruptly retired as emperor and retreated from the stress of imperial life to tend vegetables by his coastal palace. In 311, the Christian persecutions were stopped (for a time) by none other than Galerius—the one who had first urged Diocletian to violence eight years earlier. Desperate and ravaged by what seems to have been a painful cancer, Galerius asked the Christians to pray to their God for his health, and issued an edict of toleration on the condition that they did so.[15]

The God of Constantius Chlorus

Constantine's father, Constantius Chlorus, a military man so-named for his pale complexion, ruled as Diocletian's Caesar in the West from 293–305 CE. Despite Diocletian's reforms, Constantius was evidently a monotheist. Eusebius, in his *Life of Constantine*, described Constantine's embrace of the Christian deity as a turn towards "his father's God."[16] Eusebius does suggest, however, that neither Constantius nor his son knew immediately that this deity was, in fact, the God of the Christians, but worshiped him in ignorance. In Eusebius's account, "Constantine had not known his father

---

11. *Pan.* XI, 10.5, in Nixon and Rodgers, *In Praise of Later Emperors*, 95. Likewise, when a panegyrist saw Maximian in 289, he looked upon a "manifest god" (Pan. X, 2.1, in Nixon and Rodgers, *In Praise of Later Emperors*, 55).

12. Barnes, *Constantine*, 57.

13. Digeser, *Making of a Christian Empire*, 28.

14. "Like Diocletian, Constantine emphasized his role as God's agent on Earth, which strengthened his authority" (Eysturlid, "Long-Term Decline," 61).

15. White, *Emergence of Christianity*, 90. The relief was short-lived; Maximinus Daza resumed the holocaust after Galerius' death, and the persecutions would not finally end until Daza's own decline in 313 CE.

16. Eusebius, *Vit. Const.* 27.3.

until the latter's deathbed and does not know the identity of his father's God until he receives the sign and vision of Christ himself. In this he is like Moses, who is confronted by the God of his father (Exod. 3:6) and has to ask his name (Exod. 3:13-15); for Eusebius, it is Christ who also appeared to Moses at the bush . . . Neither Constantius nor Constantine is yet aware who the one God is."[17] However, "it is almost certain that the god of Constantius Chlorus . . . was in fact Sol Invictus, not the Christian God as intimated by Eusebius (whose concern was to construct a Christian pedigree for the emperor)."[18] Constantius's interest in solar monotheism may be important for supposing how young Constantine, a member of Diocletian's court, first discovered his own interest in a Supreme God. If Constantius in fact worshiped Sol Invictus, we will ultimately be pressed by the evidence to agree with Eusebius (in a sense) that Constantine eventually turned towards "his father's God."

Constantine in Diocletian's Court

Constantine joined Diocletian's court sometime after 293, and possibly as a political hostage, whose presence may have been designed to check the behavior of his father Constantius.[19] Diocletian's entourage was constantly on the move—Constantine traveled with the emperor to Babylon, Memphis, and other exotic locales throughout the empire.[20] Diocletian's court, like other late imperial courts, was not merely a community of patricians and bureaucrats, but a party of vibrant and diverse intellectuals. One such intellectual, ironically a Christian invited by Diocletian to join his court as a rhetorician in the mid-290s, would come to have profound influence on Constantine: Lucius Lactantius (ca. 250–ca. 325 CE). It is difficult to know how much interaction the two would have had during this period, but Constantine probably was exposed to some amount of Lactantius's

17. Eusebius, *Vit. Const.* 203.
18. Domach, "Conversion of Constantine the Great," 213. Digeser concurs that Constantine's "father, who was not a Christian, was probably a solar monotheist" (Digeser, *Making of a Christian Empire*, 127). See also Barnes, *Constantine*, 57.
19. It is indeed possible that Constantine, being at Diocletian's mercy while in his court, ensured the loyalty of Constantius Chlorus. See the *Origo Constantini Imperatoris* (ca. 390), which describes Constantine as "obsess apud Diocletianum et Galerium" (1.2). Barnes argues against this picture as further propaganda designed to distance Constantine from the court's anti-Christian activities; Barnes, *Constantine*, 54.
20. Potter, *Constantine the Emperor*, 67–68.

teachings, as evidenced by Constantine's later decision to appoint Lactantius to his own court in 310.

Constantine's time spent with Diocletian would have afforded him an excellent view of the tumultuous state of Roman religion. He would have witnessed the emperor's sacrifices to the Roman pantheon as *pontifex maximus*,[21] an imperial tradition with which Constantine would later break,[22] and he would have observed Diocletian's efforts to portray himself as the right arm of Jupiter and the agent of traditional paganism's revival. Constantine was certainly there when Diocletian issued his edicts of persecution against the Christians.[23] How did Constantine perceive the emperor's war on Christian monotheism?

As Barnes aptly demonstrated, Constantine later lied about his age to escape implication in the terror.[24] Though Constantine had been a mature adult in 302-3, he needed to depict himself as merely a youth incapable of intervention in order to maintain favor with his Christian subjects. We cannot know if he ever voiced disapproval or made any subterranean efforts to stop the violence while in Diocletian's court. But there is reason to believe that he probably disapproved of Diocletian's vicious reforms and waited patiently for his chance to take power and rectify them.

Constantine's first act upon gaining power in 306 was, after all, to halt persecutions against Christians, and to proclaim freedom to all religions across Britain, Gaul, and Spain. Constantine's father had himself demonstrated tolerance of Christians in 303. Is it possible that Constantine's decision to follow his father's attitude towards the Christians was related to monotheism? It has been suggested that the reason why Constantine immediately moved to stop the persecutions in 306 was because his own mother Helena was already a Christian.[25] This seems highly unlikely, and the most comprehensive study of Helena concluded that "it is safest to date Helena's conversion after 312."[26] What we do know is that Constantine's father, whom he joined in Britain and fought alongside in a campaign in 305, is reported to have been a monotheist, and a man who respected Christians. If his father was a worshiper of Sol Invictus,

21. Potter, *Constantine the Emperor*, 77-78.
22. Barnes, *Constantine*, 25.
23. Digeser, "Platonism in the Palace," 52.
24. Barnes, *Constantine*, 2-3.
25. Barnes, *Constantine*, 45. See also Faulkner, *Rome*, 273.
26. Drijvers, *Helena Augusta*, 35.

then Constantine would doubtless have been familiar with the pluriform monotheism associated with the Invincible Sun. He might have even been familiar with the sort of monotheistic thinking exemplified by Alexander Severus in the preceding generation, which seems to have identified the Christian deity with the Supreme God. Panegyric evidence from around this time also connects Constantine himself to solar religion, and quite possibly to a monotheistic ideal: a 307 CE panegyric reveals that Constantine was already being portrayed as the divinely elected agent of the sun god, here taking the form of Apollo, who had made himself Constantine's new patron and had promised him not merely a place among the tetrarchy ("concord... and social majesty"), but *"totius mundi regna."*[27] The idea of a single world ruler, at least for some who would later become close to Constantine, was directly associated with monotheism.[28] But there is a case to be made that this panegyric, as a piece of political propaganda intending to appeal to the sensibilities and aspirations of its subject, demonstrates Constantine's own growing interest in monotheism at this time.

We must keep in mind that Diocletian's tetrarchy (the "rule by four") had been publicly connected to the plural rule of the cosmos by the traditional pantheon. Indeed, tetrarchic rule was said to be merely an earthly reflection of heavenly government.[29] This was one reason why Diocletian and his co-emperors relied so heavily on Rome's continued reverence of the traditional deities: the existence of a plurality of gods justified the plural nature of their administration. In this light, we can read the 307 CE panegyric written for Constantine, in which we ostensibly detect Constantine's personal ambition towards sole rule of the earth, as a challenge to not only the tetrarchy, but to its theological foundations. As Lactantius would write in his *Divine Institutes* around this same time, it is obvious that only "one must

---

27. Pan. VI, 1.4 and 21.5, in Nixon and Rodgers, *In Praise of Later Emperors*, 215, 583.

28. Despite the lip service paid to the other regents, "it might appear that the panegyrist is setting aside the tetrarchic system ... and providing Constantine with both a unique hereditary claim to rule ... and divine sanction to be emperor of the whole empire ... these highly personal elements (a new genealogy; a personal vision) have naturally suggested that this speaker at least was giving voice to his emperor's own claims and aspirations" (Nixon and Rodgers, *In Praise of Later Emperors*, 215). Several years later, Lactantius would argue that the tetrarchic (plural) rule of the earthly empire was an inadequate and inappropriate reflection of heavenly rule, since there is only one God who is king over all. Later, in 330, Eusebius would express a theology in which Constantine was the earthly manifestation of the one *logos*.

29. See Digeser, *Making of a Christian Empire*, 27, 29–30, 34.

rule the world" because there is only one God who rules the heavens.[30] Thus both pagans and Christians seem to have already been associating sole rule with monotheism, pushing us to agree that Constantine's 307 CE panegyric, as it has recently been described, was his first public expression of "his aspiration towards monotheistic rule."[31]

Constantine's own pragmatic spirit, combined with the influences of his solar visions and the monotheism of his father, may have also led him towards monotheism during these early years. A much later speech (ca. 325) reveals the sort of practical religious thinking which may have played a role in Constantine's initial turn towards pagan monotheism. He wonders, if there were not a Supreme God, then:

> To whom first, or last, could prayers and supplications be addressed? Who could I choose as the object of my worship, without being guilty of impiety towards the rest? Again, if haply I desired to obtain some temporal blessing, should I not, while expressing my gratitude to the Power who favored my request convey a reproach to him who opposed it? Or to whom should I pray, when desiring to know the cause of my calamity, and to obtain deliverance? Or let us suppose that the answer is given by oracles and prophecies, but that the case is not within the scope of their authority, being the province of some other deity.[32]

If Constantine was interested in solar monotheism between 305–7, then it is possible that he, following the pluriform monotheism of Aurelian's cult, and even the example of Alexander Severus, might have identified the Christian deity, or at least Jesus Christ, as a manifestation of the Supreme God. Indeed, the fact that Constantine was already making pro-Christian edicts in 306 may be significant. Digeser observed that "for whatever reason" Constantine rescinded the edicts of persecution against Christians, returned Christian property, and condoned the practice of their religion.[33] While there were doubtless some "political" considerations being made here, as Drake pointed out,[34] his motivations could have also been theologi-

---

30. Lactantius, *Inst.* 1.3.11, 18.

31. Ljubomirovic, "Latin Panegyrics," 1432, emphasis added. See Eusebius's *Oration in Praise of Constantine*, delivered at the end of the emperor's life, in which Eusebius says that singular monarchy surpasses every other form of earthly government, since "there is one God, and not two, or three, or more" (3.6).

32. Constantine, *Orat.* 3; Constantine, *Oration of Constantine*, 562.

33. Digeser, *Making of a Christian Empire*, 133.

34. Drake, *Constantine and the Bishops*, 171–72.

cal: he might have admired the Christians as brave and fellow monotheists. This is a speculative theory, certainly, but it is as plausible an explanation for Constantine's pro-Christian actions in 306 as other solutions which have been put forth.

At the very least, we know what Constantine's feelings were about Diocletian's campaign against the Christian god years after the fact. Constantine would write in his *Oration to the Assembly of the Saints* around 325[35] that Diocletian had displayed "relentless cruelty as a persecutor," and ultimately suffered from "guilt" and "the affliction of a disordered mind." He writes:

> What then, did he gain by his active hostility against our God? Simply this, I believe, that he passed the residue of his life in continual dread of the lightning's stroke. Nicomedia attests the fact; eyewitnesses, of whom I myself am one, declare it. The palace, and the emperor's private chamber were destroyed, consumed by lightning, devoured by the fire of heaven. Men of understanding hearts [said] ... What madness is this? And what an insolent abuse of power, that man should dare to fight against God?[36]

Regardless of Constantine's immediate feelings about Diocletian's war on Christian monotheism, he would have at least witnessed the failure of Diocletian's pagan reforms, and Diocletian's gods, to bring about the peace and stability so desperately needed in the wake of the turbulent third century.

Constantine and Lactantius

At the time of Constantine's ascension in the West (305–6) the Christian teacher Lactantius, who joined Constantine's court in 310, was diligently constructing his *Divine Institutes*. An eloquent theological and historical riposte to Diocletian's anti-Christian reforms, the *Institutes* also mounted a sophisticated Christian attack against the faith's philosophical opponents like Porphyry. Seeing in Constantine's recognition of the Christian God's legitimacy a tremendous opportunity for change, Lactantius rededicated his immense treatise to Constantine around 310–13.[37] For Lactantius, this new

---

35. For the dating, see Barnes, *Constantine and Eusebius*, 153.
36. Constantine, *Orat.* 25; Constantine, *Oration of Constantine*, 579.
37. Digeser, "Lactantius and Constantine's Letter," 33–52.

emperor represented an incredible chance to advance Christianity, and to build an empire more suitable to it, and even an empire governed by it.

Digeser rightly understood Lactantius's *Divine Institutes* to be an erudite proposal for a monotheistic Roman state. A major dimension of Lactantius's proposal is the essential compatibility of pagan and Christian monotheism. While Lactantius is careful to make the proper distinction between a true "god" (like the Yahweh of the Bible), and any lesser deities (like the biblical angels who, for Lactantius, actually correspond to some of the pagan deities),[38] he is more than happy to lump in the ultimate (impersonal) realities of the philosophers with the Christian god.[39] Lactantius's goal was, ostensibly, to establish a monotheistic coalition able to be joined by Christians, solar monotheists, Hermeticists, and even sympathetic philosophers. As we will see, this harmony was presented by Lactantius to his patron Constantine as the solution to the primordial loss of man's original religion. While Digeser has produced the definitive study on Lactatnius's influence on Constantine's religious policies,[40] further analysis is required of Lactantius's effect on Constantine's understanding of the history of religion, and the proposed monotheistic state as the medicine for the consequences of that history.

As we will see in the following chapters, we have panegyric evidence from 311 clearly casting Constantine as a pagan monotheist before his public embrace of the Christian deity. Paul Stephenson noted in his 2010 biography that it may have been as early as 312 that Constantine, as a pagan, recognized the God of the Christians as a manifestation of the Supreme God.[41] But this could have occurred to Constantine at least as early as 310, when Lactantius began to teach Christianity to Constantine at his court in Trier, and when Lactantius was finishing the first edition of his *Divine Institutes*.[42] There is an interesting correlation between the completion of the *Institutes*, the arrival of Lactantius in Constantine's court, and Constantine's apparent shift in religious interests. Constantine had featured many traditional deities on his coins before 310; Mars, for example,

---

38. Lactantius, *Inst.* 1.7.5–12.

39. See Lactantius's affirmation that Plato, Aristotle, Antisthenes, Thales, Pythagoras, Anaximenes, Cleanthes, Cyrippus, Zeno, Seneca, and Tullius all assert the monarchy of "the Supreme God," in Lactantius, *Epit.* 1.4.

40. Digeser, *Making of a Christian Empire*.

41. Stephenson, *Constantine*, 169.

42. See Stephenson, *Constantine*, 170. See also Digeser, "Lactantius and Constantine's Letter," 33-52.

seems to have been a favorite deity.[43] But beginning in 310, his coins begin to prominently feature Sol Invictus, and other Roman deities disappear from Constantine's coins after the year 317, while Sol Invictus remains until around 320–25. Exposure to Lactantius's teaching probably convinced Constantine that the Christian deity was Sol Invictus, the Supreme God. This would provide a reason for his reported invocation of the Christian God at the battle of Milvian Bridge in 312, and the martial success which followed doubtless galvanized this belief.

Ultimately, I suggest that sometime between 305–10, Constantine became a pagan monotheist, and as early as 310, he became convinced of the compatibility of pagan and Christian monotheism. As Drake rightly concluded, Constantine was "led first to monotheism, then to Christianity."[44] But there is an overarching metanarrative which provided the context for this evolution, and one which continued to provide the theological framework for both Constantine's propaganda and his own self-image. For this we will now turn to religious historiography in late antiquity.

---

43. See Bardill, *Constantine*, 87.
44. Drake, *Constantine and the Bishops*, 190.

4

A History of Religion: The Decline of Monotheism

CENTURIES BEFORE CONSTANTINE'S REIGN, there had emerged a historiographical trend among both pagans and Christians which represented human religion in terms of what I call a decline-of-monotheism narrative. Variations of the narrative existed, but in essence it was said that the original religion of mankind had been a pure monotheism, and that the presence of this true religion on earth had provided a golden age of human prosperity. But mankind had eventually fallen into error, and into the worship of idols and many gods. Traditional worship of the Roman deities thus represented a tragic human innovation, and was the underlying cause of widespread theological confusion and social breakdown. It was not thought, however, that this primitive monotheism was entirely out of reach. If the ancient worship of the Supreme God were revived, then one might restore also the stability and prosperity which such worship engendered.[1]

On the pagan side of things, precedent is found for the decline-of-monotheism narrative in Varro. Roman scholar Marcus Terentius Varro (d. 27 BCE) had dreamt of a decline of an "original aniconic religion," which had recognized one God, into the worship of many gods and idolatry.[2] Varro cited the Jews as an example of those men who had preserved

---

1. The modern case for an original monotheism, or *Urmonotheismus*, is made by Winfried Corduan in his *In the Beginning God* (2013). Corduan builds on the work of anthropologist Wilhelm Schmidt (d. 1954), who opposed the widespread assumption that the arrival monotheism was a slow process in human religion in *Der Ursprung der Gottesidee* (1912). Most anthropologists have not been persuaded by Schmidt's vision. See Evans-Pritchard, *Theories of Primitive Religion*, 104–5.

2. See Harding, *Paul's Eschatological Anthropology*, 35. Augustine writes of Varro's belief that "for more than 170 years, the Romans of old worshipped gods without an image. 'If this practice had remained down to the present day,' he says, 'the gods would

an original, aniconic monotheism.³ Augustine recalls Varro's belief that Jupiter "is worshipped, though called by another name, even by those who worship one God only, without an image."⁴ Jupiter was, Varro thought, the God of the Jews.⁵

The first-century CE writer Plutarch likewise claimed that Roman religion was once aniconic, and ultimately that the ancient Romans had been convinced that "it was impossible to apprehend Deity except by the intellect."⁶ Frederick Brenk has argued, and rather persuasively, that Plutarch was a monotheist, not unlike to the Jewish Philo.⁷ Other Roman writers, like Virgil, Ovid, and Cicero, despite their own theological opinions, also reported that there was once a golden age when only one god was worshiped, and thus when Rome was full of justice.⁸

As for a Christian precedent for this historiography, the Apostle Paul, in the opening of his letter to the Romans (1:18–32), taught that the current paganism in the Roman world was a distortion of an aniconic monotheism originally shared by all mankind.⁹ Paul also believed that the only way to apprehend this true religion was the renewal or transformation of νοῦς (mind).¹⁰ The monotheism which Paul has in view is ultimately, and in a way surprisingly reminiscent of Plutarch, one that can and should be arrived at through the exercise of man's God-given intellect.¹¹ Reflecting on Romans 1:20–32, we find that Paul's representation of pagan past is "a history of decline, drastically moving away from its original monotheistic

---

have been worshipped with greater purity'. . . He clearly wishes it to be understood that error already existed even when there were no images . . . he would certainly have held that one God should be worshipped, and also that he should be worshipped without an image" (Augustine, *City of God*, 4.31; Augustine, *City of God Against the Pagans*, 183).

3. Van Kooten, "Pagan and Jewish Monotheism," 641.

4. Augustine, *City of God*, 4.9; Augustine, *City of God Against the Pagans*, 154.

5. Van Kooten, "Pagan and Jewish Monotheism," 641n25.

6. Plutarch, *Num.* 8.8; Plutarch, *Plutarch's Lives*, 335. See Thiessen, *Paul and the Gentile Problem*, 49.

7. Brenk, "Philo and Plutarch," 79–92.

8. Bowlin, "Tolerance among the Fathers," 25.

9. Van Kooten, "Pagan and Jewish Monotheism," 633.

10. Rom 12:2; cf. Rom 7:23–25. For analysis of Paul's use of νοῦς, see Harding, *Paul's Eschatological Anthropology*, 150–58, 225, 262.

11. Rom 1:20; 12:1–2. As Harding notes, this demonstrates that Paul was "well-versed in the Greek, mainly Platonic and Stoic discussions of 'intelligent design' that recognized the existence of God from the apparent design of the cosmos" (Harding, *Paul's Eschatological Anthropology*, 35). Cf. Cicero, *Nat. d.* 2.2.

and aniconic stance... This historiography is remarkably similar to that of the antiquarian of Roman religion, Varro."[12] For Paul, it was precisely the loss of original monotheism that precipitated the degradation of society on every level. Implicitly, then, the restoration of human society might be accomplished by its revival. After differentiating between the ancient "golden age" of human religion and current paganism, Paul ultimately "represents his own religion as a 'logical, i.e., non-ritualistic form of worship' which restores the ideal."[13] Paul's Jewish-Christian monotheism is thus not only required for the restoration of proper society, but is even now accessible through its pagan analogies. All of this thinking would have resonated with both Lactantius and Constantine.[14] As we will later see, Paul's idea that the true and primordial religion was to be apprehended specifically by νοῦς would have been especially appreciated by the emperor.

Euhemerism

In the second and third centuries CE, the tendency of Christian apologists was to support the decline-of-monotheism narrative by employing a euhemeristic history of religion.[15] The third-century BCE mythographer Euhemerus (d. 250 BCE) had long ago offered a historical explanation for the existence of the traditional pantheon: these deities, he argued, were actually historical human figures who, in the memories of their later admirers, were promoted to godhood. Such views can actually be found in earlier Greek works by Xenophanes (d. 475 BCE) and Herodotus (d. 425 BCE), though their legacy was perhaps most famously perpetuated by Euhemerus, the Roman poet Ennius (d. 169 BCE), and the historian Diodorus (d. 30 BCE).[16] Christian apologists naturally found such Greek historiography congenial to their own opinion that the traditional deities

---

12. Paul "stresses the fact that the pagans have fallen away from their original knowledge of the one God, have changed the glory of the immortal God into an image, and have altered the truth of God into a lie. This clearly implies that Paul postulates an initial golden age of pure intellectual worship without images" (Van Kooten, "Pagan and Jewish Monotheism," 637).

13. Van Kooten, "Pagan and Jewish Monotheism," 633.

14. Van Kooten, "Pagan and Jewish Monotheism," 633.

15. For an introduction to Euhemerism, see Roubekas, "What is Euhemerism?" 30–37.

16. See Euhemerus of Messene, *Sacred Inscription*; Ennius, *Euhemerus*; Diodorus Siculus, *Bibliotheca Historica*.

and their rites were the products of human invention. It also supported their view, predicated on the book of Genesis, that monotheism had been the original religion of mankind. Unsurprisingly, the Christian apologists used euhemerism to bludgeon their pagan interlocutors. As Clement of Alexandria (d. 215 CE) once mocked his opponents: "Those whom you worship were once men like you!"[17]

A typical Christian enhancement of euhemerism contended that the process by which these historical men had come to be imagined as deities was motived by demons. Sometimes the traditional gods were actually said to be demons themselves. This seems to have followed an ancient Mosaic tradition, expressed most clearly in the book of Deuteronomy, where we read that apostate Israelites who worshiped the deities of the other nations in reality "sacrificed to demons who were not God, to gods whom they have not known, new gods who came lately, whom your fathers did not dread" (Deut 32:15). Such a view was, of course, perpetuated by Paul, who warned the early Christian communities that "the things which the Gentiles sacrifice, they sacrifice to demons and not to God" (1 Cor 10:20a).

Later Christians in the Roman empire, striving against their many critics and persecutors, effectively combined these Mosaic and early Christian interpretations of paganism with the euhemeristic explanations of the Greeks, and ultimately used such notions to support a grand decline-of-monotheism narrative. As we will now see, two Christian teachers known by Constantine (Eusebius and Lactantius) were, in fact, readers of Diodorus and Ennius,[18] and with this background they presented monotheism to the emperor as the most original of mankind's religions.

The Narrative in Lactantius

Lactantius's *Divine Institutes* grandiosely carries on the tradition of the decline-of-monotheism narrative. He writes that the traditional polydeism which had long dominated the empire was an error, and that monotheism had been the original religion of Rome. He argues that pagan claims to the most ancient tradition are the result of ignorance, and he lambasts his philosopher opponents who have failed to see that religion and wisdom are interlinked and that Christianity grants access to the truth about God.[19]

---

17. Clement, *Chortatio ad gentes*, 8.152.
18. Roubekas, *Ancient Theory of Religion*, 181.
19. Lactantius, *Inst.* 1.23.5; see Stephenson, *Constantine*, 170. See also Schott,

Lactantius, true to Christian form, reinforces these arguments with an extended euhemeristic history of religion.

In Book I, Lactantius traces the development of traditional paganism backwards into the foggy era of Saturn and Jupiter (whom he takes to have been historical persons) before the fall of Troy (some 1,800 years prior to his own time).[20] Diocletian's patron deity, Jupiter, had not been a deity at all, but a man, and one who stole the worship of the true God for himself.[21] Jupiter (whom Digeser has convincingly argued is a cipher for Emperor Diocletian throughout the *Institutes*) is made the primary culprit in leading mankind into a world-without-monotheism.[22] In this way, Lactantius explains that all the cults of the world were based on error and "stupid human consensus."[23] He addresses Constantine: "When I consider the earlier state of humanity and ponder in my soul, O Emperor Constantine, it often seems equally marvelous and ridiculous that the stupidity of one age founded the various religions."[24] For him, the foolishness of their ancestors (who had imagined that historical human beings like Jupiter were deities), was to blame for the eclipse of monotheism and the sad state of world affairs.

In Book II, Lactantius travels back further to the beginning of human history, starting in the book of Genesis. Here he demonstrates that all mankind had once appreciated an original monotheism, and that this religion had remained pure until the time of the Flood. It was after Noah's son Ham lost his inheritance (which was nothing less than the pure monotheism which God had intended to preserve through him) that errors crept into human religion: the Canaanites, the descendants of Ham, were the first to corrupt their way and reject "the cult of the true God," and they simply handed their error down.[25] The Egyptians had made some advances in the recovery of true religion when they turned their attention towards the starry lights of heaven, but they ultimately fell short, having deified their pharaohs and represented divinity with idolatrous symbols of animals.[26]

Christianity, 99.

20. Lactantius, *Inst.* 1.22.27, 1.23.2.

21. Lactantius, *Inst.* 5.5.3–5.6.6.

22. Just as Jupiter had campaigned against the worship of the true God in ages past, so Jupiter's later servant Diocletian followed in his footsteps.

23. Lactantius, *Inst.* 2.1.1.

24. Lactantius, *Inst.* 4.1.1; Schott, *Christianity*, 107.

25. Lactantius, *Inst.* 2.13.7–8.

26. Lactantius, *Inst.* 2.13.11–12. For Lactantius, man was made to walk upright, so

All of these corruptions since the Flood, Lactantius argues, were initiated by the influence of demons.[27] In Book IV, he explains that the demons worshiped as deities by the pagans "are the same ones who established various cults for themselves in different regions for the purpose of casting humans down, taking false names in order to deceive . . . they took the names of powerful kings as their own, so that, under these false names, they might win divine honors for themselves."[28] As Schott observes, it is here that Lactantius "goes beyond a basic Stoic dichotomy between the state of nature and the contrivance of human civilization. Traditional cults are not only products of human history, they are also a demonic masquerade."[29] Interestingly, Lactantius even goes beyond other Christian authors by conceding that at least some of the traditional deities actually correspond not to demons but to the good angels.[30]

Lactantius ultimately differentiates between *falsae religiones* and *vera religio*—the former is the product of demons and ignorance, the latter is the product of heaven and transcends human contrivance. Like Paul, Lactantius presents Christianity as the most rational religion which restores the ideal. Jill Harries notes that:

> By rooting Christian monotheism in an earlier, Saturnian Golden Age, where true justice prevailed, Lactantius invited monotheists in general to accept that they had more in common with Christianity than with the decayed and corrupted gods of Roman polytheism. Use of this argument suggests that Lactantius may have envisaged some kind of monotheistic coalition of Christians with sympathetic non-Christians, which he could deploy against polytheism, arguing, as did many Christian apologists, that the legends about the immoral behavior of the Olympian gods, Jupiter not least, discredited their worship.[31]

---

that he might look to the heavens and ultimately perceive the transcendent Creator. See also *Inst.* 2.1.16. Schott believes Lactantius is implying that the Christians, "the devotees of the true highest God, are the only authentic humans. The devotees of the *falsae religiones*, however, are troglodytes bent under the weight of cultural detritus and demonic oppression" (Schott, *Christianity*, 101).

27. Lactantius, *Inst.* 2.16.1-3
28. Lactantius, *Inst.* 4.27.17; Schott, *Christianity*, 103.
29. Schott, *Christianity*, 100.
30. Lactantius, *Inst.* 1.7.5–12.
31. Harries, *Imperial Rome AD 284 to 363*, 97.

To further support his vision of religious history, Lactantius employs Hermetic tradition. He speaks often of the pagan prophet Hermes Trismegistus, and his disciple Asclepius, as both historical persons and philosophical authorities.[32] He believed this Hermes, sometimes called by his Roman name of Mercury, to have been a real contemporary of Moses, and one who had passed his own wisdom to the Greek sages.[33] Lactantius is clearly sympathetic to Hermes and his books, and can even be called an "admirer."[34] The contents of the Hermetic tractates *Poimandres* and *The Asclepius* are well-known by Lactantius,[35] and in his own *Institutes* he regularly and enthusiastically summons those works to support his own Christian doctrines.[36] Though modern scholars believe Hermes Trismegistus was only a syncretic blend of the Egyptian god Thoth and the Greek deity Hermes,[37] Lactantius tells us: "He was a man, yet he was of great antiquity, and most fully imbued with every kind of learning, so that the knowledge of many subjects and arts acquired for him the name Trismegistus ["Thrice-great"]."[38]

In the Hermetic book *The Asclepius*, Lactantius locates yet another portrait of paganism as a history of decline. This time, the narrative is in the form of a prophecy of Hermes: Egypt, which at the time of Hermes and his disciples was still privileged to know true religion, would one day fall into theological

---

32. See for example Lactantius, *Inst.* 2.9, 16; 4.4, 6, 8; 5.25; 7.4, 13, 18. Lactantius was not the first apologist to take notice of Hermes's theological affinity with Christianity— "Athenagoras (second century), one of the first Christians to mention Hermes, cited his Greek epithet Trismegistus and claimed Hermes as witness to a euhemeristic explanation of the gods, according to which belief in them arose from the adoration of rulers and sages of earlier times. Tertullian (born ca. 160, died after 220) called him the 'teacher of all natural philosophers'; although he admitted that Hermes' wisdom surpassed that of Plato, the Pythagoreans, and the Stoics, Tertullian nevertheless reproached him for ignorance regarding the origin of matter. A number of individual Hermetic *dicta* were handed down by Christian writers. Eusebius called Hermes the earliest harbinger of Christ and cited Philo of Byblos, who, with Athenagoras, was the first to mention the epithet Trismegistus. In the pseudo-Justinian *Admonitions to the Hellenes*, Hermes is counted among the prophets; according to this text, one should 'allow himself to be led by . . . Hermes, to knowledge of the true God'" (Ebeling, *Secret History of Hermes Trismegistus*, 43).

33. Nash, "Hermeticism," 43.

34. Nash, "Hermeticism," 43.

35. See Yates, *Giordana Bruno*, 7.

36. Lactantius, *Inst.* 1.11; 2.11, 13, 15; 4.6; 5.65; 6.25; 7.4, 9, 13; 9; 16.

37. Fowden, *Egyptian Hermes*, 22.

38. Lactantius, *Inst.* 1.6; Yates, *Giordana Bruno*, vi.

error, and then destruction.[39] As we will see in the coming chapters, the true religion of primitive Egypt, according to *The Asclepius*, resembles an inclusive monotheism in which the One God is recognized by countless names. The consequences for the loss of this holy religion are as follows: Egypt will lose influence in the world, divinity will no longer favor the land and will return to heaven, foreigners will occupy Egypt, laws will be made against true religion, and the land will be filled with tombs and corpses.[40]

This imagery would have resonated with Constantine: he had witnessed the social and political chaos caused by Diocletian's religious policies, whose recent war against Christian monotheism had been a misguided disaster, ending with his co-emperor Galerius actually begging the outlawed Christian god to heal him. Indeed, Rome, in the third century CE, had been filled with the kind of confusion, failure, and loss which Hermes had warned would travel with the decline of true religion. The imagery of Hermes's prophecy, and of the wider decline-of-monotheism narrative presented by Lactantius, would evidently stay with Constantine. In his *Oration*, Constantine attributes the ruins of Egypt which he saw on his travels

---

[39]. *Ascl.* 24.

[40]. *Ascl.* 24. Augustine would later claim that Hermes's prophecy in *Asclepius* was actually a prophecy of pagan Rome's fall to Christianity. Augustine's writings ultimately show him to be less friendly to the Hermetic works than Lactantius, using some caution as he claims Hermes for the cause of Christianity, saying: "But when Hermes predicts these things, he speaks as one who is a friend to these same mockeries of demons, and does not clearly express the name of Christ . . . he bears witness to Christianity by a kind of mournful prophecy" (Augustine, *City of God*, 8.23; Dods, *City of God*, 341–46). Though often harsh, his criticism of Hermes also appears tinged with respect. He identifies Hermes as belonging to a class of persons mentioned by Paul, who indeed knew God, "but became vain in their imaginations" (Rom 1:21-32, cf. Augustine, *City of God*, 8.23). For Hermes, says Augustine, "makes many such statements agreeable to the truth concerning the one true God who fashioned this world. And I know not how he has become so bewildered by that 'darkening of the heart' as to stumble [into idolatry]" (Augustine, *City of God*, 8.23). Lactantius ultimately cast Hermes in the same light, describing him as a teacher who "investigated almost all Truth" (Lactantius, *Inst.* 4.9). It is safe to say that the Egyptian Hermes, drawing so closely as he did towards the truth, was admired by Lactantius. Both Lactantius and Augustine after him portray Hermes as a sort of mediating figure, torn between truth (Christianity) and the pagan cults, the latter being only treasured by him, according to Augustine, while "under the influence of a demon" (Augustine, *City of God*, 8.24). Hermeticism's monotheism was nevertheless enough to earn the respect of Lactantius, and to convince him that the religion provided a bridge between Christianity and the pagan world. At the very least, Hermeticism offered further testimony to Lactantius's vision of a long-lost golden age of true religion which was in dire need of revival, a revival which now, in the wake of Constantine's ascension, might finally be achieved.

with Diocletian to the Egyptians' corrupted religion, which had eventually manifested in human sacrifice: "Therefore these nations [Egypt and Assyria] received a recompense worthy so foul a worship. Memphis and Babylon [it was declared] shall be wasted, and left desolate with their fathers' gods. Now these things I speak not from the report of others, but having myself been present, and actually seen the most wretched of these cities, the unfortunate Memphis."[41] Lactantius had also said that the ultimate end of the loss of monotheism was the arrival of human sacrifice.[42] Presumably the imagery communicated to Constantine by Lactantius remained with him even through the Arian controversy, when he openly expressed his fear of divine judgement on both himself and the empire if the Christian dispute over monotheism were not properly resolved.[43]

In Lactantius's mind, the decline-of-monotheism narrative formed the frame story in which the Constantinian drama was unfolding. Constantine's rise to power was nothing less than the Supreme God at work: Constantine had clearly been raised up by the Creator as his agent and messenger, sent to revive the ancient monotheism and to restore order to human civilization. But when did Lactantius come to this belief about the emperor? It must have been before the time of Lactantius's insertion of the dedicatory passages to Constantine in his *Divine Institutes*. Arguments for a late date for these passages have been put forth, notably by Eberhard Heck, who suggested a date between 321 and 324.[44] However, Digeser has argued convincingly from the standpoint of tone, vocabulary, and theme for a date between 310 and 313.[45]

Lactantius writes in these dedicatory verses: "This work [of putting to rest dangerous superstitions and base errors] we are now undertaking beneath the sponsorship of your name, Constantine, O greatest of emperors."[46]

---

41. Constantine, *Orat.* 16; Constantine, *Oration of Constantine*, 573.

42. "Through this subtlety and by these crafts they have caused the knowledge of the true and only God to falter among all the nations. Being destroyed by their own vices, they rage and engage in violence in order to destroy others. Thus these adversaries of mankind even devised human victims, in order to consume as many lives as they can" (Lactantius, *Inst.* 2.17).

43. Constantine, "Letter to Alexander and Arius," ca. 323–24, preserved in Eusebius, *Vit. Const.* 2.64–72.

44. Heck, *Die dualistischen Zusätze*, 143.

45. Digeser, "Lactantius and Constantine's Letter," 33–52; See also Schott, *Christianity*, 107.

46. Lactantius, *Inst.* 1.1.

Here Lactantius suggests that the Christians were now embarking on a quest to revive the truth about God in the empire, and that this was a program which had the support and approval of Constantine. "You are the first of the Roman princes," Lactantius explains, "to have repudiated errors and to have come to know and honor the splendor of the one true God."[47] Constantine is portrayed here as one in league with Lactantius; the emperor had either received Lactantius's teaching or had conducted the same history-of-religions research as his Christian advisor, and had come to the same conclusions about primitive monotheism. But had this information led Constantine to pursue a personal revolution only? Lactantius portrays Constantine's discovery of original monotheism as a global insurgency: he describes Constantine's ascension as a time when "that most happy of days dawned for the world, the day on which the most high God carried you up to the summit of power ... when you brought back justice which had been overthrown and taken away and expiated the most foul crime of the other emperors."[48] The crime of prior emperors was not only the physical persecution of Christians, but the propagation of *falsae religiones*, and the "justice" which Constantine restored was not only civil protection for Christians, but the primeval monotheism and its expected benefits for the state. For Lactantius: "This justice is nothing else but a devoted and religious worship of the one God."[49] Indeed, it was specifically "by the knowledge of the truth of God" that Constantine was "fulfilling the works of justice in every action."[50] As Lactantius says elsewhere, "Piety is nothing other than getting acquainted with God, as [Hermes] Trismegistus defined it very truly ... If it is piety to know God ... certainly he does not know justice who does not hold to the religion of God."[51]

Lactantius assures the emperor that because of his restorative work, God will reward him with a long reign, and that at the end of his life he will hand his throne to his sons in peace. The notion that political stability, particularly Constantine's position as head of state, was intrinsically tethered to the successful repudiation of theological errors and the preservation of monotheism will continue to show itself during the later Donatist and Arian conflicts.

47. Lactantius, *Inst.* 1.1.
48. Lactantius, *Inst.* 1.1; Lactantius, *Divine Institutes: Books I-VII*, 18.
49. Lactantius, *Inst.* 5.7; Lactantius, *Divine Institutes: Books I-VII*, 343.
50. Lactantius, *Inst.* 5.7; Lactantius, *Divine Institutes: Books I-VII*, 343.
51. Lactantius, *Inst.* 5.15; Lactantius, *Divine Institutes: Books I-VII*, 363.

Lactantius ultimately portrays himself as a fellow worker alongside Constantine in the cause of true religion's revival. Hitching his cart to Constantine's ox, Lactantius turns his *Divine Institutes* into only one arm of what he believed was now an *imperial* operation to restore a religious truth which at present "seems so obscure to men."[52] The original version of the *Divine Institutes* had instructed persecuted Christians to "keep calm and silent" about the truth until their vindication from God arrived.[53] The later edition, however, galvanized by Constantine's rise, includes a final panegyric to the emperor which boldly declares that now "the truth is coming forth into the clear light."[54]

According to Lactantius, Constantine was not the first man chosen by heaven to be the agent of monotheism's revival; the Supreme God had in fact worked in other eras to recover his lost worship. After Jupiter had corrupted human religion, says Lactantius, God had raised up an agent (ostensibly the man Jesus Christ though this particular text does not say so explicitly) to revive his worship on the earth:

> But God, most indulgent parent that he is, when the end of time was drawing near, sent a messenger to lead back that old age and the justice that had been routed, so that the human race would not be thrown about by great and everlasting errors. The likeness of that golden time returned, therefore, and was given back to the earth, but justice was assigned only to a few [the Christians]. This justice is nothing else but a devoted and religious worship of the one God.[55]

For Lactantius, an integral element of Jesus's mission, which at this point had been undertaken nearly three centuries prior, was to reveal this long-obscured knowledge about the unity of God.[56] Now, Lactantius concluded, it was Constantine who had been chosen by God to restore monotheism in the present age. This was Lactantius's explicit and public teaching to Constantine. He writes:

> Nor undeservedly has the Lord and Ruler of all by a love of preference chosen you as the one through whom he restored his holy religion, since you alone stood out among all as one who might

---

52. Lactantius, *Inst.* 3.1; Lactantius, *Divine Institutes: Books I-VII*, 19.
53. Lactantius, *Inst.* 7.26.8.
54. Lactantius, *Inst.* 27.1; Lactantius, *Divine Institutes: Books I-VII*, 537.
55. Lactantius, *Inst.* 5.7; Lactantius, *Divine Institutes: Books I-VII*, 343.
56. Digeser, *Making of a Christian Empire*, 34; see Lactantius, *Inst.* 1.11.5-33.

furnish outstanding examples of virtue and holiness in which you would not only equal, but even surpass (which is truly great) the glory of ancient princes whom fame numbers among the good . . . It was fitting, therefore, that in rearranging the condition of the human race, the Divine Plan should make use of you as an organizer and assistant. We beseech him with daily prayers; first, that he may guard you especially whom he wished to be a guardian of affairs; and then, that he may inspire you with the desire to persevere in the love of the Divine Name. This is salvific to all: to you for happiness, to others for peace.[57]

Though for Lactantius the beginning of Constantine's "holy reign" marked a turning of the tide, the cause of monotheism was not yet fulfilled and would require the sustained devotion of the emperor. The question remains, of course, as to whether Constantine agreed with Lactantius's portrait of pagan history, and that he should take up the role of the messiah of monotheism which Lactantius so eagerly prescribed him.

---

57. Lactantius, *Inst.* 7.27; Lactantius, *Divine Institutes: Books I–VII*, 538. Schott also recognizes that Lactantius believes Constantine "has been chosen by God to restore the ancient and natural Ur-monotheism forgotten since the development of different Euhemeristic cults among various peoples" (Schott, *Christianity*, 109). The question is: what did Constantine believe about himself?

5

Constantine as Divine Agent

WE WILL NOW BEGIN to consider whether Constantine also believed himself to be the special agent of the Supreme God, commissioned to restore universal monotheism and thus order and prosperity to the world. First, we will consider Constantine's own grand speech preserved for us by Eusebius, his *Oration to the Assembly of the Saints* (ca. 325). Here we will immediately observe that the same history-of-decline narrative found in Lactantius, Paul, and Varro provides the dramatic framework through which Constantine interprets his own activity as emperor.

The Narrative in Constantine

Constantine begins his *Oration* by explaining that human beings are naturally inclined towards the proper worship of God. In ancient times, however, human rationality had succumbed to "principles opposed to Nature," giving way to error, to the ends that "men are greedy in their withholding his rightful worship from the Lord of all."[1] Constantine, like Lactantius, takes a euhemeristic view of pagan mythology: many of the old gods were nothing but human beings and the religions they propagated were merely human developments.[2] Though this "error" was "the practice of many generations,"[3] Constantine explains that "no sooner had the radiance of the Savior's presence appeared, than justice took the place of wrong, a calm succeeded the confusion of the storm."[4] The resemblance of this passage to

---

1. Constantine, *Orat.* 1.
2. Constantine, *Orat.* 4.3.
3. Constantine, *Orat.* 1; see also *Orat.* 16.
4. As we have seen, "justice" often acts as a cipher for monotheism in the *Divine Institutes*.

CONSTANTINE AS DIVINE AGENT

Lactantius is striking: Again, Lactantius had said in his *Institutes* that God had once sent a messenger to "lead back to that old age and the justice that had been routed," and that "the likeness of that golden time returned . . . and this justice is [the] worship of the one God."[5] If Constantine agreed with Lactantius that God had once sent Jesus to reignite the flame of monotheism, did he also agree with him that the world had subsequently fallen into error once more, and again required a deliverer? Constantine indeed says that after the coming of Jesus, "the worship due to the Supreme Father and to himself should be piously performed . . . [However] once more then unholy sedition, once more war and strife prevailed . . . a craving which is contrary to nature."[6] A new agent of revival was needed, and Constantine, it is true, saw himself in the role. "I myself, then," he writes in an earlier letter to his constituents in Palestine (ca. 323),

> was the instrument whose services [the Supreme God] chose, and esteemed suited for the accomplishment of his will . . . through the aid of divine power I banished and utterly removed every form of evil which prevailed, in the hope that the human race, enlightened by my instrumentality, might be recalled to a due observance of the holy laws of God, and at the same time our most blessed faith might prosper under the guidance of his almighty hand.[7]

Here Constantine claims to not only be God's agent, but that his work has been to recall humanity back to a certain religious condition. In the final section of his *Oration*, Constantine continues to proclaim "the truth that God is the cause of the exploits I have performed," and that in his rise to power and support of Christianity, he has only followed "the commands of God," and engaged in a "holy service" towards the Deity.[8] His martial and political efforts were, he believed, the holy conduit by which "the providence of God has granted victory" to the Christian people, those few whom Lactantius had said had preserved original monotheism.[9]

The dating of Constantine's *Oration* has been disputed. Edwards dated it to Constantine's early career, around 314–15, and on these grounds used it as evidence to suggest that Constantine was not a religious syncretist,

---

5. Lactantius, *Inst.* 5.7; Lactantius, *Divine Institutes: Books I–VII*, 343.

6. Constantine, *Orat.* 1; Constantine, *Oration of Constantine*, 561.

7. Constantine, "Letter to the Inhabitants of Palestine (323 CE)," preserved in Eusebius, *Vit. Const.* 28; Constantine, *Oration of Constantine*, 507.

8. Constantine, *Orat.* 26.

9. Constantine, *Orat.* 26.

but a committed Christian and anti-pagan who immediately rejected pagan deities after 312.[10] Barnes, in a review of Edwards, swiftly corrected his dating, pointing out that Constantine's interpretation of Platonic theology (which Beatrice noticed in 2002 was acutely Hermetic) reveals a date of the 16th or 17th of April in 325.[11] What this demonstrates is that even well-into his career, Constantine both subscribed to and was motivated by the historiography of Lactantius (and other Christians and pagans), and that it continued to form the lens through which he saw himself.

The emperor's understanding of religious history depicted in his letter and his *Oration* is reinforced by another speech in Eusebius's *Life of Constantine*. Here Constantine offers a prayer to the Supreme God, describing his recent theological achievement:

> And truly our worship is no new or recent thing, but one which you have ordained for your own due honor, from the time when, as we believe, this system of the universe was first established. And, although mankind have deeply fallen, and have been seduced by manifold errors, yet have you revealed a pure light in the person of your Son, that the power of evil should not utterly prevail, and hast thus given testimony to all men concerning yourself.[12]

Digeser sees the above quotation as vague and not necessarily Christian.[13] Constantine prays against a "temples of lies" (surely against traditional polydeism and idolatry), and for "peace, undisturbed concord, and that all will be lead towards the straight path, truth, and agreement of belief."[14] Is this a pure Christianity which Constantine has in view? In this same prayer, Constantine refers to his father Constantius, a pagan monotheist, as someone who rightly and piously called on "God the Father" to bless him.[15] Digeser recognizes that Constantine's prayer could thus have a more abstract goal, like a Roman citizenry united around monotheism.[16] That Constantine believed the Supreme God had committed him to such a task, ultimately causing him, in the words of Eusebius, "to shine

---

10. Edwards, "Pagan and Christian Monotheism," 226.
11. Barnes, *Constantine and Eusebius*, 153. See Beatrice, "Word 'Homoousios.'"
12. Eusebius, *Vit. Const.* 2.57; Constantine, *Oration of Constantine*, 514.
13. Digeser, *Making of a Christian Empire*, 127.
14. Eusebius, *Vit. Const.* 2.56.
15. Eusebius, *Vit. Const.* 2.49.
16. Eusebius, *Vit. Const.* 2.49.

forth as a brilliant light in the midst of the darkness and gloomy night," will become increasingly clear.[17]

Coins and Monuments

Constantine's early coinage and architecture certainly provide powerful evidence that he saw himself as the agent of the Supreme God. As I will argue throughout the rest of this book, for Constantine, this Supreme God was a combination of Sol Invictus, the Hermetic Divine Mind, and the Christian God. With this object in view, we will begin by consulting Constantine's coinage, on which he publicly declares himself the favored partner of the Deity.

First appearing in 310, Constantine issued mints featuring Sol Invictus. Other Roman deities, like Victory and Roma (the personifications of victory and the city of Rome), disappear from Constantine's coins after the year 317, but Sol Invictus remains prominent until around 320–25. Other emperors had depicted themselves alongside Sol Invictus on their coins, with the inscription *Soli Invicto* ("To the Invincible Sun"), but Constantine elevated his intimacy with the Deity beyond his predecessors, employing the legend *Soli Invicto Comiti* ("To the Invincible Sun, my Companion"). On one medallion issued in 313 (and thus conspicuously after his reported embrace of Christianity in 312) Constantine went further still: Sol stands immediately behind Constantine, almost merging with him, under the legend "*Invictus Constantius Max Aug*" ("Invincible Constantine Greatest Emperor"). Here Constantine has directly applied the Supreme God's title to himself. As Elizabeth Marlowe writes, "the references to emperor and god flicker back and forth, one nested within the other, until the distinctions between the two begin to blur."[18]

Constantine's decision to depict himself as the Supreme God in his propaganda is significant. We recall that Diocletian had portrayed himself as Jupiter (and his co-emperor Maximian as Hercules).[19] This had served to emphasize Diocletian's message that he was the agent of the traditional pantheon

---

17. Eusebius, *Vit. Const.* 2.2. Eusebius's comment here occurs alongside a description of Constantine as God's "servant" and as a man inspired "by [God's] special guidance."

18. Marlowe, "Framing the Sun," 231.

19. Diocletian cast himself in Jovian terms, taking the name of Jupiter, and taking up Jupiter's own mantle on his coinage. See Witt, *Isis in the Ancient World*, 239. See also Barr, *Mask of Jove*, 450.

and involved in the restoration of their honor. Constantine, as Sol Invictus, was thus the agent of the Supreme God, intimately involved in the revival of monotheism. Constantine was, in effect, the anti-Diocletian.

Another image probably served to associate Constantine with the Supreme sun god: the so-called Colossus of Constantine, fragments of which are now housed at the Capitoline museum. This statue of the emperor, which would have stood roughly forty feet tall, was originally erected in the west apse of the Basilica of Maxentius near the Roman Forum.[20] The top of his head is now missing, and his temples feature large square holes. Evidently, a crown was once placed here—a radiate crown, imitating Sol Invictus.[21]

The Arch of Constantine, construction on which began in 312, likewise powerfully articulated Constantine's message that he was the Supreme God's agent. In 2006, Elizabeth Marlowe demonstrated that the arch was carefully built to align with a colossal statue of Sol Invictus (now lost) standing in Colosseum Valley.[22] The statue itself, at one point carved with the face of Nero (d. 68 CE), had long represented a blurring of the lines between the sun god and the emperor. After Nero's demise, Vespasian added a sun ray crown to the statue and rededicated it to Sol. The face was later modified to represent various emperors.[23] Now, this grand statue, with its alignment with Constantine's arch, publicly communicated Constantine's relationship with Sol.

---

20. Maxentius, Constantine's enemy, had begun construction on the building in 308. Following his defeat, Constantine completed the work in 312.

21. See Elsner, "Perspectives in Art," 263. This statue was probably originally cut as an image of Maxentius before its Constantinian renovation. Due to the reshaping, the top of the statue's head "seems too small in proportion to the overall dimensions of the face, but this would have been hidden by the addition of a metal diadem or crown; cuttings for such a headpiece are visible on both temples and on the left side of the coiffure" (Varner, *Mutilation and Transformation*, 287).

22. Marlowe, "Framing the Sun," 223–42. Pliny the Elder records the statue's height as approximately ninety-nine feet, though it may have been taller. Stephenson understands that the arch's construction was originally begun by Maxentius and that he had fashioned the colossus to wear the face of his divinized son Romulus, for whom he had also built a temple in Roman Forum. In Stephenson's view, both the arch and the colossus were later "appropriated" by Constantine. See Stephenson, *Constantine*, 141–66.

23. In 312 the statue may have even come to wear the face of Constantine, or so the firm conclusion of Stephenson. He also wonders if this is the same bronze head of Constantine now housed in the Capitoline Museums, though he does point out that its eyes and hair resemble more Constantine's style after the year 324. See Stephenson, *Constantine*, 141–66.

Marlowe's study reveals even more dramatic interplay between Sol Invictus and Constantine. Now missing from atop the arch was another approximately thirteen-foot statue of a quadriga manned by none other than Constantine himself. This was the four-horse chariot of the sun god, which Sol Invictus can be seen driving across the universe in a frieze on the eastern side of the arch. Constantine was thus portrayed as commanding the very power of the Supreme God.

Marlowe furthermore revealed that by looking at the colossus of Sol through the Arch of Constantine from various perspectives, one could gain other dimensions of this intricate propaganda. When standing in front of the arch at a distance of approximately 115 feet, the central passageway would have perfectly framed the statue of Sol standing in the background. Removing oneself to a greater distance from the arch, the top of the colossus would have eventually become obscured by Constantine's quadriga statue on the arch's top (again, blurring the lines between the Deity and his agent). But retreating to a distance of approximately 885 feet (standing near the Aqua Claudia), one's perspective would have shifted to the effect that the colossus of Sol appeared to loom over Constantine's shoulder; the Supreme God, in this "cinematic" image, looks down on his servant, protecting him and guiding him in his divine mission.[24]

Imagery such as this made it clear to Romans: Constantine operated under the provision, inspiration, and protection of Sol Invictus, the god recognized under a thousand names. In other words, Constantine had not only associated himself with solar monotheism, but was claiming to act as the special representative of this monotheistic deity on the earth. This imagery, combined with the dedicatory passages in the *Divine Institutes*, Eusebius's *Life of Constantine*, and Constantine's own *Oration*, begins to form an image of a man interested in the promotion of monotheism, and a man who believed he had been divinely inspired to do so. Again, I suggest the context for this belief is to be found in his religious historiography.

We will now better establish the nature of the emperor's early theology through an analysis of the relationship between pagan monotheism and the references to the "Divine Mind" in early Constantinian propaganda.

---

24. Marlowe, "Framing the Sun," 230.

6

The Divine Mind and Pagan Monotheism

A PROMINENT AND MYSTERIOUS feature of the propaganda from Constantine's early reign is the identification of the emperor's god as "Mind" or "the Divine Mind." We have two, perhaps three, public references to the Divine Mind and Constantine between the years 311–13 CE: the panegyric of 311, the Arch of Constantine from 312, and another panegyric in 313. This "Divine Mind" language is regularly interpreted by scholars as a deliberately vague tool used by sensitive pagans to politically cover over Constantine's embarrassing conversion to Christianity. Such analysis is overdrawn, however, and deprives this language of its religious meaning. Indeed, such explanations, as Drake rightly noted, ultimately smack of partisanship.[1] In reality, this language represents not a clever means of concealing the identity of the emperor's god, but an established theological trend in both the Hermetic tradition and solar monotheism with which Constantine was familiar. Before we investigate its presence in these traditions, however, we will need to trace the history of this theological language, beginning with Stoicism.

The Language of Mind and Monotheism

The ancient Stoics indeed spoke of *god*, for them the immanent principle governing the universe—something radically unlike the biblical God—as "mind" (νοῦς).[2] This principle not only pervaded the cosmos, but was also the rational principle within mankind; there was a fundamental link between the greater cosmic Mind and the rational mind of human beings.

---

1. Drake, *Constantine and the Bishops*, 183.
2. As has been observed, "The Stoics appear ordinarily to have spoken of 'god' as 'mind' rather than of the 'mind of god' " (Dyck, *Commentary on Cicero*, 268).

Potentially, this indwelling principle could be contemplated, and mankind enlightened. It is important to emphasize that while the Stoics also tended to call this principle "Zeus" (or "Jupiter," also *logos*, "nature," "fate," "cause," "universe"), the Stoic god was not a truly personal deity.³

This ancient Stoic conception of immanent deity as divine νοῦς is found still thriving during the twilight of the Roman Republic. Augustine records a saying from Cicero's *Hortensius* (45 BCE): "at times there was vision by the ancients, whether they were seers or interpreters of the *divine mind*, as found in sacred things and origins."⁴ And in his *De Legibus*, Cicero explains that "the highest law is the divine mind" and is "in man" (*ergo ut illa divina mens summa lex est, item, cum in homine est, perfecta est in mente sapientis*).⁵ Cicero also portrays this pervading mind as Jupiter, but this transcendent Jupiter-mind is not the personal Jupiter of the traditional pantheon, who was selfish, became angry, and cavorted with human women—nor is it anything like the biblical God.⁶ The personal language of Cicero and the Stoics (Jupiter, God, father) can be misleading, and has unfortunately launched crusades (both ancient and modern) to locate in Stoicism a nascent biblical monotheism.⁷ Seneca (d. 65 CE), for example, has suffered greatly under the pen of Christians looking to claim him as their own.⁸ Nevertheless, "his god is not, and cannot be, a personal god, though he repeatedly calls him *parens*, 'father' . . . these are hardly more than metaphors . . . Surely, Seneca's god never acquires an individual face or personality."⁹ While a despiser of the gross mythology of pagan poetry, the worship of the traditional deities of Rome was not a problem for an ultimist like Seneca. The same can be said for Cicero, who wrote that men would be wise to "preserve ancestral traditions

---

3. Indeed, "the main Stoic preoccupation was what God *does*, not what he *is* himself in absolute terms . . . no matter what the Stoic God is, it is impossible to say *what he is* in himself, since he becomes everything he does, and divine *action*, not divine *being* proper, was what Stoicism cared to pronounce" (Tzamalikos, *Anaxagoras, Origen, and Neoplatonism*, 683).

4. Augustine, *Against Julian*, 4.15.78, emphasis added.

5. Cicero, *Leg.* 3.10. For Cicero, true law has its origin in the *mens dei* (the mind of "god") or *rerum natura* (nature). As Dyck observes, in light of the established association of *mens* with *ratio*, this identification of law with the *mens dei* is not surprising (Dyck, *Commentary on Cicero*, 268).

6. See North, "Pagan Ritual and Monotheism," 38–39.

7. See, for example, the efforts of Frede, "Monotheism and Pagan Philosophy," 41–67.

8. See Setaioli, "Physics III: Theology," 389, no. 74.

9. Setaioli, "Physics III: Theology," 389.

by retaining rituals and ceremonies; and, meanwhile both the beauty of the world and regularity of celestial phenomena force us to confess the existence of an all-powerful and eternal nature which must be sustained and worshipped by the race of humans."[10]

It was in the era of Cicero and Seneca, however, that Greek philosophy was entering a new stage of syncretism. Indeed, in the first century BCE, Greek thinkers like Posidonius (ca. 135–ca. 51 BCE) and "Timaeus of Locri" (early first century BCE to early first century CE)[11] were embarking on a dynamic blend of Stoic and Platonic philosophy that would energize a new generation of religionists, notably Middle Platonists and early gnostics.[12] The divine principle of the universe, λόγος or νοῦς, which man was to contemplate in himself, was ultimately impressed into the metaphysical dualism of Platonism, and identified with Plato's transcendent principle of the One, or the Good. By at least the beginning of the common era, Roman subjects interested in personal religion had translated these ideas into theologies of a personal god. Posidonius himself speaks of a god or spirit (δαίμων) within us, intrinsically related to the transcendent god who rules the universe.[13] And here is perhaps the foundation of nearly all systems which can be approached with the "gnostic" label: mankind is to pursue knowledge of his own inner nature, by which he is connected essentially to the transcendent god above the material realm.

Among the early proponents of such theology were the Hermeticists. In 1982, Jean-Pierre Mahé published a translation of a fragment from a work entitled *Definitions of Hermes Trismegistus to Asclepius*,[14] which he dated very early, and could even place in the first century BCE.[15] There are good reasons to appreciate such an early dating, and a *terminus ad quem* within the first century CE.[16] In the fragment, we discover the following

---

10. Cicero, *Div.* 2.148–49; North, "Pagan Ritual and Monotheism," 38.

11. Timaeus of Locri may never have existed. Nevertheless, *On the World and the Soul* is attributed to him, and is representative of Middle Platonic interpretation of Plato's *Timaeus*. See Timaeus, *On the Nature of the World*.

12. For Timaeus, one of the fundamental causes of the universe is "Mind," which governs all rational beings. Posidonius believed God to be "an intelligible and fiery spirit" (Posidonius in Stobaeus, *Anthologium*, 5.7.25–26).

13. Posidonius, frag. 187.

14. Mahé, *Way of Hermes*, 99–122.

15. See Copenhaver, *Hermetica*, xliv–xlv.

16. "Since some of the aphorisms contained in the *Definitions* seem to have been known to the author of *Poimandres*, we may assume that at least the main core of this

THE DIVINE MIND AND PAGAN MONOTHEISM

saying: "Who knows himself, knows the All." As Gilles Quispel notes, this Hermetic saying "can easily be older than the *Poimandres*,"[17] which Quispel dated to the first century CE at the latest.[18]

While we do not have space to embark on a thorough inquiry into Hermetic origins and development, we may say this, at least: The Hermetic achievement was not only the identification of the Stoic mind (νοῦς) with the Platonic transcendent One, but the importation of these concepts onto a truly personal and starkly monotheistic god—the Divine Mind, the God of Light, whom the Hermeticists lovingly called "God the Father." This entity is no mere deity, but a true god who "has no parents, since he exists of himself and by himself."[19] In the Hermetica, disciples are clearly taught to worship this god,[20] and to "pray first to the Lord and Father."[21] This is not the abstraction of Stoicism.[22] Though predicated upon and ever devoted to Greek philosophy, in light of Hermeticism's offer of intimacy with a personal deity through a revealed doctrine, the Hermetic tradition stands squarely in the realm of religion.

Indeed, in Hermeticism (still often called the *religio mentis*—the religion of mind), the disciple was to obtain a loving communion of mind with the personal God of Light—*gnosis* of the great deity, and of the deity within oneself—and was promised a metaphysical union (or reunion) with his Creator after the dissolution of the body. This union with

---

collection was already extant in the first century AD. Many other parallels with the *Corpus Hermeticum*, the Excerpts of Stobaeus and various hermetic fragments suggest that the *Definitions* either antedate most of the hermetic philosophical writings which have reached us or at least do not depend directly on them. The main reason why we cannot possibly assume the reverse (i.e., that a later writer has compiled the *Definitions* by picking up various sentences from the other hermetic works) is that most often one and the same sentence of the *Definitions* simultaneously appears (albeit with different wording) in more than one hermetic text, which would be unlikely if each of these sentences had been borrowed separately from one particular writing. An early date might also be assumed for our collection of aphorisms with regard to the clarity of its style and the firmness of its thought" (Mahé, *Way of Hermes*, 101).

17. Quispel, "Hermes Trismegistus," 1.

18. Quispel, "Ascelpius," 75.

19. Lactantius's description of Hermetic theology in Lactantius, *Epit.* 1.4.

20. C.H. IX, 65.

21. C.H. V, 9.

22. Van den Broek explains that "The Hermetic doctrine of God kept close to that of the Greek philosophers, but it was not a philosophical but a religious doctrine and, therefore, the Hermetic God is often more personal and less abstract than the First Principle of philosophy" (Van den Broek, "Gnosticism and Hermetism in Antiquity," 8).

the Divine Mind did not have to wait for death, however, but could be achieved in the present through contemplation, through mystical ascent to the Light.[23] Various elaborations on these themes are present in the *Corpus Hermeticum* and in the colorful books and fragments preserved by the many authors interested in this religious tradition in antiquity. There is unfortunately not room in this study to delve into it all, and we will need to continue our focus on the Hermetic monotheism.

One element of Hermetic monotheism useful for our study is the fact that the Supreme God, like Sol Invictus, was also said to be recognizable by countless names. In *The Asclepius* we read:

> For God is the Father or the Lord of all, or whatsoever else may be the name by which he is named more holily and piously by men . . . I have no hope that the Creator of the whole Greatness, the Father and the Lord of all things [that are] could ever have one name, even although it should be made up of a multitude—He who cannot be named, or rather he who can be called by every name. For he, indeed, is One and All; so that it needs must be that all things should be called by the same name as his, or he himself called by the names of all.[24]

Even further affinity with pluriform solar monotheism can be located in this text. Speaking of Zeus, Fortune, etc., Hermes explains that:

> These hierarchies of gods, then, being thus and [in this way] related, from bottom unto top, are also thus connected with each other, and tend towards themselves; so mortal things are bound to mortal, things Sensible to Sensible. The whole of [this grand scale of] Rulership, however, seems to Him [who is] the Highest Lord, either to be not many things, or rather [to be] one. For that from One all things depending, and flowing down from it—when they are seen as separate, they're thought to be as many as they possibly can be; but in their union it is one [thing], or rather two, from which all things are made.[25]

---

23. Cf. Justin Marytr's expectation as a Christian philosopher, who wrote the he "hoped soon to gaze on God for this is the end of the philosophy of Plato" (Justin Martyr, *Dial.* 2.6).

24. *Ascl.* 20; Mead, *Thrice Greatest Hermes*, 217.

25. *Ascl.* 19; Mead, *Thrice Greatest Hermes*, 216. This passage is representative of the "monotheistic emanationism" described in the first chapter of this book: the many deities only appear to be separate but are united by an underlying principle. The two things referenced in the final clause are the one god and his demiurgical *logos*.

Lactantius's interest in Hermetic monotheism certainly involves an appreciation of names. He takes enthusiastic note of his terminological agreement with Hermes, whom he says taught of "the supreme and only God, and makes mention of him by the same names we use—God and Father."[26] The language of Hermetic monotheism provided the most direct bridge between Christian and pagan monotheism for Lactantius, and this is why the Hermetica play such a large role in his argument that the Christian deity is the best realization of the Supreme God once known by the primitive world, and since then only glimpsed by pious pagans longing for the truth.

But Hermeticism is not the only tradition with which Lactantius appreciates a terminological affinity. Lactantius says that "the diversity of titles" for God among the many pagan authors of antiquity proves no obstacle, since they are all referring to one object, but he takes special note of the use of his favorite titles "God," "Father," and "Mind" throughout pagan history. First, Lactantius recalls that the philosopher Thales had said that "God was the Mind which formed all things from water . . . Anaxagoras said that God was an infinite Mind, which moves by its own power." Aristotle, he says, also "bears witness that one Mind presides over the universe. Plato . . . plainly and openly maintains the rule of one God; nor does he name him Aether, or Reason, or Nature, but, as he truly is, God . . . And Cicero . . . frequently acknowledges God and calls him Supreme . . . he is . . . 'a Mind free and unrestrained.'"[27] Virgil (d. 19 BCE), whom Lactantius calls Maro, is praised for being "the first of our poets to approach the truth, who thus speaks respecting the highest God, whom he calls Mind and Spirit." Lactantius recalls also a time when the Senate vainly placed "Mind [*Mens*] among the gods; [but] if they had possessed any intelligence, they would never have undertaken sacred rites of this kind." This likely refers to an episode in Roman history: following a military defeat by Hannibal, an oracle had advised that a temple be built to the goddess *Mens* or *Mens Bona* ("Good Mind"). This goddess was really a personification of the attribute

26. Lactantius, *Inst.* 1.6. Lactantius notes also the Hermetic saying: "God is one, but he who is one only does not need a name; for he who is self-existent is without a name" (Lactantius, *Inst.* 1.6; Lactantius, *Works of Lactantius*, 15). Christian tradition preceding Lactantius can also be found asserting that God has no proper name: "And if we name it, we do not do so properly, terming it either the One, or the Good, or Mind, or Absolute Being, or Father, or God, or Creator, or Lord. We speak not as supplying His name; but for want, we use good names, in order that the mind may have these as points of support, so as not to err in other respects" (Clement, *Strom.* 5.12; Roberts and Donaldson, *Fathers of the Second Century*, 463–64).

27. Lactantius, *Inst.* 1.5; Lactantius, *Works of Lactantius*, 13.

which the Roman people needed to guide them to victory, and was probably only an aspect of the goddess Venus.[28] *Mens* was ultimately "a typical example of a goddess created from an abstract concept, a very Roman practice, following such examples as Concordia (304), Victoria (294), and the two temples to Spes and Fides (First Punic War), among others."[29] Indeed, Cicero lists *Mens* among the attributes which deserve deification.[30] But for Lactantius, it is absurd that *Mens* should be entered into the traditional pantheon and praised with temples in the pagan way; the Divine Mind, to him, was no abstraction, no mere attribute, and no mere deity—Mind was nothing less than the Supreme God of the Bible.[31]

By at least the fourth century, solar monotheism itself had incorporated the "Divine Mind" language. The pagan writer Maternus, a solar monotheist living in Constantine's time, wrote a vast astrological work around 336 CE, revealing much about the state of solar monotheism in the fourth century. His *Matheseos* demonstrates a vibrant solar monotheism wrapped in a combination of Neoplatonism and Stoic philosophy, and ultimately a monotheism strikingly expressed through the same language of Constantine's propaganda (which we will soon investigate). As has

---

28. The temples to *Mens* and to Venus were both recommended by the oracle, and were both consecrated on Capitoline hill in 217 BCE. The two temples were separated only by a drainage ditch. See Livy, *History of Rome*, 23.31.9: "*utraque in Capitolio est, canali uno discretae.*"

29. Orlin, *Temples, Religion, and Politics*, 102.

30. Cicero, *Nat. d.* 3.88, *Leg.* 2.19–28.

31. Christian theologians before the time of Lactantius and Constantine had described the Christian deity as *Mind*. For example, Clement of Alexandria (d. ca. 215 CE) demonstrates that some Christians had called the Christian deity "Mind, or Absolute Being, or Father, or God" (Clement of Alexandria, *Strom.* 5.12). Origen after him (184–253 CE) wrote that God is "the Mind and source from which all intellectual nature or mind takes its beginning" (Origen, *Princ.* 1.1; Green, *Gospel and the Mind*, 17).

Springing perhaps from the same well, such language and concepts would be important in the philosophy of Plotinus (204–70 CE), who identified Mind as an emanation of the One which by thinking forms the foundation of existence, and thus contains all things within it. For Plotinus, this second principle, like the first, is no personal deity— "Plotinus' divine mind is not just a mind knowing a lot of eternal objects. It is an organic living community of interpenetrating beings which are at once Forms and intelligences, all 'awake and alive,' in which every part thinks and therefore is the whole; so that all are one mind and yet each retains its distinct individuality without which the whole would be impoverished. And this mind-world is the region where our own mind, illumined by the divine intellect, finds its true self and lives its own life, its proper home and the penultimate stage on its journey, from which it is taken up to union with the Good" (Armstrong and Markus, *Christian Faith and Greek Philosophy*, 27).

been observed, the *Matheseos* "can be regarded as a summation of trends of the fourth century, one of the last great statements of the thoughts and feelings of pagan Rome."[32]

In his *Matheseos*, Maternus identifies his god as "the Sun, Best and Greatest," Jupiter's usual appellations, "who holds the center of the heavens, the Mind of the world, the moderator, Chief of all and Prince."[33] He begins his invocation of this Supreme Sun thus: "Whoever Thou art, God, who by day keeps in motion the course of the heavens . . . who strengthens the body's weakness with infusion of the Divine Mind . . . Sole Governor and Chief of all, Sole Emperor and Lord, to whom the entire force of the heavenly powers is subservient . . . Thou, Father of all and at the same time, Mother, Thou Father and Thine own Son, bound together by the chain of fate . . . Thee we worship with trembling supplication . . . May it by Thy power, whatever that may be, which guides us to that interpretation."[34]

A historical pagan association of the "Divine Mind" language in Hermeticism, the sort of solar monotheism found in Maternus, and Christianity may also be possible. Philaster (d. ca. 397), the bishop of Brescia, catalogued one-hundred-fifty-six heresies—twenty-eight Jewish and one-hundred-twenty-eight Christian—around the year 385, and his survey reveals that in the late fourth century there was a Hermetic sect in Gaul which was combining sun worship and Christianity.[35] It may ultimately be best to understand the solar monotheism of Maternus and the Hermetic monotheism as two sides of the same coin, the latter being the more philosophical, gnostic expression of solar or "light" monotheism. Evidently both pagans (like the reported Hermetic sect in Gaul) and Christians (like Lactantius) were able to discern an essential compatibility, at least on the point of monotheism, between these pagan traditions and Christianity.

In the coming sections we will consider further the "Divine Mind" language of both Maternus's solar monotheism and Hermeticism, as we introduce the propaganda of Constantine's early reign. But at this stage we can already see that Lactantius, through his court preaching, had exposed Constantine to a terminological and conceptual affinity between Christian,

---

32. Bram, *Ancient Astrology, Theory and Practice*, 2–3.

33. MacMullen, *Paganism in the Roman Empire*, 86.

34. Maternus, *Matheseos*, Liber Quintus, Praefatio, 3–4; Bram, *Ancient Astrology, Theory and Practice*, 155.

35. See Carcopino, *Aspects mystiques de la Rome*, 314; Homo, *De la Rome païenne*, 151–57.

Hermetic, and solar monotheism, which would have resonated with the emperor. And again, Lactantius also taught Constantine through his euhemeristic history that pagan monotheists and Christian monotheists have much in common, and that they should form a monotheistic coalition for the good of the empire.[36] I argue that this vision, supported by the theological language of the Divine Mind common to both Christian and pagan monotheists, stands behind Constantine's early propaganda.

The Divine Mind in Constantine's Early Propaganda

As mentioned earlier, we have two, possibly three, public references to the Divine Mind related to Constantine between the years 311–13 CE: the panegyrics of 311 and 313, and the Arch of Constantine from 312. The first example, the panegyric of 311, needs to be understood in light of the ongoing scholarly debate over Constantine's famous vision.

Scholars have long wrestled with the conflicting lines of evidence: Did the emperor's vision take place in 310 or 312? Were there multiple visions? And precisely what did Constantine see? This last question has garnered more than its fair share of attention, thanks to the contradictory reports of Constantine's historians. Eusebius says that before his battle with Maxentius, Constantine had seen a brilliant cross in the sky. The emperor and his soldiers, in the middle of the day, had looked toward the sun, seen the cross, and heard a voice saying: "conquer in this sign." After having a dream of Jesus which explained the vision, Constantine then fashioned a military standard in the shape of the symbol he had seen that afternoon—the so-called *labarum*.[37] This was the divine symbol which the emperor marched in front of his army, ensuring his miraculous victory at Milvian Bridge. But Lactantius offers a different account: it was actually during the night that Constantine had received a dream of a "heavenly sign of God," which he describes as an "intersected letter X bent around at the top."[38] Constantine was compelled by the dream, Lactantius reports, to paint this symbol on his soldier's shields. Was this a staurogram—a pictographic representation of a crucified Jesus[39]—or a Chi-Rho, the Greek monogram of Christ? How precisely did the emperor originally respond to his visionary experience?

36. See Harries, *Imperial Rome AD 284 to 363*, 97.
37. Domach, "Conversion of Constantine the Great," 210.
38. Domach, "Conversion of Constantine the Great," 210.
39. Hurtado, "Earliest Evidence," 280.

It is true that later, in the 320s, Constantine would use the Chi-Rho as a military symbol. But as far as the battle of 312, why would the Greek letters of a Chi-Rho have been used by a Latin-speaking emperor during a campaign in the Latin-speaking West? Eusebius's account does not mention any such letters. Many scholars have also pointed out that the depiction of Constantine's battle with Maxentius on his arch, constructed between 312 and 315, does not feature any sort of Christian or pseudo-Christian symbols on the accouterments of his army. Indeed, the earliest archaeological evidence we have for any Constantinian use of the explicitly Christian Chi-Rho is on the bronze coins recovered from Siscia, dating to several years after the battle in 315. Bardill has suggested that Constantine's original response to his vision was a staurogram, which he later changed into the Greek letters of the Chi-Rho.[40] But why would Constantine alter the divine talisman which he had allegedly received from Christ, and which had thus far guaranteed his victory? While the staurogram had long been used by Christians, the Chi-Rho appears to have been something of a novelty.[41] It is possible that Lactantius, writing in 315, later misinterpreted a pagan symbol, something like a six-spoked sun or star, as a Christian icon.[42] With slight modification, the language employed by Lactantius in his report of the symbol could even describe a solar disc used by sun worshipers in Constantine's Danubian homeland.[43] Alistair Kee, who focused a good deal on the *labarum*, pointed out that the very existence of the debate reveals that whatever it was, Constantine did not lead his troops against Maxentius with a simple, popular, and unmistakably Christian symbol.[44] Kee asks us not to plunge in and identify Constantine's original response to his vision as exclusively pagan or Christian; this was a new symbol of Constantine's which represented an alliance between the emperor, the "son of the sun," and the god of the Christians.[45] In the end, something like Kee's approach may be best: the whole catalogue of evidence after 312 is of a mixed character and by no means represents a clear triumph of Christianity over the pagan world. It seems reasonable to conclude that whatever sort of symbol or combination of symbols was involved, Constantine's

40. Bardill, *Constantine*, 164–66.
41. Drake, *Constantine and the Bishops*, 203.
42. Domach, "Conversion of Constantine the Great," 210.
43. Drake, *Constantine and the Bishops*, 203.
44. Kee, *Constantine Versus Christ*, 18.
45. Kee, *Constantine Versus Christ*, 20–21.

original response to his vision was likewise of a mixed character or could at least be interpreted in a variety of ways.

But then there is the equally difficult question of how many visions of Constantine we are actually dealing with. Complicating the situation further, we must consider the overlap which the alleged Christian experience(s) of 312 appear to have with an explicitly pagan vision which took place earlier in the year 310. While traveling with his army in northern France, Constantine is said to have turned aside to "the most beautiful temple in the whole world," and experienced a luminous sight: several brilliant wreaths in the sky were offered to him, accompanied by a divine message informing him that it was his destiny to rule the world. The pagan panegyrist reporting on this incident in 311 says that this had been a vision of the sun god in the visage of Apollo. Furthermore, the panegyrist says that Constantine had seen his own likeness in the sun god's face.[46] How are we to reconcile all of these accounts, each of which feature visions of heavenly symbols and promises of victory by divine figures?

We will not have room to embark on a proper inspection of this protracted controversy, but we will take note of the significant and influential contribution of German scholar Peter Weiss. First presented in 1989 before being published in 1993 and 2003, Weiss's argument has offered a powerful solution to the seemingly contradictory lines of evidence.[47] Weiss proposed that in 310, Constantine had observed a phenomenon known as a "solar halo" in the sky, an optical effect caused by sunlight refracting through ice crystals in the upper atmosphere, and which very often resembles a cross of a light.[48] Weiss furthermore proposed that Constantine had originally interpreted this as a pagan vision—as a sign of favor from the sun god. However, Constantine later interpreted this as a Christian vision, and reported it as such to Eusebius. Constantine's pagan vision of

46. "You saw yourself in the likeness of him to whom the divine songs . . . prophesized that rule over the whole world was due" (Pan. VII, 21.5).

47. Weiss, "Die Vision Constantins," 143–69, translated into English by A. R. Birley with revisions as "Vision of Constantine," 237–59.

48. I believe the several wreaths mentioned by the panegyrist of 311, which for his future reign "carried a portent of thirty years," may also correspond to the *parhelia*, or "sun dogs," which often accompany this spectacle. One of the earliest depictions of a solar halo with sun dogs, a 1520 painting in the German *Book of Miracles*, depicts three circular suns in a row. I also believe that Eusebius, in a panegyric presented to Constantine at the end of the emperor's life, refers to these same wreaths, now understood to be gifts from the Christian god: "God himself . . . awards him now with tricennial crowns made of times of prosperity . . . three circles of ten years" (Eusebius, *Vit. Const.* 6.1).

310, and the Christian vision of 312 famously described by Eusebius, are one and the same. The originally pagan experience of the sun god, far removed from the context of Milvian Bridge, had only been reinterpreted in a Christian context years later.[49]

While Weiss offered a compelling solution, we ultimately may not need to resort to such an explanation. Indeed, Constantine could have simply had more than one vision. Eusebius reports that Constantine had "thousands" of visions and dreams.[50] It is no surprise, as Drake points out, that Constantine was an extremely "vision-prone emperor in an age that expected its rulers to manifest these kinds of ties with a divine being."[51] Drake furthermore observed that the ongoing debate over which reported vision (310 or 312) was more genuine "is a good example of how misleading it can be to make [his conversion] hinge on the single event of 312, because the debate ignores the most important feature of these two visions, which is the remarkable consistency between them: in the one, Constantine sees Apollo, a solar deity; in the other, he sees a cross superimposed over the sun. In both, the guarantee of success is an important element, as is the sense of a close personal relationship."[52] Ultimately, I believe Drake was right when he colored the long debate over the nature of the vision(s) a "diversion."[53] Indeed, how the vision(s) were interpreted by Constantine and by those around him matters far more than what he actually saw.[54] In this light, we should focus our efforts not on crosses and monograms and halos, but on which god Constantine believed had assured him total victory.

In 2011, Barnes agreed with Weiss's conclusion, that Constantine had reinterpreted an originally pagan experience as a Christian vision. But Barnes hastily claimed that "in 312 [Constantine] declared that he had come to the conclusion that the god who had revealed himself was not Apollo, but the God of the Christians."[55] It is just as plausible, however,

---

49. Of course, we are not forced to conflate the visions. Constantine could very well have had two visions, one in 310 and one in 312. But Weiss's scenario has certainly presented the most comprehensive solution.

50. See Nicholson, "Constantine's Vision of the Cross," 309.

51. Drake, *Constantine and the Bishops*, 188.

52. Drake, *Constantine and the Bishops*, 189–90.

53. Drake, *Constantine and the Bishops*, 198.

54. Drake, *Constantine and the Bishops*, 198.

55. Barnes, *Constantine*, 80.

and I believe more so, that Constantine believed the sun god *was* the god of the Christians.

The panegyric of 311 no doubt refers to this great solar deity which Constantine had encountered in his 310 vision, and provides the earliest extant reference to the "Divine Mind" in relation to Constantine. The poet refers first to the wise plans which Constantine had devised in his own mind, but then he says that "things sent from heaven come swiftly to earth, for thus does that Divine Mind which governs the entire earth create immediately what it conceives." He then identifies this Supreme Deity as "the ally and comrade of his majesty." Here there is an important connection made between the mind of Constantine and the supreme Mind of the cosmos, which is, as we will see, a predominant theme of both Maternus's *Matheseos* and the Hermetic *Asclepius*. As has been furthermore observed, this is "the first affirmation of monotheism in the panegyrics."[56] Though Eusebius would later report that it was in the following year after this panegyric was written (312) that Constantine would turn to monotheism, the evidence continues to suggest that Constantine, as a pagan, was already a monotheist.

We must keep in mind that a panegyric, by nature, intends to appeal to its subject's tastes. The panegyrists "couched their requests in language that the emperors wanted to hear."[57] Constantine had certainly made his penchant for solar monotheism well-known, at the very least by his publicized relationship with the sun god described in the panegyric of 307, his solar-themed vision of 310, and then by his solar (monotheistic) coinage beginning circulation in that same year. Going further, I suggest that Constantine had either personally promoted Sol Invictus as the Divine Mind in some public way, or that solar monotheism had already begun to be cast by its adherents in this language, as found so visibly in Maternus (ca. 336). Regardless, the pagan identification of Sol Invictus as the Divine Mind must have been current sometime before 311, otherwise the 311 panegyrist would not have described the Divine Mind as the personal "ally and comrade" of Constantine, which is precisely how the emperor's coins had officially designated Sol Invictus since 310.

Ultimately, this "Divine Mind" language, able to be appreciated by Hermetic, solar, and Christian monotheists, as well as by philosophical ultimists,

---

56. Pichon, *Ecrivains profanes*, cited in Nixon and Rodgers, *In Praise of Later Emperors*, 280. For a possible contender for the "earliest" mention of monotheism in imperial panegyrics, cf. Pan. XI, 14.2 (291 CE), which refers to the traditional, personal Jupiter in terms of the Stoic panentheism.

57. Digeser, *Making of a Christian Empire*, 28.

was designed to "tap into a wider monotheistic discourse."[58] There is no need to follow the scholarly tendency to see the panegyrist's reference to the Divine Mind as merely a cover shielding a delicate public from the emperor's appalling conversion to Christianity. For Constantine, this was a reference to the Supreme God—Sol Invictus, the Divine Mind, the god of the Christians—a deity to which all of Rome should, in his mind, be able to rally.

The second reference to the "Divine Mind" is arguably located on the Arch of Constantine, under construction in Rome from 312–15. Constantine's solar monotheism, so dramatically proclaimed in the arch's imagery and careful architectural staging, provides the theological backdrop for its massive central inscription: "*quod instinctu divinitatis mentis magnitudine*" (often translated as "with inspiration of divinity and greatness of mind"). Glen Bowersock has suggested that the phrase *mentis magnitudine* "may be interpreted more plausibly as the *divina mens* than as the *mens* of Constantine himself."[59] Others have nevertheless argued that *mentis magnitudine* refers to Constantine, appealing to the panegyrist of 313's usage of similar language to refer to the greatness of Constantine's own mind.[60] In light of Constantine's penchant for Hermeticism, this flexibility may be deliberate.

In the Hermetica familiar to Constantine, the identification of the human mind as the proper means of divine communion is a major theme, as is the dramatic enhancement which the human mind is said to experience upon achieving unity with God. Indeed, Hermes speaks of men who "have won such rapture that they have obtained a share of that Divine Sense of intelligence which is the most Divine of Senses, found in God and man's reason."[61] The special intelligence gained through this communion of mind is ultimately cast in terms of illumination, and in ways typical of solar monotheism: "For as the world is illuminated by the Sun, so is the mind of man illuminated by that Light; nay, in [still] further measure . . . once the [Higher] Sense hath been commingled with the soul of man, there is at-onement from the happy union of the blending of their natures; so that minds of this kind are never more held fast in errors of darkness."[62]

Regardless of whether or not we conclude that such thinking provides the background for the arch's inscription, we should at least agree with the

58. Harries, *Imperial Rome AD 284 to 363*, 156.
59. Bowersock, "From Emperor to Bishop," 302–3.
60. Barnes, *Constantine*, 19–20.
61. *Ascl.* 7; Mead, *Thrice Greatest Hermes*, 203.
62. *Ascl.* 10; Mead, *Thrice Greatest Hermes*, 214.

majority of scholars that the arch refers to Constantine's inspiration by a god.[63] The question is, which god? In light of Elizabeth Marlowe's evidence, it must be the Supreme God, the Invincible Sun, so powerfully portrayed as the personal god of the emperor in the arch's architecture.[64] Ralph Novak, while rightly noting that "there are no Christian symbols on the Arch of Constantine," still described the inscription as a "vague reference" to Constantine's "unnamed patron deity," designed to politically obscure the identity of the emperor's "still rather disreputable" Christian god.[65] But such assessments ignore the fact that the arch, with its meticulous architecture, as well as its detailed frieze of Sol, boldly proclaims Constantine's relationship with the pagan deity Sol Invictus, and thus with pagan monotheism. Martin Wallraff, on account of the arch being "full of solar symbols," rightly concluded that even in the year 315, the year of the arch's completion, we can be sure that "Sol Invictus was at least as important to Constantine as Jesus Christ."[66] Barnes, however, in 2011, completely ignored Marlowe's architectural evidence, and quickly brushed Wallraff aside.[67] He furthermore claimed that Constantine had *nothing to do with the arch*—it was the "non-Christian Senate" who had proposed the inscription and had cleverly concealed the emperor's true deity.[68] Bardill rightly notes, however, that "even assuming that the Senate took the lead, it is unlikely to have undertaken a construction or composed an inscription of which the emperor might disapprove."[69] Constantine's own religious preferences were indeed the impetus for the "Divine Mind" language in both the panegyrics and the solar-themed arch, but such language was not designed to preserve the

---

63. See Bardill, *Constantine*, 224, who also reflects on Noel Lenski's intriguing suggestion that the god who inspired Constantine was "not named" on the arch as a deliberate strategy to prevent the god from being invoked by Constantine's enemies, who might draw the god's favor away (224–25). However, as Bardill notes, there are other similar instances in which the Supreme Deity is not named, for example, Licincius's letters to the governors in 313 refer to a "Supreme Deity" (*summa divinitas*) and to "whatever deity there is in the seat of heaven" (*quicquid divinitatis in sede caeleste . . . possit existere*). Licinius' army also prayed to the "Supreme Deity . . . Holy God." Bardill agrees that Licinius would have personally believed this deity to be Zeus, but notes that the prayer would have proved acceptable to both pagans and Christians in his army (Bardill, *Constantine*, 226).

64. See Marlowe, "Framing the Sun," 223.

65. Novak, *Christianity and the Roman Empire*, 161.

66. Wallraff, "Constantine's Devotion to the Sun," 256.

67. Barnes, *Constantine*, 23.

68. Barnes, *Constantine*, 19.

69. Bardill, *Constantine*, 224.

THE DIVINE MIND AND PAGAN MONOTHEISM

pagan world from the shocking advent of Christianity—it was language already typical of both pagan and Christian monotheisms. If some "political" purpose did energize its design, it was surely the unity of the pagan and Christian worlds beneath the banner of the Supreme God.

Finally, we turn to the pagan panegyric of 313. Here, the poet reflects on Constantine's great victory over his enemies: "Truly Constantine, you have some secret communion with the Divine Mind itself (*illa Mens Divina*), which having delegated our care to the lesser gods, deigns to reveal himself to you alone."[70] The poet also says that Constantine was given council by "divine will" (*divinum numen*) and "guided by divine inspiration" (*divino monitus instinctu*).

Hermeticism may also shed light here: in the Hermetica known by Constantine, such intimate, even "secret" communion was a prize gained only by special election. Hermes says that "Some, then, though they be very few, endowed with the Pure Mind, have been entrusted with the sacred charge of contemplating Heaven."[71] That especially pious and fortunate individuals alone have the mental capacity for communion with the Divine Mind is found not only in the Hermetica, but probably in the panegyric of 313 to Constantine: here Constantine, bypassing the lesser deities, had established a special relationship with the Divine Mind, attaining a mystical union with the sun god, the God of Light, Sol Invictus. This special communion, achieved by (Constantine's) mind alone, had imparted heightened intelligence and wisdom (Hermes calls this "true reason"[72]). This is how Constantine was understood to have outsmarted his enemies and established his reign. To quote the 313 panegyric, he was "guided by divine inspiration" (*divino monitus instinctu*). To quote the inscription on the arch, he was able to deliver Rome from her tyrant precisely "because he, inspired by the divine" had therefore a "greatness of his mind."

As Bardill noted in the 313 panegyric, "the orator has no shame in claiming more than one god, although these many gods are inferior to the Divine Mind, with which the emperor is privileged to have a connection."[73] Noteworthy also is the poet's reference to "the Greatest Creator of the universe," who goes by "as many names as there are languages of mankind." The pluriform monotheism associated with Sol Invictus is manifest here, and is

---

70. Pan. XII, 5 in Nixon and Rodgers, *In Praise of Later Emperors*, 296.
71. *Ascl.* 9: tr. Mead, *Thrice Greatest Hermes*, 206.
72. *Ascl.* 7.
73. Bardill, *Constantine*, 226.

likewise reminiscent of the monotheism of *The Asclepius*. Hermes's reference in that text to "the Creator of the whole Greatness" certainly reminds us of the 313 panegyrist's reference to "the Greatest Creator of the universe," but even more striking is the alignment between the Constantinian and the Hermetic gods' ability to be "called by every name."

What about the solar monotheism of Maternus, who lived during Constantine's reign? Describing the great "Creator," Maternus calls his god "that highest divinity, the ruling God who has organized all things under the rule of law." He furthermore says that "by the same law Divine Mind is transfused into earthly bodies, that descent is allotted through the Sun . . . For the Divine Mind is diffused throughout the whole body of the universe as in a circle."[74] Maternus also reveals that "God the Creator of man" has animated mankind "by the breath of the Divine Mind."[75] He repeatedly attests that "the spirit of the Divine Mind has poured itself into the [human] body."[76] As in *The Asclepius*, and in the 313 panegyric, we find here a pagan monotheism in which all other deities are subjected to a single power, a Supreme Deity cast in the language of "Divine Mind" who grants divine inspiration to his worshipers. All of this aligns with the Constantinian sources, and in a powerful way: Maternus speaks of himself as one having "a mind infused with divine inspiration" (*sed animus divina inspiratione formatus*); the 313 panegyrist likewise says that Constantine was "guided by divine inspiration" (*divino monitus instinctu*).

In a fascinating passage, the 313 panegyrist appears to speculate on whether the divine inspiration came from Constantine himself, or from "a certain force or Divine Mind which is infused into the whole world and mixed with all the elements" (*quaedam vis Mensque Divina . . . quae toto infusa mundo*), or from "some Power above all the heavens who looks down upon this work of his from the higher citadel of nature" (*Aliqua supra caelum Potestas . . . quae . . . ex altiore naturae arce despicias*). The panegyrist's apparent speculation in the quotations above has been a source of scholarly debate: was the poet unsure of Constantine's evolving theology? Was he uncertain if he should represent Constantine himself as a god? Or perhaps the poet was leaving Constantine's religion ambiguous, as is so often argued by scholars, in light of the emperor's conversion to Christianity? Fourth-century solar monotheism may again prove

---

74. Maternus, *Matheseos*, Liber Primus, 5.7, 9–10.
75. Maternus, *Matheseos*, Liber Quartus, 1.3, 6.
76. Maternus, *Matheseos*, Liber Quartus, 1.1.

helpful: Maternus the sun-worshiper, like the 313 panegyrist, appears to refer to the Supreme Deity with an air of diffidence, addressing him as "Whoever Thou art" and then referring to "Thy power, whatever that may be." This is immediately reminiscent of the 313 panegyrist, who likewise described Constantine's deity as "A certain force or Divine Mind . . . Some Power." If Maternus represents the kind of solar monotheism in vogue in Constantine's day, there may be no need to look any further than solar monotheism itself for the religious background of Constantine's coins, monuments, and inscriptions. Ultimately, in the above analysis we have discovered at least two pagan sources—fourth-century solar monotheism (exemplified in Maternus), and Hermeticism—which can account for all of the language and concepts of the early Constantinian sources. There is no need to follow the many modern scholars who describe these sources as deliberately vague tools carefully designed to politically cover over the emperor's embrace of the Christian deity.

Charles Odahl argued that Constantine, whom he describes as "a sincere believer in the Christian Deity," would have appreciated the language of the panegyrics and the arch because of the deliberate lack of reference to pagan deities.[77] But this language *does* describe pagan theology. Odahl, supporting his portrait of Constantine as an orthodox Christian, ultimately ascribes any syncretism in the panegyrics to the panegyrists, who he says looked to unite devotees of solar syncretism and Christian monotheism around Constantine.[78] But any syncretism in these early sources is surely Constantine's: the panegyrics, the arch, and the coinage by nature intended to reflect *Constantine's* theological proclivities, and were achieved with his approval. The meticulous architectural association of Constantine with Sol Invictus on his arch, for example, was far more than a Senatorial fancy which a Christian Constantine (grudgingly?) accepted in the name of tolerance or political tact—it was a bold theological statement: Constantine was the agent of the Supreme God, the deity he believed was currently worshiped by all monotheists—both pagan and Christian.[79] Such a statement, cast as it was in the language of the Divine Mind which Constantine had come to appreciate through solar monotheism and Hermeticism,

---

77. Odahl, *Constantine and the Christian Empire*, 123.
78. Odahl, *Constantine and the Christian Empire*, 123.
79. As Drake put it, "If Constantine truly rose to power—or truly believed he rose to power—by the direct intervention of deity in his personal life, it makes no sense to say that he would put that experience aside when deciding how to deal with such mundane obstacles as senatorial opinion" (Drake, *Constantine and the Bishops*, 19).

would serve as a banner for the enterprise imagined for him by Lactantius: a coalition of pagan and Christian monotheists united against idolatry for the good of the empire.

7

Constantine's Dream

IN THE MIDDLE OF the nineteenth century, Jacob Burckhardt convinced many that Constantine's turn to Christ was a purely "political" enterprise. Today, Burckhardt's specter continues to urge modern investigators down similar paths. But the still-popular idea that a conniving and insincere Constantine thought he could "gain political power" or even "control the empire" through a public conversion to Christianity seems increasingly outlandish in light of the research which has demonstrated that only ten percent of the Roman population belonged to this persecuted sect (at the very most).[1] Prejudiced by the knowledge of Christendom's later triumph, it is easy for us to buy in to unqualified narratives about "political power" without subjecting them to the sort of tests they deserve. Put in a different context, such stories rapidly lose their appeal. Indeed, what would we think if today a political commentator asked us to believe that a modern Muslim dictator, whose Muslim government had been harshly persecuting its minority Hindu population, publicly faked a conversion to Hinduism in order to "take control" of his Muslim nation? Would we not be compelled to look for other motivations?

To think that we can neatly extricate political and theological concerns in an era in which proper devotion was believed to assure political success is probably misguided. At least in Constantine's life, the evidence seems clear enough: the tangled mesh of politics and religion was a knot tightly woven. Edwards once keenly observed that "there are men in whom sincere and scrupulous piety conspires with the most incontinent of political and material ambitions. Constantine's religion shaped his policy and his policy shaped his religion."[2] Constantine was certainly a

---

1. Kreider, "Converted but Not Baptized," 47, 57.
2. Edwards, "Pagan and Christian Monotheism," 224.

master of politics, and clearly played to win. But the question remains as to how Constantine's concerns as a political pragmatist interfaced with his decision to champion the Christian version of monotheism. Indeed, while I have treated Burckhardt's approach as inadequate, and have emphasized Constantine's theological motivations for turning to Christianity, it has not been my intention to suggest that Constantine's public promotion of the Christian religion after 312 was entirely without practical or even "political" dimension. If my suggestion is right—that Constantine's turn to Christianity was "sincere," and did not involve an immediate turn from paganism, and was motivated by a desire to restore a universal monotheism on the earth, then questions about pragmatism and "politics" make a surprising return. Indeed, if Constantine wished to restore monotheism, and before 312 was already a monotheist, then why did he not simply continue in his solar monotheistic tradition? What did Christianity offer his quest which the cult of Sol Invictus or Hermeticism did not? Furthermore, as Peter Kaufman once so poignantly asked, "What would have tempted someone in late antiquity to join a persecuted sect?"[3]

Practical Concerns

As we have seen, pagan monotheisms typically allowed their followers to continue to venerate a host of other deities and did not require them to completely renounce other forms of faith.[4] The ability of pagan monotheism to interface with other cults had been its strength in the previous era, but Constantine's needs were much more radical. Having come to the belief that the many deities of the world's religions were the product of human error, he wanted Romans everywhere to abandon their misguided worship and to turn away from falsehoods. For a pragmatic monotheist like Constantine, the ideal and most rational faith was a monolatrous one. Thanks probably to Lactantius's emphasis on the decline-of-monotheism narrative, he longed for the simple religion of the golden age: the worship of one god only with no idols. If Constantine truly intended to lead his whole empire back to mankind's original religion, then the streams of pagan tradition which had thus far supported Roman monotheism would probably have seemed incapable of theologically uniting the empire. On the other hand, the famously aniconic Christian expression of

3. Kaufman, *Redeeming Politics*, 14.
4. Mitchell and Van Nuffelen, *One God*, 7.

monotheism—the teachings of Jesus and his Apostles—must have seemed like the purest form of his religious ideal.

It remains right to say that Constantine's decision to promote Christianity was both theological and practical, but the practical concerns themselves were theologically driven. Again, the line between Roman religion and public life was immeasurably thin, and Constantine's project was as much sociocultural as it was theological. Leading the empire back to monotheism meant turning many Romans from their usual habits and preferences. The emperor required a tradition which could not only lead the way theologically, and towards a monotheistic praxis in line with his own values, but one which could maintain social cohesion both during and after the turbulence of change.

In this light, no other Roman monotheism appears to have been able to satisfy Constantine's quest better than Christianity. Mithraism, though arguably still distinguishable from the cult of Sol and still popular at this time, was too secretive a tradition and apparently exclusive to males; the monotheistic worship of Apollo or Helios may have been difficult for the common Roman to distinguish from the traditional worship of those gods; even Hermeticism, with its personal God of Light, was nevertheless a deeply gnostic religion, perhaps too esoteric to capture the wider empire. The Jews, it was clear, had already forfeited their place as God's emissaries of truth by their wanton murder of Jesus—the messenger who God had originally sent to enlighten the world with monotheism.[5] But what about the cult of Sol Invictus, probably the "most intelligible and popular manifestation" of pagan light-monotheism?[6] Could the cult of Aurelian's god alone, without the aid of Christianity, have achieved Constantine's dream of theological unity?

At least in Rome, the number of official religious centers for Sol Invictus had already been surpassed by Christian centers by the time of

---

5. Constantine, though he could not deny that the Jews worshiped the Supreme God, saw their disastrous rejection and murder of God's Christ as reason enough to completely separate from them; see Eusebius, *Vit. Const.* 3.18. Theodoret also records the emperor's disdain for the Jews, who, through the killing of Jesus, "have impiously defiled their hands with enormous sin, and are therefore deservedly afflicted with blindness of soul . . . Let us then have nothing in common with the detestable Jewish crowd; for we have received from our Savior a different way" (Theodoret, *Hist. eccl.* 1.9). For a survey of Constantine's relationship with the Jews, see Carroll, *Constantine's Sword*, 155–229.

6. Edwards, "Pagan and Christian Monotheism," 220.

Constantine.[7] Indeed, Christianity boasted an organized network of hundreds of churches and bishoprics across the empire, and by the close of the second century CE, the Christian world had been operated by "uniform and theologically justified authority structures, and bishops exercised joint activity through synods."[8] By the late third and early fourth century, when Constantine observed Christianity from Diocletian's court, the Christians "had an elaborate system of internal governance, with the bishops of major cities (Alexandria, Antioch, Rome) exercising suzerainty over all the local churches in a region."[9] These bishops had emerged as a stabilizing and progressively influential force. If the religious revolution Constantine had in mind were ever to take hold and endure, it would require unified and stable leadership. As Drake observed, the bishops had already appropriated the authority of the martyr and the duties of the apologist, and had given their movement an effective organization.[10] If gaining influence in the empire "meant commanding sufficient resources to ensure that one's interests could not be ignored, then the disasters of [the third] century made clear that the church was ready to become a player."[11] In addition to securing the necessary moral high ground, by the time of Constantine's ascension, Christianity had also proven its ability to produce educational literature on a wide scale, disseminating theological arguments across the Roman territory in Greek, Latin, and Syriac.[12] If one were looking for an engine which could not only spread monotheism in the empire, but had the organizational potential to maintain social and theological cohesion, it was the Christian organism.

Beyond these practical considerations, I suggest that Constantine would have been attracted to what he initially understood to be a basic Christian ideal of religious tolerance—a vital ingredient for his plan to win over his fellow Romans to the truth.[13] The Christian arguments with which the

---

7. In the last two centuries, four temples to Sol Invictus had been built in Rome: at the Campus Agrippae, the Circus Maximus, on the Quirinal, and in Tastevere. See Hijmans, "Temples and Priests of Sol," 381–427. On the other hand, Optatus of Milevis tell us that by the year 300 CE there were more than forty Christian Basilicas in Rome (*On the Schisms of the Donatists*, 2.4).

8. Johnson, *Among the Gentiles*, 173.

9. Johnson, *Among the Gentiles*, 173.

10. Drake, *Constantine and the Bishops*, 110.

11. Drake, *Constantine and the Bishops*, 110.

12. Johnson, *Among the Gentiles*, 174.

13. See Drake's arguments for tolerance as an inherent principle of the Christianity

younger Constantine was most familiar were certainly those of Lactantius, who had championed tolerance in light of Diocletian's violent reforms. The other Christian voices which Constantine would have heard during his time in the imperial court would likewise have been sighing for tolerance under the weight of the persecutions. By 306, religious tolerance of all Christians and pagans was the official policy of Constantine, as made clear by his edict of that year. But how does Constantine's pronounced spirit of tolerance in his early reign pair with the idea that Constantine was on a quest to transform the empire into a monotheistic state? Why not outlaw traditional (non-monotheistic) religion immediately?

Aside from the troublesome and unattractive politics which would have traveled with such a tactic, the answer lies in both Lactantius's and Constantine's own preference for religious tolerance and their understanding of monotheism as a natural and rational religion. Lactantius, building on Cicero's ideals, had taught Constantine that "it is inappropriate to threaten the use of force or penalties to defend any sort of religious worship."[14] He writes that "Unless it comes from the heart spontaneously, it is blasphemy when people act under threat of proscription, injustice, prison or torture. If those gods get worshiped like that, they are not fit to be worshiped for the single reason that they want to be worshiped like that . . . We by contrast make no demand that our God, who is everyone's God [whether they like it or not], be worshiped by anyone unwillingly."[15] Indeed, "Lactantius wanted to persuade the pagans of the fourth century, not coerce them."[16] Both Lactantius and Constantine, in their historiography, portray monotheism as the original, most intuitive form of devotion; no one was to be forced into monotheism (Constantine would not follow in the tyrannical footsteps of the tetrarchy). True religion would, over time, come to be realized by way of reason. If monotheism could only

---

in Constantine's view, despite the principles of certain bishops who found themselves in the seats of influence (Drake, *Constantine and the Bishops*, 72–84); there was indeed an impulse towards "cooperation and inclusion," and one that existed alongside an equally important impulse towards "rigor and exclusion." These impulses "represent an internal tension in Christianity which at all times has been an important dynamic for the movement" (Drake, *Constantine and the Bishops*, 85). At the very least, the imperial tutor Lactantius "argued that refraining from the use of force by exercising forbearance (*patientia*) was a cornerstone of the Christian faith" (Digeser, *Making of a Christian Empire*, 118).

14. Digeser, "Lactantius, Porphyry, and the Debate," 142.
15. Lactantius, *Inst.* 20.8; Lactantius, *Divine Institutes*, 324.
16. Lefebure, "Reign of God," 129.

be set as a beacon on a hill, the world would eventually flock to its light. For Constantine, there probably seemed no better beacon than Christianity, with its organization, familial spirit, educational capabilities, apparent spirit of tolerance, and unyielding devotion to the Supreme God—a devotion recently proven in the fires of the Great Persecution.

Christians as a New Race

Other theological factors likely played a role in Constantine's preference of Christianity. The emperor was, I believe, ultimately led to identify the Christians as his chosen priestly class by both Christian and pagan tradition. In Constantine's eyes, not only did both Christian and pagan oracles dream of a world restored to primitive monotheism, they both dreamt of the Christians themselves: a new race of men who embodied true religion and virtue, a heaven-born people standing tall amidst the error-laden masses.

For centuries, Christians had already been described as a "new race," or frequently as "the third race." There is some fog surrounding how this language initially came about, and who was the first to use it, and precisely which categories originally composed the "three races" in view (Greeks, barbarians, and Christians; or pagans, Jews, and Christians).[17] The notion that Christians represent a third race of people may have its prototype in the New Testament (1 Cor 10:32; 12:2; Gal 3:28; 1 Pet 2:9). And in the second century, Christians like Aristides, Justin Martyr, Melitio of Sardis, and the writers of *Hermas* and the *Epistle to Diognetus* were all describing Christians in racial terms.[18] Melitio once wrote to Marcus Aurelius complaining about the persecution against "the race of the God-fearers."[19] Justin, in his arguments against Trypho the Jew, explained that "After that righteous one [Jesus] was slain, we sprouted up afresh as another people [*laos heteros*], and shot forth as new and thriving ears [of wheat] as the prophet said: 'And many peoples [*ethne*] shall flee to the Lord in that day to become a people [*laos*] ...' [Zech 2:15]. But we are not only a people, but also a holy people [*laos hagios*], as we have already proved."[20] In the early third century, Clement regularly cast Christians in racial terms—*genos, ethnos,* and *laos*. For him, Christians

---

17. For a more comprehensive study, see Lieu, *Image and Reality*, 164–77.
18. Lieu, *Neither Jew nor Greek?*, 72–73.
19. Recorded in Eusebius, *Hist. eccl.* 4.26.5.
20. Justin Martyr, *Dial.* 119.3; Justin Martyr, *Dialogue with Trypho*, 245, parentheticals mine.

are the *trito genei*, the third race which worships in a way distinct from pagans and Jews.²¹ Tertullian on the other hand would later argue against such identifications, warning that this language painting Christians as a new and separate *genus* produced too sharp a distinction between Christians and other Romans, leaving them prone to persecution.²² Tertullian concluded that this language about a third race was only a negative epithet used by their pagan enemies to exclude them. As Harnack ultimately surmised, this racial language was both a self-descriptor used by Christians, as well as an appellation employed by their critics.²³

In the fourth century, both Lactantius and Eusebius continue this tradition. True to his mission to build bridges between the Christian and pagan worlds, Lactantius portrays both Israelite and pagan prophets as pointing to the future race of Christians. He writes that while the biblical prophets like Isaiah spoke of a future testament between God and the house of Judah, this house was not really the Jews, but the Christians, whom Lactantius calls "sons of the Jews."²⁴ The pagan *Sibylline Oracles* also, which describe the Jewish people as "The divine race of the blessed, heavenly Jews,"²⁵ also have Christians in view here, men who have been "called by [God] out of the Gentiles" and have been "enlightened" by "the light of wisdom."²⁶

In the theology of Eusebius, we similarly find that the brilliant *logos* of God emanates from the Supreme God like a ray of sunlight, reaching out to all races of the earth (*ethnos*), "be they Greeks or barbarians."²⁷ Interestingly, Eusebius eventually came to teach that this *logos*, which had once manifested so brilliantly in Jesus, now dwelled especially in the person of Constantine. In effect, the emperor himself became the vehicle of divine revelation which radiated out to cure the ignorance of the world. His work specifically was to reveal to the masses the knowledge of the highest power.²⁸ By this illumination of the *logos*, which Eusebius, like Lactantius, finds

---

21. Clement of Alexandria, *Strom.* 6.41.7. Here Clement also notes that "the one and only God was known by the Greeks in a pagan way, by the Jews in a Jewish way, but by us in a new a spiritual way." See Ashwin-Siejkowski, *Clement of Alexandria*, 8.

22. Buell, *Why This New Race*, 154–55.

23. See notice of Harnack's study in Horrell, "Race, Nation, People," 151.

24. Lactantius, *Inst.* 4.29.10.

25. *Sibylline Oracles*, 5.249; Terry, *Sibylline Oracles*, 127.

26. Lactantius, *Inst.* 4.29.5–11.

27. Eusebius, *Praep. ev.* 1.1.6.1–10.

28. "The work of the *logos* is not simply to make men rational, but to make them capable of responding to God's redeeming call. In imitation, the sovereign, [says Eusebius,]

prophesied in the "divine oracles" of the pagans, men of all backgrounds are transformed into the people of God.[29]

In Constantine's own writings, the Christians are clearly "the newborn race."[30] The emperor concurs with earlier Christians like Justin Martyr that this new strain of humanity had commenced at the coming of Jesus in the first century.[31] He furthermore agrees with Lactantius that this people had long ago been envisioned by pagan poets and prophets, like the great Virgil. Jesus's first advent had "enlightened the world," and it was at that time, Constantine says, that "the mystery of our most holy religion began to prevail, and as it were a new race of men commenced: of which, I suppose the prince of Latin poets thus speaks: 'Behold, a new, a heaven-born race appears.'"[32] Constantine cites several other passages from Virgil, including one which reveals that the ancient Sicilian Muses also had the Christians in mind when they "sound[ed] a loftier strain."[33]

All of this is important for understanding why Constantine would identify the Christians as the ones who could lead the Roman world back to the true God. For him, the Christians were nothing less than a special people divinely appointed for the task, a priestly class, and one long dreamt of even by pagan prophets. Was it the teachings of Lactantius which had convinced him of this?[34] If so, when? Clearly for Christians like Lactantius this identification of the Christians as the long-awaited heavenly race of both biblical and pagan prophecy was a necessary component of the larger decline-of-monotheism narrative, and was doubtless preached by Lactantius. Thus, Constantine could have become convinced of the special role of the Christian race as early as 310, when Lactantius began teaching from the

'like some interpreter of the Logos of God, summons the whole human race to knowledge of the Higher Power, calling in a great voice that all can hear and proclaiming for everyone on earth the laws of genuine piety (II.86).' The Emperor is part of the natural order and part of the scheme of salvation for the world. In this he passes from the realm of the contingent to the necessary" (Kee, *Constantine Versus Christ*, 135).

29. Iricinschi, "Good Hebrew, Bad Hebrew," 75.

30. Constantine, *Orat.* 20.

31. Justin Martyr, *Dial.* 119.3.

32. Constantine, *Orat.* 19. Cf. Virgil, *Ecl.* 4, *Pollio*; Constantine, *Oration of Constantine*, 575.

33. Virgil, *Ecl.* 4, *Pollio*; Constantine, *Oration of Constantine*, 575.

34. Lactantius, like Constantine, also makes use of Virgil, and passages which describe different races of men, for example when he cites the poet's expression, "And the earth-born race of men raise its head from the hard fields'" (Lactantius, *Inst.* 2.11, citing Virgil, *Georg.* 2); cf. Constantine's citation of Virgil's reference to the "heaven-born race."

Institutes in his court. At the very least, by 312 Constantine had ostensibly been persuaded that he should not only embrace the Christians, but that he should favor them and ultimately award them special place and privilege as Rome's divine counselors and judges.

Indeed, we must pay special attention to Constantine's decision to assign special judicial powers to Christian clergy. As John Dillon observed:

> Constantine seems to have regarded bishops with such veneration that he conferred on them judicial powers that approached that of praetorian prefects or his own: the rulings of bishops were considered sacred—*sancta*—and, like the emperor's, inappellable. Constantine had such confidence in the judgment of bishops that he decreed that a case had to be transferred to the bishop even against the wishes of one of the parties.[35]

Why did Constantine so trust the bishops with the empire's justice? As we have seen, in both Constantine and Lactantius, "justice" often acts as a cipher for monotheism. According to Lactantius, in primordial, pre-Saturnian times, because the Supreme God was still known to man, there had existed no dissention, no avarice, no lust, no violence, no discord among relatives.[36] Though that golden age had passed away, for Constantine, when Jesus first appeared and established the Christian movement, "justice took the place of wrong," and monotheism was partially restored to the earth. And in Lactantius, too, Jesus had been sent to "lead back to that old age and the justice that had been routed . . . and this justice is [the] worship of the one God."[37] But Lactantius explains that this "justice was assigned only to a few," that is, to the new heaven-born race recently inaugurated.

By their monotheism, the bishops had already demonstrated to Constantine that they could see through error. Being the heaven-born race, they were naturally inclined to reason and justice. Lactantius had taught that it is impossible for anyone to know true justice outside of monotheism, for "it is plain that he is ignorant of justice who does not possess the knowledge

---

35. Dillon, *Justice of Constantine*, 256.

36. Lactantius, *Inst.* 5.5. See also *Inst.* 5.8: "Be just and good, and the justice which you seek will follow you of her own accord. Lay aside every evil thought from your hearts, and that golden age will at once return to you, which you cannot attain to by any other means than by beginning to worship the true God. But you long for justice on the earth, while the worship of false gods continues, which cannot possibly come to pass . . . But if God only were worshipped, there would not be dissensions and wars, since men would know that they are the sons of one God" (Lactantius, *Works of Lactantius*, 308).

37. Lactantius, *Inst.* 5.7; Lactantius, *Divine Institutes: Books I–VII*, 343.

of God. For how can he know justice itself, who is ignorant of the source from which it arises?"[38] While Lactantius agreed with Cicero that "true justice lay in upholding divine law, Lactantius thought that this could not be achieved unless one acknowledged the greatest God."[39] If even the wise Plato, Socrates, and the other great philosophers had not really known true justice, according to Lactantius, then how much less could the pagan judges of Rome? All of this sheds light on why Constantine would have trusted the Christians with the judicial powers that he did; it also sheds light on why Constantine saw Christianity and her bishops as so vital to the restoration of true religion and the civic prosperity which accompanied it.

Ultimately, it is clear that Lactantius had taught Constantine that "monotheism [could] return Rome to the virtues of the Principate, with its uncluttered calculus of one God and one emperor," and that Constantine joined him in believing that "Above all, Christians [could] carry the educated elite along this path, an elite whose own commitments place them just a short step away from this salvific restoration."[40] Like the (now missing) quadriga statue atop Constantine's arch, Constantine elected to drive the chariot of monotheism across the empire himself, a chariot pulled by Christian horses. But the Christian organism would not prove as reliable (or tolerant) an engine as Constantine's dream of universal monotheism required. Constantine became increasingly aware of this fact around 313, as he came face to face with the Donatist controversy.

The Dream Is Threatened

Less than one year after his support of Christianity emerged publicly, Constantine's dream of universal monotheism, and even his own spirit of religious tolerance, would begin to fail him. In 313, Constantine was moved to personally intervene in the raging disputes in northern Africa over which group of Christians were "the true church." Eventually, Constantine's military would march on the disputing Christians, compelling them to unify, and a number of them, including some church leaders, would be killed in the violence.[41] Pursuing further strong-arm tactics during the subsequent Arian controversy, Constantine would outlaw Arianism, exile Christians

---

38. Lactantius, *Inst.* 5.15; Lactantius *Works of Lactantius*, 325–26.
39. Digeser, *Making of a Christian Empire*, 58.
40. Bowlin, "Tolerance among the Fathers," 25.
41. Leithart, *Defending Constantine*, 160.

who disagreed with his views, destroy Arian writings, and promise capital punishment by "beheading immediately" anyone found with dissident literature.[42] Where was the tolerance Constantine had displayed in his earlier edicts, like the famous "edict of Milan" just issued in 313, in which he and his co-emperor Licinius returned all confiscated property to Christians, and assured all peoples of the empire, Christian and otherwise, the right to practice their religion as they saw fit without molestation?[43]

It seems to me that the turmoil of the Donatist and Arian disputes had shocked and horrified Constantine; he believed such intolerance and disruption among the Christian bishops would destroy his dream of universal monotheism, and thus the stability and prosperity its success promised the realm. This prompted an anxious shift in policy. Ultimately, the Donatist and Arian disputes each demonstrate different dimensions of Constantine's anxiety, and his evolving methods for dealing with religious conflict.

The circumstances of Constantine's involvement in the Donatist crisis are revealed to us in his own letters on the subject. Speaking of the Christians who had separated themselves and proclaimed their movement the "true church" (and the others apostates), Constantine writes:

> I consider it by no means right that contentions and altercations of this kind should be hidden from me, by which, perchance, God may be moved not only against the human race, but also against me myself, to whose care, by his heavenly decree, he has entrusted the direction of all human affairs, and may in his wrath provide otherwise than heretofore. For then shall I be able to remain truly and most fully without anxiety, and may always hope for all most prosperous and excellent things from the ever-ready kindness of the most powerful God, when I shall know that all, bound together in brotherly concord, adore the most holy God with the worship of the catholic religion, that is his due.[44]

Why might God move against the human race, and against Constantine? Evidently, the emperor believed that the recent disputes could lead

---

42. Constantine, "Letter to the Churches (325 CE)," preserved in Socrates Scholasticus, *Hist. eccl.* 1.9.

43. See Constantine's edicts of 306 and 313 CE (Milan), jointly issued with the pagan Licinius, emperor of the East. This latter edict was essentially aimed at Maximinus Daia, Caesar of the East, who had renewed persecution of Christians after Galerius had stayed them in 311.

44. Constantine, "Letter to Ablavius (314 CE)," preserved in Optatus of Milevis's *Against the Donatists*; Alexander, "Rethinking Constantine's Interaction," 64.

to the interruption of the Christian's proper (monotheistic) worship to the Supreme God. This was, in his mind, a disastrous proposition. In another letter, Constantine would exempt Christian clergy from civil labors and responsibilities which might interfere with their ability to worship, and the reason provided is important: "The setting at naught of divine worship . . . has brought great dangers upon public affairs, and its lawful restoration and preservation have bestowed the greatest good fortune on the Roman name and singular prosperity on all the affairs of mankind (for it is the divine providence which bestows these blessings)."[45] The bishops, he says, "when they render supreme service to the Deity . . . confer incalculable benefit on the affairs of the state."[46] Note Constantine's claim that "divine worship" (the monotheistic worship of God "that is his due") had recently been "restored," implying its earlier loss. Constantine thus continued to interpret his activity through the prism of the decline-of-monotheism narrative: if the steady stream of proper worship rising from the earth to the Supreme Deity were interrupted, then darkness would return, as it had in former times.

But in 313, Constantine had yet to fully comprehend the situation in Africa, as evidenced by his sending of reparations to Caecilian, an anti-Donatist, and his conspicuous lack of gifts for the Donatists, which greatly aggravated the conflict.[47] The belligerents dug in, unimpressed by Constantine's meddling, and Donatus himself asked the important question: "What has the emperor to do with the church?"[48] By 314, a frustrated Constantine was taking matters into his own hands, calling the Council of Arles to settle the matter. But as the bitter unrest continued, Constantine became painfully aware of not only the savage sectarianism coursing through the Christian religion, but of his own inability to rally the Christians around their shared monotheism. If even the Christian monotheists could not unite on this point, how could the rest of the empire? The beacon of Christianity was dimming rapidly, and Constantine became desperate. He wrote in 315 about the sectarians:

---

45. Constantine, "Second Letter to Anulinus (313 CE)," preserved in Eusebius, *Hist. eccl.* 10.7.1–2; Ledegang, "Eusebius' View on Constantine," 63.

46. Constantine, "Second Letter to Anulinus (313 CE)," preserved in Eusebius, *Hist. eccl.* 10.7.1–2; Ledegang, "Eusebius' View on Constantine," 63.

47. Frend, *Donatist Church*, 144–45.

48. Optatus, *Against the Donatists*, 3.3.

Those same persons who now stir up the people in such a war as to bring it about that the Supreme God is not worshipped with the veneration that is his due, I shall destroy and dash in pieces . . . I shall also make these persons see what worship and what kind of worship is to be given to the Divinity . . . What can be done by me more in accordance with my constant practice, and the very office of a Prince, than, after having driven away errors and destroyed all rash opinions, to bring it about that all men should show forth true religion and simplicity in concord, and to render to Almighty God the worship which is his due?[49]

Here we see Constantine believed that by publicly endorsing and supporting monotheism he had driven away the theological errors of former times, and that it now remained his duty to show mankind the truth of monotheism, to the end that all the world would be united under one simple opinion. The "simplicity" on which his desired concord would be founded is certainly the basic truth that there is one Supreme God. For Constantine, the monotheistic worship "which is his due" need not be concerned with particulars, that is, with whether or not Yahweh, Jupiter, or Sol are properly reverenced according to the specific traditions and interpretations of man which had heretofore supported them—such details would only get in the way and hamper Roman unity. Since general monotheism was Constantine's chosen bonding agent for uniting the disparate religious groups of the empire, he could not tolerate the Donatists or any other sectarians proclaiming themselves the only true way to God.

By 317, Constantine was issuing an edict promising death for any Christian who continued to cause disturbances. Another edict soon followed, ordering the confiscation of Donatist property. As mentioned earlier, many Christians, including several bishops, were eventually killed by Constantine's military.[50] From his letters we can observe how deeply Constantine was shaken by the idea that the Christian institution, which should have been the shining light of proper worship in the empire, might actually destroy his dream, and consequently his God-given reign. Seven times Constantine describes the Donatist situation as "madness." More research certainly needs to be done on the psychological effects of the years 313–17 on Constantine. The emperor no doubt recognized in this period, and in a dramatic way, exactly what sort of religionists he had attached himself to

49. Constantine, "Letter to Celsus (315 CE)," preserved in Optatus of Milevis's *Against the Donatists*; Leithart, *Defending Constantine*, 84.

50. See Leithart, *Defending Constantine*, 160; Barnes, *Constantine and Eusebius*, 60.

and so visibly supported since the previous year of 312. Constantine discovered that the Christian world was a radically stubborn one, resistant to imperial hopes of unity, and rather unlike the stable bastion of tolerance and monotheism which Lactantius had led him to believe could facilitate a golden age of rational religion.

It is possible that the miserable years spent dealing with the Christian infighting caused Constantine to realize a need to more stringently define his own theology. He had, after all, publicly identified which Christians belonged to the *true faith* by his repudiation of the Donatists—where did his own doctrine fall on the spectrum of Christian orthodoxy? Speculation aside, what is evident from the sources is that Constantine's penchant for and proficiency in acutely Christian theology would visibly progress from roughly 317–24. Constantine's *Oration*, delivered probably in April of 325,[51] reveals a man who has advanced remarkably in his knowledge and appreciation of Christianity, far beyond the scarce and impartial references to "our God" found in his 314 letter after the Council of Arles. However, as we will soon observe in the next section, the Christianity of Constantine was still, even through the year 325, thought by him to be compatible with his pagan background. Though by 324 Constantine appears to have pivoted to some degree against traditional paganism, namely against idols and blood sacrifice,[52] he evidently still believed the pagan world and the Christian world, at least in regard to monotheism, could discover some compatibility. Indeed, Christian theology, for Constantine, could still be interpreted through a framework of Hermeticism and pagan monotheism, and this fact will come dramatically into view in his remedy for the Arian controversy.

If the Donatist dispute over ecclesiastical legitimacy disturbed Constantine's vision of Christianity ushering in a universal monotheism, then the Arian controversy, boiling over by 324, was its complete undoing. Now the Christians were arguing publicly about monotheism itself! Constantine wrote to Alexander and Arius, who were quarreling over the metaphysical relationship between God and Jesus, begging them to keep their dispute private. He also expressed his waning hope that they would have one day spread their religion to the whole world, and he begs them to realize that such quarrels over the particulars of monotheism are not important—what

---

51. Barnes, *Constantine and Eusebius*, 153.

52. By 325, Constantine has at least progressed towards aniconism. He writes: "under Divine direction, I have disencumbered as it were of the heavy weight of foul idol worship" ("Letter of Constantine to Macarius, 325 CE").

matters is that they both worship the same Supreme God, as he himself does. He ultimately suggests they follow the example of the pagan philosophers who, though disagreeing on "certain points," are "recalled to harmony of sentiment by the uniting power of their common doctrines."[53]

In the opening of this letter, Constantine reveals information vital to the present study. He first demonstrates a continued use of solar imagery to frame discussions of Christian monotheism; he speaks of "the power of Divine light, and the law of sacred worship [monotheism], which, proceeding in the first instance through the favor of God, from the bosom, as it were, of the East, have illumined the world by their sacred radiance."[54] Regarding his personal objectives relative to monotheism before the year 313, he explains: "My design then was, first, to bring the diverse judgements formed by all nations respecting the Deity to a condition, as it were, of settled uniformity; and, secondly, to restore to health the system of the world, then suffering under the malignant power of a grievous distemper." This was, he claims, the "twofold reason" for all of his religious activity before his discovery of the Donatist controversy in 313. I suggest therefore that Constantine's edicts of tolerance, his monotheistic propaganda, and his public embrace of Christianity in 312 be read in precisely this light, as part of a theological quest to establish a single opinion about God (monotheism) on the earth, reconciling the diverse theologies of "all nations," and thereby "restoring" the former order of the world, which, being apart from this "uniform" condition, had fallen into misery.

But again, the Christians had not proven the stable beacon of monotheism originally so integral to Constantine's plan. The emperor was a hardheaded man, however, and would not allow Christian infighting to hamper his agenda. Already in a letter in 315, he demonstrates a willingness to take matters into his own hands. It is "I," he says, who "shall make these persons see what worship and what kind of worship is to be given to the Divinity," and "[I shall] bring it about that all men should show forth true religion and simplicity in concord."[55] If Christian leadership was not up to the task, he himself would teach the human race what kind of (monotheistic) worship was due to God, and thus through his example,

---

53. Constantine, "Letter to Alexander and Arius (ca. 323–24)," preserved in Eusebius, *Vit. Const.* 2.64–72; Constantine, *Oration of Constantine*, 516.

54. Constantine, "Letter to Alexander and Arius (ca. 323–24)," preserved in Eusebius, *Vit. Const.* 2.64–72; Constantine, *Oration of Constantine*, 516, parentheticals mine.

55. Constantine, "Letter to Celsus (315 CE)," preserved in Optatus of Milevis's *Against the Donatists*; Alexander, "Rethinking Constantine's Interaction," 79.

"all men" would "see" (by way of reason) the truth and become united under a universal monotheism ("simplicity of concord"). The emperor's frustration with Christian leadership, and his anxiety for the fulfillment of his divine mission, never left him after 313. In 335, two years before his death, Constantine was still discouraged by the failure of the bishops to properly demonstrate true worship and harmony to the world, and he continued to draw a distinction between himself and them. Constantine ultimately portrays himself as a champion sallying forth to complete his mission for monotheism despite the failures of Christian leadership. He writes: "Even the barbarians now through me, the true servant of God, know God and have learned to reverence him . . . [while the bishops] do nothing but that which encourages discord and hatred and, to speak frankly, which leads to the destruction of the human race."[56]

---

56. Constantine, "Letter to the Bishops at Tyre (335 CE)," preserved in Athanasius, *Apologia Secunda*, 86, emphasis added; Drake, *Constantine and the Bishops*, 4.

8

Nicaea and *Homoousios*

FOR PERHAPS A DECADE before the great Council of Nicaea in 325 CE, even as the Donatist controversy raged, a christological crisis had festered in Egypt. Arius, a presbyter from Alexandria, and his bishop Alexander had entertained a public disagreement about the nature of Jesus and his relationship to God. Arius held that the Father and the Son were distinct beings, and that "there was a time when the Son was not."[1] This contravened with his bishop, and perhaps more importantly with Alexander's spirited deacon Athanasius, who claimed the Son was "eternally generated." Arius defended his own unitarian subordinationism as traditional Christian doctrine.[2] But who was right? When Arius said that the Father and Son were separate in essence, was he an innovator or a theological conservative? And what was the relationship between God and his Son Jesus? The controversy soon became a major scandal and caught the attention of Constantine.

The emperor, deeply troubled by the discovery of yet another Christian controversy, sent his advisor, the Christian bishop Hosius of Cordova (d. 359 CE), to investigate.[3] Upon his recommendation, an imperial call was made for a council of bishops to settle the matter.

---

1. Arius's views as described in Socrates, *Hist. eccl.* 1.5.

2. "Many of the earlier Church Fathers, including Justin Martyr, Clement and Origen—the last two Alexandrians themselves—treated Jesus the Son as somehow derivative of the Father . . . When Arius claimed that he was following 'our faith from our forefathers, which we have learnt from you,' these were the formidable theologians whose work he could draw on" (Freeman, *Closing of the Western Mind*, 165). See also Williams, *Arius: Heresy and Tradition*, 256–57.

3. Hosius, like Lactantius, was an important Christian voice in Constantine's ear. Odahl describes him as "a man of high morality and great learning, [who] was highly respected in both the Christian Church and Roman society." He points out that "a new Latin translation of Plato's *Timaeus* was dedicated to him, and he seems to have been well versed in both classical philosophy and Christian theology," and he suggests that

In this chapter we will consider Constantine's participation in the Council of Nicaea (325 CE), and his famous connection to the Nicene Creed's keystone philosophical term *homoousios*. Understanding Constantine's involvement will ultimately provide valuable insight into both the evolution of the emperor's personal theology and his continued belief in the essential harmony of Christian and pagan monotheism.

The Word *Homoousios* before Nicaea

Special attention in this investigation must be paid to *homoousios*, the controversial Greek term used in Nicaea's creed to officially define the relationship between God and the Son of God. Scholars have long debated the origins of the word, but what is widely accepted by historians is Eusebius's eyewitness report that the term was proposed by none other than Constantine himself. Bernard Lohse summed up the remaining problem of origins this way: "The decisive catchword of the Nicene confession, namely, homoousios ('of one substance'), comes from no less a person than the emperor himself. *To the present day no one has cleared up the problem of where the emperor got the term.*"[4]

In his landmark investigation, Christopher Stead catalogued every pre-Nicene occurrence of the word *homoousios*, revealing the term's link to Gnosticism.[5] Indeed, modern scholarly consensus on the historical usage of the word is that the first persons to use the term in a theological context were gnostics.[6] There are no pre-gnostic examples of the word, and Pier Franco Beatrice, in his own landmark study, confirmed that the Christian gnostics were in fact the first to introduce the term into the wider Christian world.[7] But what did this term mean to the early gnostics of the late first and early second centuries CE?

Hosius "probably mentioned to the emperor that the Platonic concept of a first and second Deity was somewhat similar to the Christian belief in God the Father and his Son the Word" (Odahl, *Constantine and the Christian Empire*, 112–13). That such things were mentioned to the emperor is certain. However, as we will see, we can more confidently pin such conversations on Lactantius.

4. Lohse, *Short History of Christian Doctrine*, 51–53, emphasis added.
5. Stead, *Divine Substance*, 190–91.
6. Stead, *Divine Substance*, 190–202.
7. Beatrice, "Word 'Homoousios,'" 248, 263.

NICAEA AND *HOMOOUSIOS*

In these circles, the term was first used "to describe 'the relationship between beings compounded of kindred substance' and was 'used alongside notions of emanation.'"[8] Stead reveals that in the majority of the earliest cases, "the notion of 'ousia' that is implied is either material or conceived in physical terms. It thus means roughly, 'made of the same ... kind of stuff.'"[9] Stead continues: "When [*homoousios*] first appears it is not used to express the Christian theology of the Trinity ... [it] go[es] back to pre-Christian times."[10] If this is true, then where did Christian gnostics first learn to use this term?

Beatrice explains that the Christian gnostics had first drawn the word directly from Hermetic sources.[11] The earliest use of the word in extant literature is found in the important Hermetic tractate *Poimandres*, which dates to the first century CE at the latest.[12] Here the word is used to define the relationship between a monotheistic God—God the Father or "Mind" (νοῦς)—and his emanations. Especially noteworthy is the first of these emanations, the *logos*, who is cast as a second god and called "the Son of God."[13] In the text, God the Father says: "I am the Mind (νοῦς), the first God . . . And the brilliant *logos* that issued forth from the Mind is the Son of God . . . You must understand that what hears and sees inside of you is the *logos* of the Lord, his Son, but the Mind is God the Father. And they are not divided from each other, because they are united by life."[14] We then read that "the *logos* of God . . . was united with the Mind of the Demiurge. For the *logos* was of one-substance (ὁμοούσιος) with the Mind."[15] We already detect here in this pagan document the language of Nicaea: God and his Son-Logos are *homoousios* (consubstantial). It is easy to understand why Beatrice ultimately pursued the gnostic world for clues about the origins of Nicaea's language.[16]

---

8. Ezigbo quoting first J. N. D. Kelly, then Lewis Ayres, in *Introducing Christian Theologies*, 155.
9. Stead, citing G. L. Prestige, in *Divine Substance*, 190.
10. Stead, *Divine Substance*, 190.
11. Beatrice, "Word 'Homoousios,'" 263.
12. Quispel, "Asclepius," 74–75.
13. *Poimandres*, 6.
14. *Poimandres*, 6.
15. *Poimandres*, 10.
16. Beatrice, "Word 'Homoousios,'" 243.

In the Valentinian (Christian gnostic) philosophy of the second century, *homoousios* typically means "made of the same element" or "belonging to the same order of beings," whether made of spiritual, psychic, or non-spiritual matter.[17] It was thus used by Christian gnostics to describe God's relationship with the created world, and generated beings' relationships to each other. In most instances it is used to describe a generated thing's relationship to its source, and is naturally used in conjunction with notions of emanation. The word did not necessitate an organic connection between the emanation and its source, nor an equality of status, though it did not prohibit these things.[18] In its earliest theological usage, entities which are *homoousios* are regularly presented as unequal, and in terms of subordination. Indeed, virtually all of the theological applications of the term *homoousios* before Nicaea refer to "two or more beings" who "severally have (and do not 'jointly constitute') a single *ousia*; that is . . . they have the same generic or specific characteristics, or the same material constitution."[19]

In the third century, the vast majority of instances of *homoousios* are still found in quotations of and references to gnostics, and in ways typical of the earlier appearances of the term. In Origen, for example, *homoousios* is used to refer to the Valentinian doctrines about classes of beings. The evidence related to Origen's own use of the word *homoousios* in his doctrines is highly suspect: the term only occurs in Rufinus's admittedly corrupted translation of Origen's work. Rowan Williams and R. P. C. Hanson are both convinced that Rufinus inserted the word in order to prove Origen's (Nicene) orthodoxy.[20] Beatrice thinks, and only "with all due caution," that it's possible Origen may have used the term analogically.[21] Regardless, as Williams writes, "Origen certainly did not teach that the Son is 'from the ousia' of the Father' . . . he did not usually employ *ousia* to describe the substance of God."[22] Indeed, we must ask: if Origen really did freely utilize *homoousios*, why were later Origenists, like Eusebius, so wary of it? While certain elements in Origen might be viewed as foreshadowing Nicaea (like

---

17. Stead, *Divine Substance*, 193.

18. Stead, *Divine Substance*, 201.

19. Stead, *Divine Substance*, 248, 247.

20. Williams, *Arius: Heresy and Tradition*, 136; Hanson, *Search for the Christian Doctrine*, 185.

21. See Beatrice, "Eusebius and Marcellus," 173; Beatrice, "Word 'Homoousios,'" 250–51.

22. Hanson, *Search for the Christian Doctrine*, 185.

the eternal generation of the Son), "however one accounts for these obscurities, it seems unlikely that Origen could have signed the Nicene Creed of 325, in which the Son is declared to be from the *ousia* of the Father, and therefore *homoousios* with him."[23]

It has sometimes been thought that if the word did not originate in Origen, then it must have been an established term among the Sabellians of the third century. Evidence for Sabellian usage is said to be located within the orbit of the so-called "two Dionysii" controversy, in which some Libyan Sabellians are purported to have used the language as a term of identification between the Father and the Son. Luise Abramowski and Uta Heil argue, however, that the documents of the Dionysii controversy are fourth-century forgeries, and that these were drawn up to support Athanasius's defense of Nicaea.[24] Athanasius appears to report that the Sabellians used the word in a Nicene sense—but Sabellians in Athanasius's day, we should keep in mind, were using the word *monoousious*, not *homoousios*. It is true that Basil of Caesarea tells us that in the third century Dionysis of Alexandria had rejected the word *homoousios* explicitly because the Sabellians were employing it in order to blur the distinction between the Father and the Son. Indeed, in 268 at Antioch, the word was officially banned because the council thought it implied Sabellianism.[25] Thus, the third century use of the word in non-gnostic Christian circles is probably to be connected in a limited way to Sabellianism, and largely to a group of Libyan bishops experimenting with it as a term of personal identification.

In the late third and early fourth centuries the word was still in use in gnostic circles. After the time of Plotinus (d. 270 CE), who had experienced a good deal of contact with gnostics in Rome and had even written a treatise against them, pagan philosophers can also be found using the word to describe "things of the same order."[26] Indeed, for Neoplatonist

---

23. Edwards, "Origen." See Origen's comments on John: "The Saviour is here called simply light. But in the Catholic Epistle of this same John we read that God is light. This, it has been maintained, furnishes a proof that the Son is not in substance different from the Father. Another student, however, looking into the matter more closely and with a sounder judgment, will say that the light which shines in darkness and is not overtaken by it, is not the same as the light in which there is no darkness at all" (Origen, *Comm. Jo.* 2.18; Menzies, *Gospel of Peter*, 336).

24. Beatrice, "Word 'Homoousios,'" 254. See Abramowski, "Dionys von Rom," 240–72; Heil, *Athanasius von Alexandrien*, 22–71, 210–31.

25. Prestige, *God in Patristic Thought*, 207.

26. Stead, *Divine Substance*, 215.

successors of Plotinus like Porphyry (d. 305 CE), all perceptible things were *homoousios*.[27]

By the time of the Arian controversy, Manichaeism, a gnostic religion, had already embarked on its meteoric rise towards becoming a major world faith. The Manichaeans had evidently made much use of *homoousios*, and I believe it had formed a distinctive element of their theology by at least the early fourth century. The Manichaeans evidently "regarded the divine substance as quasi-material, and held that the Son was begotten of the Father by cutting the paternal substance in two sections."[28] Thus in the years prior to Nicaea, the Manichaean, Valentinian, and Hermetic use of the term can largely be seen as having traveled along the same axis of meaning: it referred to the sharing of substance between two or more beings, typically between an emanated entity and its source, and it carried materialistic connotations.

Homoousios: Not a Matter of Debate

It must be pointed out that the theological use of *homoousios* was not originally a matter of debate between Arius and his bishop Alexander. In fact, Arius's letter to Alexander, and the way he denounces the term as a definition of relationship between the Father and the Son, even gives the impression that he knows his opponents did not approve of it either. Arius made it clear that he and his friends personally rejected it as a vehicle for defining God and Jesus, and Arius attached the use of that model, not surprisingly, to gnostics. In his confession of faith, Arius reveals that the term *homoousios* was in use by the Manichaeans of his day, and he declares that he and his allies "are not prepared to affirm that the Son is homoousios with the Father."[29] Ultimately, Arius casts *homoousios* as something widely known to be inappropriate or alien to the catholic faith, and in light of the above survey, this seems correct.

Supporting Arius's negative portrait of the term is the fact that the use of *homoousios* had already been rejected by an earlier catholic council, the Synod of Antioch, in 268 CE. The reports are murky, but the council had evidently been convened to solve the problem of Paul of Samosata, a dynamic monarchian bishop who reportedly had some connection to the

27. Porphyry, *Sentences*, 33. See Stead, *Divine Substance*, 215–16.
28. Prestige, *God in Patristic Thought*, 210.
29. Arius, *Thalia*, in Athanasius, *Syn.* 15

word. It has been noted by historians that this council rejected not only Paul's theology, but also the word *homoousios*.[30] And as Hanson points out, this fact ultimately caused "considerable embarrassment to those theologians who wanted to defend its inclusion in an official doctrinal statement" at Nicaea.[31] The rejection of *homoousios* at Antioch is good evidence that before Nicaea the use of the term was not well-established among the catholics, and was seen as foreign to the catholic faith.

Theologically speaking, why would Arius (and those of his opponents he presumed shared his sentiments before Nicaea) reject *homoousios*? In his letter to Alexander (ca. 320), Arius first strongly condemns Valentinian emanationism, which involved the idea that the Son is a materialistic projection from the Father's substance.[32] Arius also strongly condemns the Manichaean teaching that the offspring is "a *homoousios* portion" of the Father. Towards the end of his letter, Arius links *homoousios* to emanationism (again, not surprisingly), and these elements to the idea that God is material, and that the Son is a part of the Father's material. Knowing how indebted the East was to Origen and his famous insistence that God's essence was *immaterial*, it is not surprising that Arius would openly denounce such thinking. For Arius, the use of the phrase "from the Father," and *homoousios*, suggested that God is material, and divisible, and changeable.[33] The general distaste in the East for materialistic emanationism and the word *homoousios*, which typically carried such connotations, is why Arius brings these items up in his defense to Alexander—he is demonstrating that he is not subscribing to theological elements which they mutually condemn. As G. L. Prestige once wrote, "We may therefore conclude that, down to the Council of Nicaea, *homoousios* meant 'of one stuff' or 'substance'; and that, when it was applied to the divine Persons, it conveyed a metaphor drawn from material objects, just as hostile critics alleged."[34]

---

30. "It must be regarded as certain that the council rejected the term *homoousios*" (Chapman, "Paul of Samosata," x).

31. Hanson, *Search for the Christian Doctrine*, 195.

32. Arius, "Letter to Alexander (ca. 320)," 1.2, preserved in Athanasius, *Syn.* 16. As we will see in the coming sections, Arius is also rejecting the theology of Western third-century theologian Tertullian, d. 240 CE.

33. See Prestige, *God in Patristic Thought*, 209–10.

34. Prestige, *God in Patristic Thought*, 209.

The Bishops and *Homoousios*

Athanasius, Eusebius of Caesarea, and Marcellus of Ancyra were all ultimately able to sign on to the language of the Nicene Creed. The fact that each of these theologians held to vastly different theologies indicates that they were each interpreting the controversial *homoousios* language in different ways. We certainly get this sense from Eusebius, who in a letter to his constituents works diligently to explain away his signature, emphasizing his personal interpretation of the creed.[35] But why would the bishops ever agree to using such a controversial term, even if it could be understood in different ways?

It seems obvious that the value the council members found in this foggy language was in its ability to oust the trouble-maker Arius, who had made his disapproval of this article public. While *homoousios* had typically carried materialistic connotations, and indeed smacked of the Gnosticism which Arius attributed to it, it could still be given different meanings, and we know this at least by its aforementioned limited appearance in Sabellian circles in the third century as a term of identification. Depending on how one understood the term *ousia*, it is true that the bishops could have understood *homoousios* in a variety of ways, and Dale Tuggy has catalogued at least nine possible interpretations of the word which would have been available to the bishops at Nicaea.[36] With this flexibility in view, and since the anti-Arians knew that Arius had publicly denounced the word and would never accept it, *homoousios* appears to have made the perfect tool for getting rid of Arius while at the same time not placing too tight of theological restrictions on themselves.

Barnard highlighted the "ambiguity of the terms used in the creed," and ultimately concluded that "the bishops had understood *homoousios* in different ways; for anti-Arians, such as Athanasius, it meant the personal identity of the Son with the Father, so excluding Arianism; for others it merely carried the idea of a broader identity; still others were confused but signed the creed at the Emperor's behest. Everyone read his own theology into the Creed and there were no 'Nicene' theologians as such."[37]

---

35. Rubenstein, *When Jesus Became God*, 83.

36. 1. Same individual entity; 2. Same universal essence; 3. Same individual essence; 4. Same haecceity; 5. Same kind of matter; 6. Same portion of matter; 7. Same parts; 8. Similar beings; 9. Self and his action. See Tuggy, *What is the Trinity?*, 71–93.

37. Barnard, *Council of Serdica 343 A.D.*, 19–20.

Considering the controversial career of the word *homoousios* after the Council of Nicaea, scholars have made the following suggestion: the reason why Nicaea's so-called champion, Athanasius, deliberately avoided even speaking of *homoousios* for fifteen years after the council was because Athanasius knew that the term stood under an "evil odor," and he did not wish to provoke a hostile public by waving it around.[38] What was the reason for such an odor, and why would the Christian public be hostile to it? Indeed, why did Eusebius feel the need to explain away his agreement to the word to his presumably hostile constituents?[39]

As we have seen, the term *homoousios* had its origins in pagan and gnostic theologies.[40] And again, the term had already been banned long before Nicaea by a well-respected Christian council in 268 CE.[41] Why would Constantine insert this controversial and unorthodox language into the creed? Even if it did have the power to exclude a perceived troublemaker, why would the bishops ever sign onto it while it remained beneath such an evil cloud? Is there any evidence that Constantine consciously retrieved the word from pagan and gnostic sources?

Constantine and *Homoousios*

In 2002, Beatrice demonstrated that Constantine indeed drew the term from his Hermetic background, placing special emphasis on the presence of the word *homoousios* in *Poimandres*.[42] Again, in *Poimandres*, the first God, God the Father, and the *logos* his Son are distinguished as two entities. Both possess the same divine perfection (or divine nature), and the *logos* had proceeded from the Father. The word *homoousios* worked specifically to describe their relationship as one of kindred substance.[43] The affinity

---

38. Kelly cited in Barnard, *Council of Serdica 343 A.D.*, 87.
39. Rubenstein, *When Jesus Became God*, 83.
40. Stead, *Divine Substance*, 190, 201–2, 204.
41. "There was some suspicion of this word on the part of the orthodox because of its earlier association with Gnosticism and even Manicheism. Even its defenders experienced some embarrassment about this term because of its identification with the condemned ideas of Paul of Samosata [in 268 CE]" (Erickson, *God in Three Persons*, 82–85).
42. Beatrice, "Word 'Homoousios,'" 243–72; see also Beatrice, "Eusebius and Marcellus," 172–78.
43. See *Corpus Hermeticum* 1.6, 10. In gnostic circles, as Ezigbo notes, this term was originally used "to describe 'the relationship between beings compounded of kindred substance'" (Ezigbo, *Introducing Christian Theologies*, 155).

with the Nicene Creed is certainly striking, but is there any way to connect the theology of Constantine to *Poimandres*?

In his *Oration*, written probably only months before Nicaea, Constantine justified his own Christian theology by invoking Plato. He says: "For Plato himself . . . declared, with truth, a God exalted above every essence, but to him he added also a second, distinguishing them as two, though both possessing one perfection, and the being of the second deity proceeding from the first."[44] But was it truly *Plato* to whom the emperor appealed? As Beatrice revealed, Constantine's explanation "evidently has no relation at all with Plato's real doctrine.[45] Indeed, "the Plato recalled by Constantine is just a name used to cover precisely the Egyptian and Hermetic theology of the 'consubstantiality' of the Logos-Son with the Nous-Father."[46] In other words, Constantine's is a Hermetic interpretation of Plato.

Digeser pointed out that none of the places in which Constantine spent time as a member of Diocletian's court—Nassius, Salona, Trier, Babylon, Memphis, Nicomedia—are known for being home to Hermetic circles, but as Digeser admits, "it is extremely difficult to pinpoint where Hermetic circles do exist in the third and fourth centuries."[47] Concluding that there must have been a close advisor or teacher who introduced Constantine to Hermeticism, both Beatrice and Digeser naturally agreed that the emperor's Hermetic source was Lactantius.

Indeed, we have already seen how Lactantius familiarized Constantine with Hermeticism through his *Divine Institutes* and taught him that it was essentially compatible, in its monotheistic doctrine, with Christianity. Lactantius enthusiastically quotes from *Poimandres* fourteen times,[48] and in the Greek edition of the *Asclepius*, too, which he also cites, we discover a doctrine of *consubstantiality* between the Father and Son.[49] Most importantly, we locate in Lactantius a reference to Plato which mirrors Constantine's reference in his theological justification: Lactantius says that

---

44. Constantine, *Orat.* 9. Toom translates this as "the god above being, then made a second subordinate to this one (θεον . . . τον ὑπερ τον ουσιαν . . . ὑπεταξε δε τουτω και δευτερον)," (Toom, "Constantine's *Summus Deus*," 120).

45. Beatrice, "Word 'Homoousios,'" 265.

46. Beatrice, "Word 'Homoousios,'" 265.

47. Digeser, "Platonism in the Palace," 52.

48. Lactantius, *Inst.* 1.11; 2.11, 13, 15; 4.6; 5.65; 6.25; 7.4, 9, 13; 9; 16.

49. The word *homoousios* appears in fragments of the lost Greek version of *Ascl.* 19–20; see Digeser, "Platonism in the Palace," 51.

"Plato spoke about the first god and the second god,"⁵⁰ and he concludes that Plato was only following the ancient teaching of Hermes.⁵¹ With Lactantius's grand purpose of establishing a kinship between Platonism, Hermeticism, and Christianity in view, it becomes easy to believe that he would, as Constantine's religious advisor, have shared these sentiments and insights with the emperor. Professor Beatrice ultimately postulated that "in the years of the outbreak of the Arian controversy, Lactantius might have played a decisive role in influencing Constantine's Hermetic interpretation of Plato's theology and consequently the emperor's decision to insert *homoousios* into the Creed of Nicaea."[52]

We will now consider further evidence which connects Constantine to Graeco-Egyptian theology, both before and after Nicaea.

The Divine Mind and the Valley of the Kings

In 326 CE, ostensibly less than one year after the Council of Nicaea, Constantine enabled a pagan mystic named Nicagoras to take a trip to Egypt. Nicagoras traveled to the Valley of Kings, the famous burial site of ancient pharaohs, and made a point to visit the underground tunnels called the Syringes. Whether Constantine had personally commissioned this journey, or only sponsored it, is still unknown. Regardless, while Nicagoras was there, he left inscriptions on the stone: his trip to Egypt, he says, mimicked the same trip Plato had once made there hundreds of years earlier. Indeed, Greek legends said that Plato had traveled to Egypt to learn the Egyptians' secret theology, and now Nicagoras had been enabled by Constantine to follow in his footsteps. Nicagoras mentions Constantine by name in his inscription. He writes: "I . . . Nicagoras . . . investigated the tombs many lifetimes after the divine Plato from Athens, and I marveled and gave thanks to the gods and to the most devout emperor Constantine who made this possible for me."[53]

Constantine, by enabling Nicagoras's journey, may demonstrate an interest in a link between Plato and Egypt. We recall, of course, that Hermeticism is largely a fusion of Platonism and Egyptian religion, and we

---

50. Lactantius, *Epit.* 37,4.
51. Lactantius, *Epit.* 37,4.
52. Beatrice, "Word 'Homoousios,'" 266.
53. Inscription in Valley of Kings, Thebes, Egypt (*IGLT* 1265), cited in Lee, *Pagans and Christians*, 90.

are reminded also of Constantine's Hermetic reading of Plato. To further substantiate the connection between Nicagoras's trip to the Nicene *homoousios*, we must consider yet another inscription, this one found in the underground tunnels beneath the Valley of the Kings. Engraved on the stone walls was the Greek word *homoousios*, and the full inscription once again reminds us of the Nicene Creed: "There was a unique Mind . . . from him [came] the intelligent *logos* . . . [the] eternally incorruptible Son, reflection of the intelligent Father, one with the Father. Distinct from the Father only by name, but one with the Father and one from one . . . *homoousios*, eternally incorruptible."[54]

The affinity with both Nicaea and Constantine's Hermetic reading of Plato is obvious. The Hermetic tradition continues to provide the most direct link between Constantine and the word *homoousios*, and other Egyptian sources provide further evidence along these lines: at the Egyptian fortress of Ombos, for example, we find the inscription: "They call the *logos* 'Son of God' and 'God-Logos': a shared divinity is in the Son and in the Father."[55] And in another writing from Coptos we read about God and his Son-Logos: "The two are one, the Father and the illustrious Son."[56] As Beatrice observes, the corpus of evidence demonstrates "that the specifically theological use of homoousios should be traced back to its real Egyptian, pre-Christian roots."[57] And it is ultimately "very likely," he concludes, "that it was Lactantius who led Constantine towards the Christian reinterpretation of the Hermetic theology with which they were both acquainted."[58] Constantine's doctrine at Nicaea thus represents a Hermetic doctrine which had been "reworked in a Christian sense" by the emperor and his advisor.[59]

---

54. This inscription, originally composed by a priest of Heliopolis named Antiochus, was copied from the walls of the Syringes by a fifth-century Monophysite writer, who included it in the fifth oracle of his *Theosophia*. For a reconstruction, see Beatrice, *Anonymi Monophysitae Theosophia*, 22; see also Beatrice, "Word 'Homoousios,'" 261.

55. *Theosophia* 1.41. See Beatrice, *Anonymi Monophysitae Theosophia*, 21.

56. *Theosophia* 1.42.

57. Beatrice, "Word 'Homoousios,'" 263.

58. Beatrice, "Eusebius and Marcellus," 176.

59. Beatrice, "Eusebius and Marcellus," 176.

Constantine's Christology at Nicaea

We now turn our attention towards Constantine's personal use of *homoousios*, and to his understanding of the relationship between the Father and the Son at the time of Nicaea. Prior to the council, the emperor had admonished the Christians not to trouble themselves (and the empire) with christological nuances. He wrote to the quarreling Alexandrians that "We must . . . avoid being talkative in such matters."[60] But Constantine would ultimately refuse his own advice on speculating about what is "beyond comprehension."[61] Indeed, the emperor had developed his own opinions on the nature of Jesus Christ and his relationship to the Supreme God, opinions now maturing with his growing attachment to Christianity and his own involvement in her conflicts, and supported by some fair amount of imperial philosophical education. He would have preferred, of course, that the technical distinctives of his and every other monotheists' doctrine of God be kept private, and doubtless his own views would have remained confidential if the labor of Nicaea had not forced them into the open.

It is true that we may never be able to arrive at a definitive understanding of Constantine's Christology during this period, thanks to the insufficiency of the available sources and the political complexity of their context. Some have even argued that Constantine was deliberately misleading or vague in his christological pronouncements in order to "prepare for the establishment of a hoped for consensus at the grand Council of Nicaea."[62] Nevertheless, I do believe that a clearer picture than what has heretofore been drawn is attainable. What do the available sources tell us about the emperor's "gradually more precise" Christology?[63] In Constantine's *Oration*, the emperor says that his own doctrine agrees with the doctrine of the great Plato, who he says had taught the following "sound" sentiments "with truth":[64]

- There are two gods, "distinguished numerically as two."

---

60. Eusebius, *Vit. Const.* 2.69.
61. Toom, "Constantine's *Summus Deus*," 113.
62. Toom, "Constantine's *Summus Deus*," 116.
63. Toom, "Constantine's *Summus Deus*," 104.
64. "For Plato himself . . . declared, with truth, a God exalted above every essence, but to him he added also a second, distinguishing them as two, though both possessing one perfection, and the being of the second Deity proceeding from the first" (Constantine, *Orat.*, preserved in Eusebius, *Vit. Const.* 9).

- Both possess "one perfection."
- The "being of the second god proceeded from the first."
- The second deity is the "obedient agent" of the first God.
- The second deity, the Son and *logos*, is also to be "named" God.

Constantine himself speaks of the relationship between the Son and Father in the following way:

- God "has no origin, and therefore no beginning."
- The generation of the Son "was accompanied by no diminution of the Father's substance."
- Everything has a cause, and "the Father is the cause of the Son"
- The Son has an "eternal nature"

Eusebius, in his letter to his constituents describing the results of the Nicene Council, reflected further on Constantine's use of *homoousios*.[65] He says that the emperor in a speech had explained the following to the bishops:

- An *ousia* is not like a human body.
- The generated Son is not severed or divided from the Father (meaning he is an emanation whose production in no way diminished the Father's substance).
- The divine nature is:
  - Immaterial
  - Intellectual/exists in a spiritual realm

65. "[Constantine] interpreted [*homoousios*] not in the sense of the affections of bodies, nor as if the Son subsisted from the Father, in the way of division, or any severance; for that the immaterial and intellectual and incorporeal nature could not be the subject of any corporeal affection, but that it became us to conceive of such things in a divine and ineffable manner. And such were the theological remarks of our most wise and most religious emperor ... Additionally, it did not seem out of place to condemn the statement 'Before he was begotten he did not exist,' because everyone confesses that the Son of God existed before he was begotten according to the flesh. At this point in the discussion, our most pious Emperor maintained that the Son existed before all ages even according to his divinely inspired begetting, since even before the act of begetting was performed, in potentiality he was with the Father, even before he was begotten by him, since the Father is always Father, just as he is always King and always Savior; he has the potentiality to be all things, and remains exactly the same forever" (Eusebius, "Letter to his Constituents").

- Incorporeal/not in a body
- The Son preexisted his birth in Mary, being generated "before all ages."
- The Son-Logos was immanent in God, and "potentially" with the Father. God had been eternally a Father in the sense that he had the *potential* to be a Father, as he has the potential to be "all things."
- It is wrong to say that there was a time when God *became* the Father of the Son because God is immutable and never changes.
- We should ultimately conceive of the Son's relationship to God in a "divine and ineffable manner."

In light of all this testimony, I believe I can begin to articulate Constantine's personal theology at the time of Nicaea in the following way. For him, there had first existed a transcendent, immaterial, and solitary God, who at some point emanated out of his individual immaterial substance a second entity, the *logos*. There was no literal eternal generation per say—the *logos* was immanent in God and did not literally exist as a distinct entity until his generation (still it must be said that God was *in a sense* eternally a Father, due to his "potential" to be a Father, and because God is immutable). This second being was made of the same immaterial stuff as the first God, though his generation did not diminish the substance of the first God in any way. There were ultimately two gods, *homoousios* (made of the same kind of stuff), and the Son was the subordinate agent of the Father. In this way, Constantine's Christology, perhaps unsurprisingly, resembles that of his advisor Lactantius, who preached that God had "made" and "created" a "second god."[66]

Nicaea's creed, however, clearly anathematizes anyone who says that the Son was not eternal (in other words, that there was a time when God was not a Father). Given the emperor's Christology, how could he endorse such a creed? Through Eusebius's letter, we see that even Constantine appears to have read the language of the creed in his own way for the sake of unity. During the proceedings, he could see that the majority of the bishops wanted to say that the Son existed eternally and that God was eternally a Father, so he, like Eusebius and others, interpreted the language to accommodate his views.

Sara Parvis has argued in the opposite direction, that "Constantine *had always* been adamant that the Son had no temporal beginning," and

66. Lactantius, *Inst.* 4.6.4.

she points to two passages from Constantine's *Oration* in which the Son is said to have an "eternal (ἀΐδιος) cause" and to be of "eternal (αἰώνιος) nature."[67] But a closer look reveals that we need not read these passages to the effect that Constantine believed the Son himself had literally and personally existed from eternity.

In the first passage, Constantine says that the Son was generated not through a sexual union, but by "the effect of an eternal cause"—and he argues that because "nothing exists without a cause, of necessity the cause of existing substances preceded their existence . . . the Father is the cause of the Son, and the Son the effect of that cause." For Constantine, the Father was the preceding cause that generated the Son *in the same way* that Christ was the preceding cause that generated "the world and all things that it contains." In other words, the preceding eternal cause that effected the prolation of the Son was the Father. Regarding the second passage quoted by Parvis, Constantine says that "when the time came for him to assume a terrestrial body . . . an eternal nature received a beginning of temporal existence: a sensible form of a spiritual essence, a material manifestation of incorporeal brightness, appeared." Certainly, the divine *nature* of the Son was derived from the eternal nature of the Father, and in this way it could be said that the Son had an "eternal nature." This need not mean that the Son himself *personally* existed *alongside* the Father from eternity. It was the "eternal nature" which received a "beginning of temporal existence," not the "eternal Son."

A helpful analogy may be found in Tertullian, who had believed that there was a time when the Son did not personally exist, but nevertheless recognized that the Son's divine material was eternal, having been derived from the Father.[68] In other words, for Tertullian, the substance or nature of the Son was eternal, but the personality of the Son was not.[69] In the same way, for Constantine, the Son had a divine and eternal nature, being derived from the essence of the eternal Father, but before his begetting before all ages, he existed only *potentially* with God. In this way, we are able to harmonize these quotations from the emperor's *Oration* with Eusebius's testimony of Constantine's speech.

---

67. Parvis, *Marcellus of Ancyra*, 130, emphasis mine; see Constantine, *Orat.* 11.

68. "There was a time when there was no sin and no Son, when God was neither judge nor father" (Tertullian, *Herm.* 3.18). See Tuggy, "Tertullian the Unitarian."

69. See Bunsen, *Hippolytus and His Age*, 463.

Tarmo Toom argues, however, that Constantine's christological analogies describing the Son as a "word from the mind" actually "imply the co-temporality of the mentioned elements. By implication, they can also imply the co-eternality of the Father and the Son."[70] This analogy indeed does not necessarily imply co-eternality, or that God was truly an eternal Father. Analogically speaking, if the word has not yet been spoken, then one is not yet truly a "speaker"—one is only a potential speaker because of the presence of the word within him. Again, for Constantine, God was potentially a Father from eternity past, as Eusebius attests, and it is for this reason he could be called an eternal Father in virtue. It is perhaps true that an immanent word within a mind might be said to be co-temporal in some sense, but Constantine, when speaking of the Son, is describing a spoken word—this is the immanent word (*logos endiathetos*) which has become the proceeding word (*logos prophorikos*)—a distinct entity which, having been spoken out, now truly exists alongside God. The word may be eternal, and eternally within God, but the independent personality of the Son is not eternal and not identical to God.

Toom also argues that because Constantine rejected the anthropological analogy of birth for describing the generation of the *logos*, then he must have believed that there was no "temporal gap" between the Father and the Son.[71] But what Constantine clearly rejects is the materialistic implications of such an analogy, not necessarily its temporal implications; he rejects specifically the idea that the generated Son took with him a portion of the parent, which occurs during human childbirth. Constantine could furthermore reject the human birth analogy because in his view the preexistent Son does not have a Mother, and this is an argument which Toom also recognizes in Constantine.[72] Toom ultimately fails to take into account Eusebius's letter referring to Constantine's explanation that the Father can be understood as eternally a Father because the Son

---

70. Toom, "Constantine's *Summus Deus*," 120.

71. Toom, "Constantine's *Summus Deus*," 120.

72. That the Son was generated through a mystical union of a heavenly Father and Mother, or through a cooperation of masculine and feminine elements in God, was a speculation of some Christian gnostics. Several texts, including the Gospel of Thomas, the Gospel of Philip, and the Apocryphon of James suggest the Holy Spirit is the "Mother" of Jesus (or the true mother). See Barnstone and Meyer, *Gnostic Bible*, 34. As Toom reports, Constantine argues that "the begetting of the 'child' has to match with the fact that the eternal Son does not have a Mother—although the temporal, incarnated Son has a mother" (Toom, "Constantine's *Summus Deus*," 120).

was always potentially with the Father, but this should not be ignored and ultimately must be reconciled with the emperor's views in *Oration*. Constantine's sentiments in *Oration*, however, also continue to pull him toward a more subordinationist Christology.

In his praise of Plato's doctrine, which he clearly identifies as "sound" and "truthful," Constantine agrees that "the God above being, then made a second subordinate to this one."[73] Toom says that if Constantine had stopped there, then he would have been a subordinationist. But Toom points out that Constantine says both the first and second god "shared one perfection and the essence of the second god received its concrete existence from the first," which Toom believes represents a theology compatible with "later trinitarian orthodoxy."[74] In other words, Toom takes all of this to mean that for Constantine the Father and Son are two personalities abiding within the same single instance of the divine *ousia*, and that the Father has only logical (not ontological) priority over the Son. But as we have seen, in its earliest theological usage, entities which are said to be *homoousios* are regularly presented as unequal, and in terms of subordination. The word did not necessitate an organic connection between the emanation and its source, nor did it imply an equality of status, though it did not prohibit these things.[75] Indeed, virtually all theological applications of the term *homoousios* before Nicaea refer to "two or more beings" who "severally have (and not 'jointly constitute') a single *ousia*; that is . . . they have the same generic or specific characteristics, or the same material constitution."[76] Constantine's belief that the Father and Son are *homoousios*, that the first and second gods share an *ousia*, by no means implies a "trinitarian" or "orthodox" doctrine of God. The emperor's position that the first god has always *potentially* been the father of the second subordinate god is certainly outside the bounds of later orthodoxy.

Toom is probably right, however, that the articulation of Constantine's doctrine of God "retained a certain deliberate vagueness, which suited the always expedient pontifex maximus of every religion and sect of his empire,"[77] and that his "utterances were perhaps deliberately designed to

---

73. Toom, "Constantine's *Summus Deus*," 120.
74. Toom, "Constantine's *Summus Deus*," 121.
75. Stead, *Divine Substance*, 201.
76. Stead, *Divine Substance*, 248, 247.
77. Toom, "Constantine's *Summus Deus*," 103.

be heard according to one's religious preference."[78] Nevertheless, I believe Constantine held to a subordinationist Christology at the time of Nicaea which he had to privately square with the Nicene statement about the Son being eternal, and he was certainly not the only one who did so. Eusebius provides a helpful analogy in this regard: historians have long recognized that Eusebius, "while freely recognizing that the Son exists 'before all ages,' 'before eternal times,' etc., he consistently refuses to concede that He is co-eternal with the Father."[79] Though Eusebius did not believe in the eternal generation of the Son,[80] when describing the incarnation he could still speak of "the eternal Son of God [becoming] visible on earth."[81] If Eusebius, who did not believe in the eternality of the personal Son, found a way to not only sign the creed, but to speak of the Son (at least his divine nature) as "eternal" in some sense, then so could Constantine.[82] There are ultimately good grounds for concluding that while Constantine's Christology traveled along a similar axis as Eusebius's in regard to the Son's generation, he had (along with Eusebius) interpreted the creed to fit his theology for the sake of concord at Nicaea.

Timothy Barnes argues that we should date Constantine's *Oration* to just months before Nicaea in 325, and points out that Constantine's reference

---

78. Toom, "Constantine's *Summus Deus*," 122. Fox portrays Constantine as somewhat clumsy and ignorant of Greek theology, describing his doctrine as coming "dangerously close at one point to language which Arius would have permitted: we can only relish the irony and reflect that these words are one more proof that the speech was not thoroughly revised in later years" (Fox, *Pagans and Christians*, 654). Such a portrait does not, I believe, give adequate credit to Constantine.

79. Kelly, *Early Christian Doctrines*, 226. In Eusebius we find that "since the Father is alone ἀγέννητος 'everyone must admit that the Father is prior to and pre-exists the Son'" (Kelly, *Early Christian Doctrines*, 226).

80. See Rankin, "Arianism," 978: "[Eusebius] could, with Origen (and Paulinus of Tyre), describe the Logos as a 'second God'. Subordinationism was for him the only way to guarantee and appropriate distinction of Persons. The son is God, but not the one, true God . . . The Son worships the Father as God; therefore, the Father is God of the Son . . . Unlike Origen, however, for Eusebius there is no eternal begetting. The begetting of the Son is not without a beginning. The Son is not co-eternal with the Father (*Demonstratio Evangelica*, 5.1.20). The Father is alone unoriginated." See also Beatrice, "Eusebius and Marcellus," 169.

81. Eusebius, *Orat.* 17.

82. In the view of some early Christian fathers, time appears to be a byproduct of the movement of the celestial bodies. See Novation, *On the Trinity*, 1; Pseudo-Justin, *Exhortation to the Greeks*, 33. Time is thus a creation and part of the natural world, and could not precede the demiurgical *logos*. But the *logos*, being generated before time, is still necessarily after the Father, who is the source of all.

to a "second god" would have been popular among theologians who were sympathetic to "Arian" ideas in the early 320s, and that these sentiments disappeared after Nicaea.[83] But we must not make the mistake of assuming that Constantine would have abandoned his subordinationist theology after hearing the Nicene debates. Eusebius's letter reveals that Constantine did not ultimately feel too much pressure to fundamentally alter his own views about the Son's generation, but he did publicly assent to certain creedal statements in order to establish a consensus—on the condition, of course, that the bishops also assented to certain of his own preferences, namely his affinity for the Hermetic-gnostic term *homoousios*. Thus we are not forced to restrict the dating of the *Oration* to before Nicaea on the grounds of Constantine's Christology—it could very well belong, as Harold Drake once supposed, to "the last period of Constantine's reign."[84] Drake ultimately observed that Eusebius had attached this speech to his biography of Constantine "as an example of the emperor's developed thought . . . It seems clear, then, that Eusebius took the *Oration to the Saints* as a valid guide to Constantine's thinking at the very last stages of his reign and scholars [should not] try to limit its use merely to one period or another."[85]

Whatever *homoousios* had originally meant, or even what it meant to Constantine personally, for the sake of unity (which we must not forget was always Constantine's chief prize), the emperor appears to have allowed the word to be interpreted in new ways at Nicaea, as evidenced by his stripping

---

83. Barnes, "Monotheists All," 153–54.

84. Drake, "Suggestions of Date," 348.

85. Drake, "Suggestions of Date," 349. It is possible, however, to make the case that in the final years of his life (ca. 333–37) Constantine came to believe in the eternal generation doctrine in the same sense as Athanasius. There is one letter, preserved by Athanasius, in which Constantine seems to frame his doctrine in these terms (see Constantine's "Letter to Arius (ca. 333)," in Athanasius, *De Decretis*); it is unknown, however, and to my knowledge has not been considered whether or not Athanasius has faithfully reproduced this document in the context of his own polemical writing against Arius. At the very least we can say that the above summary represents Constantine's theology around the time of Nicaea, and this assessment is reinforced by another letter from that same year of 325 (November or December): Here the emperor says that it is God the Father who is without beginning, that "the Son always existed *in the Father*" (a statement consistent with Constantine's reported belief in the Son's *potential* existence in God), and finally that the Son was begotten in a going-forth which involved no division—he did not take a portion from the Father's being ("Constantine's Letter to Nicomedia [325 CE]"). This is, I believe, the sense in which we are to understand Constantine's insistence in his *Oration* that the Son was not divided from the Father—his prolation did not divide or diminish God's substance.

the term of its usual material sense. This might even be said to represent Constantine's (and Nicaea's) great theological achievement—the shift in the meaning of *homoousios* away from its typical materialistic connotations towards immateriality. And it is right to say that Constantine, in addition to enabling this shift in meaning, also enabled other interpretations of this language by encouraging the bishops to think of it in a "divine" and "ineffable" way. This leads us to believe that Constantine, though intent on using forms familiar to him, was ultimately setting up a useful mystery. Indeed, for the many attendees who held to a diverse range of christological views, the meaning of *homoousios* was necessarily ambiguous. It may have had a specific sense for Constantine, but there was no agreement among the bishops—nevertheless, it *would* force the rejection of Arius, who had publicly rejected the word as gnostic and unscriptural. But again, the manner of its implementation at Nicaea could still leave room for those who wanted to privately interpret it in their own way. The "inexpressibility" of Constantine's *homoousios* indeed left the door wide open to a variety of different theologies, and thus to as much theological unity as could be achieved in the aftermath of an Arian censure.

Aftermath

After Nicaea, some of the anti-Arian bishops revealed that during the council they had been "reduced to silence in order to preserve peace."[86] As Beatrice concludes, "This means that all the leaders of the anti-Arian party were unwillingly forced to accept Constantine's decision in favor of homoousios, but that none of them was really interested in the addition of this new word."[87] Arian signatories like Eusebius of Nicomedia, we know, later confessed to Constantine that in signing the creed they had only been "subscribing to the heresy from fear of you."[88] It was thus a problem for Arians and anti-Arians alike, both at the council and in its wake.[89]

---

86. Eustathius of Antioch, in Theodoret, *Hist. eccl.* 1.8.3.

87. Beatrice, "Word 'Homoousios,'" 256.

88. Nicetas Choniates, *Treasury of Orthodoxy*, 5.7–9. Philostorgius, *Church History*, 2.7–7b. See Chandler, *God of Jesus*, 199.

89. "Moreover it is clear that both before and after the council there were many Greeks who regarded the *homoousion* as a treacherous neologism: who but Constantine could have induced them to accept it with such unanimity in 325?" (Edwards, "First Council of Nicaea," 563).

Constantine, on the other hand, had evidently been convinced that Christian doctrine could be interpreted through pagan theological forms, specifically through those of Hermetic monotheism. He furthermore shared the concern of the anti-Arians and hoped that through the use of such Hermetic categories he could preserve the divinity of the Son, keeping him on the side of the divine Father, and that he could simultaneously enable a theological consensus. By doing away with the materialistic notions of the term, and by instructing the bishops to think of it in a "divine and ineffable manner," the bishops then accepted it in its ambiguity for political reasons, namely to oust Arius and to please the emperor.

Eusebius of Caesarea appears to have reluctantly accepted it because for him, it did not ultimately contradict his famous doctrine of *two ousiai*.[90] Though Eusebius was hesitant to assent to it for the many reasons described above, in its original Hermetic-gnostic meaning (describing two beings of kindred substance) it appears surprisingly conducive to Eusebian theology. The modalist bishop Marcellus of Ancyra would write against Eusebius and the Arians, strongly arguing that they were in fact crypto-Hermeticists and gnostics, evidently because Eusebius's doctrine was akin to the Hermetic doctrine of two gods.[91] It is interesting that Marcellus, in his dramatic critique, stops short of directly criticizing the word *homoousios*, perhaps because of Constantine's authorship, and the fact that the emperor was the real crypto-Hermeticist actively infusing Christian confession with borrowed and alien elements. But Marcellus's critique of his opponents' alleged crypto-Hermeticizing may help us to explain why Constantine reacted so harshly towards Marcellus.[92]

---

90. See Hanson, *Search for the Christian Doctrine*, 185. See also Beckwith, *Hilary of Poitiers on the Trinity*, 16.

91. "These then teach three hypostases, just as [the gnostic] Valentinus the heresiarch first invented in the book entitled by him 'On the Three Natures.' For he was the first to invent three hypostases and three persons of the Father, Son, and Holy Spirit, and he is discovered to have filched this from Hermes and Plato" (Marcellus of Ancyra, *On the Holy Church*, 8–9; Logan, "Marcellus of Ancyra," 95). The God of Marcellus is a monad; it is not possible that there is more than one hypostasis. Marcellus "totally rejects the idea of a possible agreement of the Bible with Platonism. Instead he wants to develop a theological discourse based exclusively on the exegesis of the Scriptures" (Beatrice, "Eusebius and Marcellus," 181).

92. See Parvis, *Marcellus of Ancyra*, 130. See also Beatrice, "Eusebius and Marcellus," 184, who also sees that "Marcellus' personal attack on the members of the *Eusebian Alliance* did not find favour with Constantine who had been engaged for quite some time in reconciling the opposing parties, and in the end Marcellus was deposed at the synod of Constantinople in 336."

Bishop Hosius, the man Constantine had originally summoned to investigate the Arian controversy, left Constantine immediately after the Council, deeply disappointed in its result. The bishop, once the important advisor of the emperor, seems to have stayed relatively silent until the death of both Constantine and his opponent Eusebius. After both his old master and his theological foe had passed, Hosius returned with Marcellus and reformulated a creed *without* the word *homoousios*.[93] Perhaps we should read this as Hosius's and Marcellus's revenge on Constantine's theological innovation, which had been accepted by Eusebius, their common enemy.[94]

Constantine's Nicaea can be seen as reflective of his quest for universal monotheism, not merely in the concerns which precipitated the gathering, but in its final product. The creed illustrates that Constantine not only believed common theological ground could be discovered between the majority of Christian monotheists, but that pagan monotheism, in the form of Hermeticism and Hermetic readings of Plato, could point the way to that common ground. Constantine's personal conviction that Christian doctrine could be communicated through the terminological forms of pagan monotheism is reminiscent of his teacher Lactantius, and evidently this pluralistic vision, paired with both the emperor's inexorable influence and *homoousios*' ability to expel perceived troublemakers, was enough to override any ecclesial concerns about the word *homoousios*, public or private.

If the ongoing Donatist problem had not made it sufficiently clear, the frail theological alliance achieved at Nicaea made the tenuous nature of Christendom's unity undeniable. Going forward, Constantine's strategy for resolving intra-Christian disputes would need to change. His suppression of Christian "schismatics" and "heretics" soon paced beyond the Donatists and the Arians. By 326 CE, he was victimizing Novationists, Valentinians (gnostics), Marcionites, Paulinists (unitarians), and Montanists by outlawing their assemblies and confiscating their property. "The unity of the Christian movement," it was now clear, "was to be maintained by the power of the empire."[95]

But important questions remain: did Constantine's growing intolerance for perceived Christian dissidents spill over into his treatment of

---

93. The Council of Sardica in 343 CE, influenced by Marcellus and Hosius, dropped Constantine's *homoousios* in favor of *mia hypostasis*. Hosius continued his campaign against the word in the creed developed at Sirmium in 351 CE, also called the "formula of Hosius," which condemned both *homoousios* and *homoiousios*.

94. See Beatrice, "Word 'Homoousios,'" 271.

95. Grant, *Augustus to Constantine*, 249.

traditionalist pagans? Exactly how *Christian* was Constantine? Despite his christological musings and significant involvement in official councils and pronouncements of the church, does the rest of the evidence pointing to his sustained connection with the pagan world permit us to call him a Christian? And what do his official religious policies, his later propaganda, and his famous baptism tell us about his relationship with the Christian religion both before and after Nicaea?

9

Constantine's Program

IN 312, FOLLOWING THE battle at Milvian Bridge, Constantine entered the city of Rome carrying his brother-in-law's head on a pike. The people turned out to greet their new master and celebrated with cheers his victory over Maxentius, whom Constantinian propaganda had labeled a "usurper." Making the customary journey down the Via Sacra towards the Roman Forum, Constantine's chariot was followed by a host of senators eager to show their support—each of them doubtless imagining what this abrupt change might mean for the empire and their own careers. Continuing down the path, Constantine would have passed the still incomplete construction of Maxentius's basilica, which Constantine would later finish and adorn with a forty-foot solar-themed statue of himself. Next he would have passed the massive bronze doors and porphyry columns of the temple which Maxentius had built for his deified son, Romulus. It was clear that the rule of Maxentius was one dramatically cut short, and, as the songs would later say, not by the sword of Constantine alone, but by the hand of the Supreme God. This point would form the axis on which all Constantinian propaganda would turn for the next quarter of a century. But how many in the Roman crowds that day were fully aware of it? They would know soon enough. As Constantine finally entered the Forum, the masses cheered his victory, his name, and the dawn of a new era. But I cannot help but think that Constantine's face remained stern amidst the fanfare, his mind trained squarely on his next steps. Despite the trumpets of victory, he knew his revolution had only just begun.

Constantine's immediate task was to initiate the religious insurgency for which his god had commissioned him. Knowing that he would be challenging not only the theological assumptions and praxis of the tetrarchy, but of countless Romans, Constantine needed to immediately rally to himself the coalition of monotheists who would support both his restoration program and his rule. At the same time, he needed to demonstrate his program's link to Roman tradition and identity. How would Constantine's personal theological journey shape his official religious policies? Did the emperor, at any point during his reign, compel the empire to follow in his righteous footsteps? Did he make all sacrifice illegal, as some scholars have resolutely proposed, effectively outlawing traditional paganism? As we will see, reading Constantine's actions in light of the emperor's quest for primitive monotheism helps fill in the gaps.

A Policy of Intolerance or Concord?

The emperor's official religious policies are perhaps the most contentious area of Constantine scholarship. Claims that he either outlawed traditional pagan religion in the empire, or made life extremely difficult for pagans, are regularly lobbed at those who have found the reports about his sudden and complete "conversion" in 312 unconvincing. We will now embark upon a brief investigation of these claims, and will ultimately attempt to reconcile the reports of his actions against traditional Roman paganism with our broader narrative about Constantine's quest for monotheism.

First, we must define our terms. What is *religious tolerance*? A policy of tolerance is one which officially disagrees with certain religious ideas or groups, but because of some guiding principle, permits the existence of such groups without actively working to remove or otherwise transform them. In such a policy, there is no expectation that these ideas or groups will ever change.

A policy of *intolerance* is one which officially disagrees with certain religious ideas or groups and *does not* allow them to exist. Such a policy actively works to remove or otherwise transform them. In this approach, there is a pointed expectation of change.

A policy of *concord*, however, while it is similar to one of tolerance in that it is guided by a principle which permits the existence of unfavorable religious ideas and groups, also "works toward ultimate conversion and unity."[1] As Digeser explains, "A state has adopted a policy of concord if (1) its attitude of forbearance is dictated by some moral, political, or even religious principle and (2) it expects that by treating its dissenters with

---

1. Digeser, *Making of a Christian Empire*, 110.

forbearance it is creating conditions under which they will ultimately change to conform to what the state accepts."[2]

As we have seen, Lactantius's ideal policy for his proposed monotheistic state set forth in his *Divine Institutes* is one of concord. Guided by the principle that conversion cannot be forced, Lactantius advocates for freedom of religion—both Christian and non-Christian religion—with the expectation that eventually things will change. I argue that Constantine's own policy, ostensibly building off of Lactantius's model, was likewise one of concord. Constantine certainly disagreed with the traditional cults, and he eventually came to publicly despise their idolatry and especially their blood sacrifices, nevertheless, as I will argue, he permitted them to exist.

It is true that at several junctures he took isolated and limited action against certain pagan sites and practices, and we will discuss these incidents in the following section. But at this point we may already recognize how antithetical an aggressive policy of intolerance would have been to all the advice of his counselor Lactantius. It seems difficult to believe that Constantine would agree with Lactantius that the Supreme God had made man reasonable, and that monotheism was the most natural and rational theology,[3] but then suddenly disagree with his advisor that man should be allowed to exercise his natural reason, and should instead be compelled to monotheism by force. Yet this has been the unflinching position of some scholars, and their arguments that Constantine enacted an aggressive policy of persecution against pagans must be considered.

Prohibition of Pagan Ritual?

Constantine, having noticeably matured in his Christian theology by 325, had come to disdain both idolatry and blood sacrifice. The emperor's increasing contempt of idols is certainly in keeping with his adoption of the decline-of-monotheism narrative. Like Lactantius and other writers, Constantine now identified the setting up of "false idols" as a practice which "seduce[s] from the service of the true God."[4] The biblical king Nebuchadnezzar's idolatry, he says, was "unlawful worship."[5] Constantine finally ridicules the human

---

2. Digeser, *Making of a Christian Empire*, 111.

3. See Constantine's "Letter to the Eastern Provincials in Eusebius (324 CE)," preserved in Eusebius, *Vit. Const.* 2.48.

4. Constantine, *Orat.* 11.

5. Constantine, *Orat.* 17.

sculptor who, "as if forgetful of himself, idolizes his own creation, and adores it as an immortal god, while yet he admits that himself, the author and maker of the image, is a mortal man."[6] He criticizes also those who might think "that some special power resided in images formed and fashioned by human art; and hence your reverence, and diligent care lest they should be defiled: those mighty and highly exalted gods [are] thus dependent on the care of men!"[7] For some Hermeticists, humans were indeed understood to be "creators of gods," agents capable of calling down a portion of the divine essence into a material idol in order to produce a living deity.[8] Certainly Constantine would have learned to despise such idols through exposure to the biblical monotheism of the Christians, but we must not forget that some Roman pagans had already understood that man's original religion was aniconic. Again, the Roman scholar Varro (d. 27 BCE) had mourned the decline of an "original aniconic religion," and, longing for a return to a "more pure" religion in Rome, even said that the most ancient Romans had worshiped without images for nearly two centuries.[9] While Christianity remains the most obvious source, and while it is difficult to know how widespread Varro's opinion was in the early fourth century, we should not preclude the pagan world from having had some influence on Constantine in this regard. Whatever Constantine's previous opinions on idols before his public embrace of Christianity in 312, it is clear that by 324–25 he had come to utterly reject idolatry. He concludes in his *Oration* that those who "worship images of their own devising, made in the likeness of men or other living beings," belong to "the unthinking portion of mankind."[10]

Regarding Constantine's disdain for blood sacrifice, some scholars have suggested that it was first manifest in a dramatic refusal to offer the customary sacrifice to Jupiter on Capitoline Hill after his defeat of Maxentius in 312. This is often interpreted to mean that Constantine had truly "converted" to Christianity and already turned away from the pagan world in that year. But the whole Capitoline scenario is an argument from silence.[11] It is true that

6. Constantine, *Orat.* 4; Constantine, *Oration of Constantine*, 563.
7. Constantine, *Orat.* 22; Constantine, *Oration of Constantine*, 578.
8. See *Ascl.* 23–24, 37–38.
9. Harding, *Paul's Eschatological Anthropology*, 35. See Augustine, *City of God*, 4.31.
10. Constantine, *Orat.* 9; Constantine, *Oration of Constantine*, 567.
11. Fraschetti made the argument that "on the basis of the most absolute lack of any positive documentation, it is difficult, very difficult, to suppose that on the occasion of his first advent in Rome, Constantine had ascended to the temple of Jupiter Optimus Maximus" (Fraschetti, *La conversione*, 76, translation mine). There is one late fourth-century

the earliest records of the 312 celebration show no evidence that Constantine's procession stopped at the Temple of Jupiter, but Moralee has recently demonstrated that new emperors did not always ascend Capitoline Hill, and for a variety of political reasons.[12] In the end, whether this contested story is true or not may matter very little. We know for certain, at the very least from his letter to Sapor around 324, that sometime between the battle at Milvian Bridge and Nicaea, Constantine did come to refuse blood sacrifices—a revolutionary development for any emperor at any time.[13] Does this signal a complete turn from paganism to Christianity? Would either Constantine or his subjects have interpreted a refusal to sacrifice to Jupiter (for example) as undeniable apostasy from Roman paganism?

Other interpretations are available. First, Constantine could have refused sacrifice to Jupiter on the hill, not because he was an orthodox Christian who wanted nothing to do with paganism, but because he was a monotheist who believed in the decline-of-monotheism narrative. After all, he had learned from both Lactantius and a host of pagan writers that Jupiter, the god of the tyrant Diocletian, was no god at all, and had actually been a historical human figure who stole the true god's honor for himself. The Hermetic *Asclepius*, used by Lactantius, reveals that some pagan monotheists already thought that Jupiter, chief of the traditional Roman pantheon, was in reality beneath the Supreme God and only king of the lesser deities.[14] But how

---

account, composed roughly eighty years after the fact by the pagan historian Eunapius (d. 414), who in his *Historia* says that at one point the emperor did visit the temple on Capitoline Hill, and at other times he decided not to (this text is preserved for us in the pagan Zosimus's *Nea Historia*, ca. 498–518 CE). However, Eunapius writes that Constantine's first refusal took place in the year 313 and at the Secular Games, not in 312 during his victory celebration. Moralee's recent investigation of traditions surrounding Capitoline Hill (2018) regards the Eunapius account as polemical and spurious; see Moralee, *Rome's Holy Mountain*, 42, 124–25. It has often been pointed out that the pagan author of the 313 panegyric, the earliest account we have of the celebration, not only omits any mention of a Constantinian trip up the Capitoline that day, but also says that some Romans in the crowd chided Constantine for entering the palace "too quickly." This may suggest he had left some important business undone. The whole scenario is impossible to prove, however, and several good points have been made to the contrary; see McCormick, *Eternal Victory*, 101 no. 93.

12. Moralee, *Rome's Holy Mountain*, 32–42.

13. In his letter to Sapor, Constantine explains that he personally "recoil[s] with horror from the blood of sacrifices, from their foul and detestable odors" (Constantine, "Letter to Sapor, King of the Persians (324/325 CE)"; preserved in Eusebius, *Vit. Const.* 4.9–13; Constantine, *Oration of Constantine*, 543).

14. *Ascl.* 19.

did Constantine, a Roman emperor, get away with refusing to participate in traditional cult? Would the people have ever tolerated an emperor who showed such disrespect for deities like Jupiter?

When Constantine entered Rome in 312, we must not forget that he came armed with not only a contempt for Jupiter, but with a strong public commitment to the Roman god Sol Invictus. His penchant for Sol, in light of the preceding numismatic and panegyrical evidence, had obviously spread far beyond his own army and entourage by this time. Indeed, when the senators organized the construction of Constantine's arch in 312, they did not have to guess which god or what religious themes were important to him. The god Constantine brought with him down the Via Sacra was the well-known god of his own father, the emperor Constantius Chlorus, and had been the famous patron and protector of the great emperor Aurelian, the one to whom Aurelian had built lavish temples in Rome and had given the title "Master of the Roman Empire."[15] When Elagabalus had dragged his great stone from Syria into Rome in the previous century, his push for monotheism had not enjoyed the support of this great legacy. But in 312, Constantine's god was undeniably Roman.

Furthermore, we know that some pagan monotheists had already scorned blood sacrifices in favor of "rational" worship. In the Hermetic *Asclepius*, "the one and only God should be worshipped by noetic means. Indeed burning as much as a grain of incense when praying is a sacrilegious act (*Asclepius* 41)."[16] As Digeser points out, Constantine's rejection of blood sacrifices "would have pleased Neoplatonists and Hermeticists as much as Christians."[17] Simon Corcoran even goes so far as to say that in Constantine's day "for many pagans sacrifice was not a key issue, indeed it was already disapproved," and for this he cites Porphyry's arguments in his *De abstinentia*.[18] In my view, this sort of thinking represented only a minority of Romans. Nevertheless, in this light, I see no reason why Constantine could not have already begun to develop disdain for sacrifices as a non-Christian monotheist before 312.

---

15. MacMullen, *Paganism in the Roman Empire*, 86.

16. Athanassiadi and Frede, *Pagan Monotheism*, 13.

17. Digeser, *Making of a Christian Empire*, 169.

18. Corcoran also notes that "When Julian 'the Apostate' later indulged in lavish sacrifices, even his admirer Ammianus thought this unnecessarily ostentatious and immoderate" (Corcoran, "From Unholy Madness to Right-Mindedness," 79–80). See Ammianus Marcellinus, *Res Gestae*, 22.12.6–7; 25.4.17.

Constantine's public disregard for the long tradition of sacrifice doubtless surprised and angered many. But this was a risk he had been willing to take. Beyond reasons of personal preference, I do see a larger game afoot. Leithart was right to point out that "Diocletian's empire was built on sacrifice, his persecutions inspired by failed sacrifice. As soon as he defeated Maxentius, Constantine made it clear that a new political theology was coming to be, a political theology without sacrifice."[19] But Constantine, in refusing blood sacrifice, was not only honoring the Supreme God with the pure and rational worship of the golden age, he was obliterating one of the greatest roadblocks to unity between the pagan and Christian worlds.

Evidence of Persecution?

Among Constantine scholars, a debate has endured over whether or not Constantine, regardless of his own feelings, ever imposed an official ban on sacrifice in his empire. If he did, does this indicate that Constantine, as a Christian, ultimately took an aggressive "anti-pagan" stance, as argued by Barnes and others?

After a long and bloody conflict, Constantine finally defeated his co-emperor Licinius in the year 324.[20] Eusebius tells us that Constantine, having ascended to total power over the empire, subsequently banned Roman officials from preceding official business with sacrifice.[21] In his following chapter, Eusebius recalls another declaration of Constantine's which, regardless of whether or not he had access to the full text of the purported edict, the bishop certainly understood to include the total banning of new cult-objects and pagan sacrifice.[22] This point has provided a major substrate for Barnes's

---

19. Leithart, *Defending Constantine*, 66.

20. Before Constantine killed him, Licinius may have been encouraged by his brother-in-law towards monotheism. "Undoubtedly inspired by Constantine," writes Odahl, "Licinius had a dream on his journey in which an angel told him to seek aid from the 'Highest God.' [Licinius's opponent] Maximin, in contrast, took a vow that if his forces should win, he would utterly destroy the Christians . . . Before the battle, Licinius led his army in prayer to the *Summus Deus*" (Odahl, *Constantine and the Christian Empire*, 120). While having jointly issued the so-called Edict of Milan with Constantine in 313, giving freedom to Christians and all Romans to worship the *Summus Deus* in their own way, his tolerance of Christians (perhaps for their connection to his rival Constantine) appears to have run out towards the end of his rule. According to Eusebius, persecutions of Christians were finally enacted in his territory (Eusebius, *Hist. eccl.* 1.3).

21. Eusebius, *Vit. Const.* 2.44.

22. Eusebius, *Vit. Const.* 2.45.

vision of the emperor as an aggressive anti-pagan. Barnes's interpretation of Eusebius has, however, been forcefully challenged.[23]

One reason to doubt the existence of a Constantinian law totally banning sacrifice, which would have effectively halted the exercise of traditional paganism and even encouraged the persecution of pagans, is the fact that we have no such law recorded in the *Theodosian Code*. Another reason is found in Constantine's own *Letter to the Eastern Provincials*, also quoted by Eusebius.[24] Dating to the spring or summer of 325, the letter reaffirms the need for peace in the empire, and that tolerance should be awarded to both Christians and pagans. Constantine declares:

> Let those in error, as well as the believers, gladly receive the benefit of peace and quiet. For this sweetness of fellowship will be effective for correcting them and bringing them to the right way. May none molest another; may each retain what his soul desires, and practice it . . . Those who hold themselves back [from the truth], let them keep if they wish their sanctuaries of falsehood.[25]

As has been suggested, in this letter Constantine was probably responding to localized intolerance of pagans initiated by overly-aggressive Christians who were galvanized by, but not quite content with, their recent political success.[26] Constantine's envoy thus represents an appeal to return to the broadly tolerant state envisioned by the earlier edict of 313 (the so-called Edict of Milan, jointly issued by Constantine and the pagan Licinius). Most importantly, revealed in this letter is Constantine's policy of concord: traditional cult was allowed to remain, despite the emperor's fierce disagreement with it. "For it is one thing to undertake the contest for immortality voluntarily," he writes, "[it is] another to compel it with punishment." He furthermore says that he has written these words to publicly clarify his policies, "because I hear some people are saying the customs of the temples and the power of darkness have been taken away. I should, indeed, have advised this very thing to all men, if the violent opposition of wicked error were not immoderately embedded in some souls."[27] He

---

23. See Errington, "Constantine and the Pagans," 309–18.

24. Eusebius, *Vit. Const.* 2.48–60.

25. Constantine, "Letter to the Eastern Provincials (324 CE)," preserved in Eusebius, *Vit. Const.* 2.48–60; Lenski, *Constantine and the Cities*, 232.

26. Errington, "Constantine and the Pagans," 118.

27. Constantine, "Letter to the Eastern Provincials (324 CE)," preserved in Eusebius, *Vit. Const.* 2.48–60; Drake, *Constantine and the Bishops*, 303.

ultimately "pray[s], however, that they too may receive the same blessing, and thus experience that heartfelt joy which unity of sentiment inspires."[28] Indeed it may be, Constantine concludes, "that restoring the sweetness of fellowship . . . will prevail to direct them to the straight road."[29] As Drake rightly surmised, "Rumor or misunderstanding had prompted some persons to believe that Constantine had or would act against pagan rites. To set the record straight, and either to prevent or stop acts of violence against the temples from occurring, Constantine issued a clear statement of policy."[30] This policy is certainly one of concord, not intolerance. All of this moves powerfully against those who have argued so earnestly that Constantine was an aggressive anti-pagan crusader, effectively banning paganism by outlawing traditional sacrifice.

Eusebius's *Oration in Praise of Constantine*, delivered to the emperor at the end of his life in 335 and read aloud in a mixed company of pagans and Christians, reinforces this assessment.[31] The bishop explains to the assembly that Constantine's god is one who is able to be approached, and in fact is approached, by everyone. He says that "the entire family of mankind . . . though diverse in their opinions about other matters, unanimously agree on this alone: calling on the one and only God in obedience to the logic implanted in them, the uninstructed impulse of their own minds."[32] This suggests that Constantine's sentiments, even at the end of his reign, must have continued to mirror Lactantius's in regard to religious tolerance, since it was ostensibly public knowledge that the emperor regarded monotheism as the most natural and rational religion, and thus one which need not be compelled. Constantine, says Eusebius, "demonstrates a pious spirit in every action of his life, and imparts to all his subjects the knowledge of the one who is everyone's Sovereign Lord."[33] And Constantine imparts this knowledge not by the spear, but by the shepherd's staff. This emperor is no religious tyrant like Diocletian. Constantine takes not the role of the butcher but of the shepherd of the Roman people, guiding them and influencing them through his own

---

28. Constantine, "Letter to the Eastern Provincials (324 CE)," preserved in Eusebius, *Vit. Const.* 2.56.

29. Constantine, "Letter to the Eastern Provincials (324 CE)," preserved in Eusebius, *Vit. Const.* 2.56.

30. Drake, *Constantine and the Bishops*, 303.

31. For the dating, see Drake, "De Laudibus Constantini," 345–56.

32. Eusebius, *Laud. Const.* 1.3, translation mine.

33. Eusebius, *Laud. Const.* 5.8, translation mine.

example to use their God-given senses to commune with the Divine Mind. As Eusebius tells the court, their pious emperor, whom he likens to a "radiant sun" benevolently touching each of his subjects with his rays, has replaced the sacrifice of firstborn lambs with an offering of human souls to God, the "souls of the flock which is in his care, those rational creatures whom he leads to the knowledge and righteous worship of God."[34]

Still, the rest of the evidence offered by those who believe Constantine to have been an anti-pagan tyrant must be carefully considered. It is true that Eusebius provides a catalog of Constantine's actions against pagan sites and rituals, including the cleansing of a future church site of elements of Aphrodite's cult,[35] and the shuttering of cult prostitution in Phoenicia and certain healing rituals in Cilicia.[36] But when Eusebius recounts these movements against specific pagan sites and practices, no mention of any general law against sacrifice is made, and at any rate such a law would not have accounted for all of these actions.[37] Constantine's activity can thus be interpreted in a variety of ways: for example, several of these instances might be reflective of local municipal problems or matters of taste and public decency.[38] It is interesting that Eusebius says Constantine's decision to close down a ritual prostitution complex had taught the local citizens "to practice self-control."[39] Were issues of morality and decency and other civic concerns, rather than rival doctrines of God, indeed at the heart of Constantine's actions? In this light, and as T. G. Elliott and R. Errington have skillfully contended, it appears that in his reference to a total ban of sacrifice Eusebius deliberately created a false impression of Constantine's actual and "long-term" policy.[40]

Later references to Constantine's policies have also been important to this debate. For example, Libanius, a pagan born in 314, made a grand plea to preserve pagan temples in 386 to the emperor Theodosius. Here Libanius reflects positively on the general peace of Constantine's reign, and ultimately says that Constantine "made absolutely no changes in the traditional forms

---

34. Eusebius, *Orat.* 2.6, 3.4, translation mine.
35. Eusebius, *Vit. Const.* 3.26.
36. Eusebius, *Vit. Const.* 3.55–58.
37. Errington, "Constantine and the Pagans," 313.
38. Errington, "Constantine and the Pagans," 317.
39. Eusebius, *Vit. Const.* 3.55.5.
40. Elliott, "Eusebian Frauds," 169; Errington, "Constantine and the Pagans," 315.

of worship."[41] While he does admit that Constantine raided the treasuries of pagan temples in order to build his new city of Constantinople, Libanius nevertheless confirms that the temple rituals carried on.[42] Barnes, however, has concluded that Libanius simply lied, citing Libanius's own reference in his *Autobiography* to an uncle of Crispinus of Heraclea who "risked death by his ostentatious paganism and 'mocked that evil law and its impious enactor.'"[43] But does this refer to some law of Constantine, or to a law of this sort later enacted by his sons Constans and Constantius II in 341? In 341, the two brothers certainly portrayed their own total ban on sacrifice as only reinforcing the law of their father,[44] and at first glance this seems like good evidence that such a ban had indeed been executed by Constantine. But if this is true, then Constantine's original ban had ostensibly not been very well-enforced, as suggested by the need of his sons to reaffirm, and in the harshest and most lucid language, an empire-wide ban on sacrifice. But even if a total ban had indeed been signed by Constantine sometime in 324, it might have only lasted a few months before being "quietly superseded" by the *Letter to the Eastern Provincials*.[45] Constans and Constantius II, much more prepared to publicly repudiate the pagan world than their father, might have been selective in their citation of their father's commands. Ultimately, Libanius, in his plea to Theodosius, had clearly found Constantine's public record useful for encouraging Theodosius to adopt a similar policy of tolerance towards paganism. Constans and Constantius II, as well as Eusebius, were on the other hand "using Constantine as a rhetorical tool to bolster anti-pagan programs. This makes it difficult to know which authority to trust."[46]

Most modern scholars have ultimately concluded that in Eusebius's description of Constantine's total ban on new cult idols and sacrifice, "Eusebius must be generalizing on the basis of isolated attacks on pagan cults."[47] Thus most scholars believe that Constantine continued a program of religious

41. Libanius, *Autobiography*, Orat. 30.6; Bradbury, "Constantine and the Problem," 120–39.
42. Libanius, *Autobiography*, Orat. 30.6.
43. Barnes, *Constantine*, 6.
44. *Codex Theodosianus*, 16.10.2.
45. Errington, "Constantine and the Pagans," 315.
46. Lenski, *Constantine and the Cities*, 232.
47. Bradbury, "Constantine and the Problem," 122.

tolerance throughout his reign, though perhaps one punctuated from time to time with the fruits of his impatience and passion.

But what of Kevin Wilkinson's evidence from Palladas, so enthusiastically employed by Barnes to justify his essentially Eusebian portrait of Constantine as a Christian emperor marching proudly against the pagan world?[48] Wilkinson had argued that some of the writings of Palladas, a pagan Greek epigrammatist, were, contrary to prevailing opinion, produced between 325–35, and that they are representative of what must be general pagan sorrow at the victory of Christianity in Constantine's empire.[49] The pagan Palladas writes: "We Hellenes are men reduced to ashes, holding to our buried hopes in the dead; for everything has been turned on its head."[50] Barnes takes this to mean that traditional pagan religion had essentially "already perished" beneath Constantine's "serious attack" on paganism.[51]

However, some scholars have doubted Wilkinson's evidence, portraying his claim to have redated Palladas to the time of Constantine as "much less strong than he presents it."[52] Regardless, it all bears surprisingly little weight for the basic thesis of this book. Even if it were true that Constantine had enacted a significant and even permanent ban on new idols and traditional sacrifices, evoking dismay from pagans like Palladas, such changes could still fit into a Constantinian quest for universal monotheism: his rejection of cult idols would be understandable in light of the aniconic spirit driving Jewish, Christian, and some strains of pagan monotheism, while his removal of blood sacrifice might represent a risky but necessary obliteration of a chief roadblock preventing unity between Christians and pagans. Again, Constantine's banning of blood sacrifices "would have pleased Neoplatonists and Hermeticists as much as Christians."[53] Thus Constantine might have been progressively purging the pagan world of its base accouterments, contracted long ago in ignorance, and now inappropriate in light of the restoration of true religion. Digeser points out that "nothing in the definitions of tolerance or concord requires a state to allow everything religious

---

48. Barnes, *Constantine*, 16.

49. Wilkinson, "Palladas and the Age of Constantine," 36–60.

50. Palladas, *Anth. Gr.* 10.90; Wilkinson, "Palladas and the Age of Constantine," 36–60.

51. Barnes, *Constantine*, 16.

52. Dijkstra, Review of *New Epigrams of Palladas*, 370–73.

53. Digeser, *Making of a Christian Empire*, 169.

that it finds harmful. Even the more liberal constitutions can justify some sanctions against religion: The United States Constitution guarantees freedom of religion, but this guarantee does not protect every practice or action that is called religious."[54] Indeed, Mormon fundamentalism, for example, is allowed to exist in the United States, but its polygamous practices are not. As Digeser concluded, "[Constantine's] legislation sought to promote monotheism, especially Christianity, without eliminating the opportunity for polytheists to continue their practices, but some things were now seen as harmful that had not been in the past."[55] If certain traditional pagan rites were being removed, it would not be surprising that traditional pagans like Palladas would express dismay.

If during his reign Constantine did reject the pagan world entirely, which I believe is demonstrably false, there is still another way of reconciling such a conclusion with our general thesis about the emperor's quest for universal monotheism. Constantine, shocked by the Christian intolerance featured in the Donatist and Arian controversies between 313–24, might have sharpened his own Christian theology and at the same time come to believe that his initial religious latitude, and his hopes that the bishops would act as a beacon for true religion, were inadequate forces for change. He might have taken matters into his own hands and tried to accelerate the empire's conversion to monotheism—by 324 a progressively Christian monotheism. If we discover that Constantine was indeed a sincere and orthodox Christian whose shifts in policy we are forced to interpret as a total rejection of the pagan world (pagan monotheism included), this still would not preclude pagan monotheism and a quest for primitive monotheism as the original motivation for Constantine's embrace of Christianity.

In the end, our central thesis about the reasons for Constantine's conversion is able to stand firmly beside a variety of interpretations of his later policies on idolatry and sacrifice. On the one hand, if it were once-and-for-all proven that Constantine made no significant changes in pagan worship in the empire, this might only be representative of his belief (and that of Lactantius) that the world should not be coerced into monotheism. On the other hand, if it is proven that he did indeed make sweeping changes to pagan worship, it would still seem to affect very little the plausibility of a Constantinian quest for a monotheistic state supported by Christians and pagans. Such a thing would require significant and unprecedented reforms,

54. Digeser, *Making of a Christian Empire*, 119.
55. Digeser, *Making of a Christian Empire*, 128.

and those reforms would doubtless arrive through experimentation and compromise. The alleged policy shift(s) regarding traditional pagan rites taking place between 324–25 could be read in this light.

Our thesis about monotheism and the reasons for Constantine's conversion escapes this particular debate unscathed. We ultimately must not make the mistake of thinking, as some earnest and brilliant scholars have, that public actions against traditional paganism—its shrines, its idols, and its blood sacrifices—prove indisputably that Constantine, in his turn towards Christianity, was completely detaching himself, and the empire, from the pagan world. For Constantine, that world still had much to offer and admire.

10

Constantine the Christian

WHAT DOES IT MEAN to convert to a religion? At the beginning of this book we considered A. D. Nock's definition of conversion as "the reorientation of the soul of an individual, his deliberate turning from indifference or from an earlier form of piety to another, a turning which implies a consciousness that the old was wrong and the new is right."[1] At present there seems little reason to look for a better definition, but we must be careful which psychological paradigm of religious conversion we pair it with. If we embrace the older paradigm, we might look in vain for "a sudden 180-degree turn in religious outlook" in the life of Constantine.[2] The contemporary paradigm, however, allows us to recognize Constantine's experience with Christianity as an extended search for meaning. As we have seen in previous chapters, there is no proof that Constantine turned his back on pagan monotheism after his alleged vision in 312, and thus identifying his reported experience in that year as a sudden 180-degree turn from "an earlier form of piety to another" with "a consciousness that the old was wrong and the new is right" is not helpful. But determining whether or not it is as appropriate as it seems to identify Constantine's conversion to Christianity as a "gradual conversion" requires several things. We must first establish that persons in late antiquity were capable of conceiving of such a religious experience; and we must furthermore observe more than one turning point in Constantine's faith in order to establish a series of awakenings; and finally we must locate an endpoint for the conversion process, a point when he had truly forsaken his former life as a pagan and joined the Christian community.

1. Nock, *Conversion*, 7.
2. Drake, *Constantine and the Bishops*, 187.

The Contemporary Paradigm in the Fourth Century

Lactantius's concept of conversion has a good deal of affinity with the concept of "gradual conversion" so often discussed in the contemporary psychological paradigm. As has been observed, for Lactantius, "conversion is not a sudden event but a series of steps toward illumination."[3] These serial awakenings will ultimately lead to a dramatic change, but since "many are the steps by which one is raised to the abode of truth," Lactantius writes, "to be carried upward to the highest place is not easy for anyone, no matter whom." He continues:

> Now, the first step is to become aware that untrue religions exist and to abandon impiously worshiping things made from human hands; the second, certainly, is with the rational soul to observe that there exists one single greatest God . . . the third is to become acquainted with . . . his minister and messenger whom he dispatched to earth.[4]

In this way, Lactantius is able to see all Romans as not only potential Christians, but indeed many Romans as already somewhere in the process of becoming Christian.[5] Pagan monotheists, like the Hermeticists, would thus be very close to being Christians, in fact they now "needed merely to admit that the figure they had learned to call Hermes was really Christ."[6] Of course, if Lactantius were to recognize anyone as a true Christian, that individual must at the very least have forsaken idolatry, the worship of many deities, and cult sacrifices. Interestingly, Hermeticists would have already been traveling down a similar road as they advanced through their own religion: in *The Asclepius* we learn that Hermeticism had showed some disdain for the offering of incense and sacrifices to God.[7] "It is also likely," says Digeser, "that a Hermetist would learn to think differently about these 'gods' as he or she proceeded towards *gnosis*. As initiates came to focus increasingly upon their relationship with the One, they might learn . . . that it is wrong to worship a plurality of gods."[8] It is ultimately very possible, as Digeser argues, that "Lac-

---

3. Digeser, *Making of a Christian Empire*, 78.
4. Lactantius, *Wrath of God*, 2.1–2; Digeser, *Making of a Christian Empire*, 79.
5. Digeser, *Making of a Christian Empire*, 79.
6. Digeser, *Making of a Christian Empire*, 83.
7. *Ascl.* 41.1-5.
8. Digeser, *Making of a Christian Empire*, 70; see C.H. X, 24; *Ascl.* 38. In the Hermetica, man is placed above the gods in the divine hierarchy, and this is evidenced by

tantius would consider as Christian those Hermetists who saw Christ as an incarnation of Hermes-Thoth, the *logos*."⁹

Lactantius's concept of gradual conversion presented in his writings seems to represent a shift (and again, one resembling contemporary paradigms) away from earlier conceptions of Christian conversion, like those conjured by the dramatic and sudden conversion of the Apostle Paul in the New Testament.¹⁰ As Digeser observed: "Although converts in antiquity must have experienced a wide range of situations that led them to Christianity, most Christian authors before Lactantius understood conversion as a sudden, swift change brought about as an act of God, not a gradual illumination."¹¹ Interestingly, Lactantius, as well as "Hermeticists and Neoplatonists both envisioned three stages that would allow them to achieve *gnosis* and become one with God,"¹² and "These similarities . . . are interesting especially because the *Divine Institutes* parts company in this regard from all previous writings about the process of conversion."¹³

Lactantius also represents a shift from previous Christian writers in his assertion that conversion can and will (provided the right conditions) be individually achieved through man's natural reason.¹⁴ Miracles, exorcisms, visions, or any such divine spectacles are not necessary elements of the conversion process for Lactantius. In general he anticipates that pious pagans will come to the truth by way of a conscious searching and longing—through an individual *quest* for God. In Lactantius's view, because monotheism is inherently rational, and because true conversion must involve a conscious act of free will, indeed a series of such acts, violence or any

---

man's ability to actually call down the divine essence to fill material idols, turning them into living gods. Man is above the gods because he is the Supreme God's greatest creation and is a creator of gods.

9. Digeser, *Making of a Christian Empire*, 83, emphasis hers.

10. "In Luke's book of Acts, conversion is understood to be a gift from God because it happens in response to an extraordinary event (2:1—4:4) . . . the author of a sermon attributed to Clement witnessed a Christian performing a miracle and wanted to emulate that person (*Hom. Clem.* 7.8). These images of sudden change continue in the literature of the Latin church . . . [while] Greek authors [place] emphasis on the role of rational argumentation, their customary use of protreptic may show that they saw conversion as the exercise of a choice or a judgment rather than a process of gradual transformation" (Digeser, *Making of a Christian Empire*, 80–81).

11. Digeser, *Making of a Christian Empire*, 80.

12. Digeser, *Making of a Christian Empire*, 81, emphasis hers.

13. Digeser, *Making of a Christian Empire*, 83.

14. Digeser, *Making of a Christian Empire*, 89.

sort of coercion is an unacceptable means of evangelism. The true and good religion must be realized through "words rather than wounds," he says. Thus "we [Christians] teach, we prove, we explain."[15]

These theological standards provide the underpinning for Lactantius's policy of concord which he proposes should govern the monotheistic state described in his *Institutes*, theological standards which would likewise provide the basis for Constantine's religious policies.

Transition

Peter Leithart succinctly claimed, in his 2010 polemic, that what had happened to Constantine in 312 was "a religious conversion."[16] Likewise Charles Odahl, reflecting on the emperor's realization that the Christian god was the *Summus Deus*, says that it was "at that moment" that Constantine became a Christian convert.[17] The evidence does not allow us, however, to confine the emperor's conversion to a single night in October, or even to the year 312. Indeed, for decades after his victory at the bridge, the emperor lived a life in two worlds.

After the year 312, it is clear that Constantine had not closed himself off from traditional paganism entirely. One famous piece of evidence is his continued use of pagan *haruspices*, who gained his approval in 320 to perform ritual examination of the entrails of sacrificial beasts in order to interpret lightning strikes.[18] It is true that after 312 Christianity appears to have entered his policies in a significant way: gladiatorial games were abolished; Christian leaders were awarded rights long enjoyed by pagan priests; gifts and construction projects benefiting the Christians abounded. And eventually a new attitude towards traditional paganism did emerge within his policies: imperial construction funds, for example, were directed to Christian projects and withheld from the construction of new pagan temples.[19] But Constantine evidently continued to tolerate pagan sacrifice (while making his personal distaste for sacrifices known).[20] It is true that he

15. Lactantius, *Inst.* 5.19.8, 14.
16. Leithart, *Defending Constantine*, 96.
17. Odahl, *Constantine and the Christian Empire*, 106, 117.
18. See Lenski, *Constantine and the Cities*, 232.
19. Gerberding and Cruz, *Medieval Worlds*, 28.
20. Brown, *Rise of Christendom*, 60. See Constantine's "Letter to Macarius (325 CE)," preserved in Eusebius, *Vit. Const.* 3.53.

eventually pillaged and shuttered several pagan sites,[21] but the pillaging may have had less to do with Christianity and more to do with raising money for the construction of Constantinople.[22] As has been observed, "even the pagan emperors had been willing to melt down statutes fashioned out of precious metals in order to pay for armies or palaces."[23] It is probably significant that Constantine destroyed statues which could be melted into gold and silver ingots, but left the brass, wood, and marble statuary alone, and even committed them to the decoration of his new city.

In 330, when Constantinople was dedicated, the goddess Tyche was officially invited to dwell in the city. Several prominent pagans and philosophers were in attendance. And Constantine decorated yet another statue of himself in the solar imagery of Sol Invictus, giving himself the radiate crown, and placing the statue atop the grand column in the city's forum. While Eusebius reported that Constantinople was a purely Christian city and completely without pagan temples and statues, the city did feature pagan elements.[24] Wilkinson observes a range of such elements, from the "quasi-pagan monuments like the new Tychaion, to the appearances of Victories and other conventional figures, to the Helios imagery of Constantine's statue in the Forum. The presence of these and similar features cannot be denied and may seem to contradict Eusebius's claim." Indeed, as Wilkinson concludes, "if 'pagan' and 'Christian' are to be treated as pure categories, then there can be no doubt that Constantinople contained a 'mixed' or even 'contradictory' religious environment."[25] Wilkinson noted also the suggestion of Krautheimer, that "because Constantine himself was avowedly Christian, whatever he endorsed in the realm of public religion in his city was also perforce Christian."[26]

Nevertheless, it is true that Constantine's public interest in the traditional deities of the Roman pantheon had visibly dwindled by 317, as evidenced by their disappearance from his coinage in that year, while Sol Invictus remained on his coins until 325, when he too disappeared. Sol was eventually replaced with imagery emphasizing Constantine himself, often

21. MacMullen, *Christianizing the Roman Empire*.
22. Kirsch, *God Against the Gods*, 184.
23. Kirsch, *God Against the Gods*, 184.
24. Eusebius, *Vit. Const.* 3.47.
25. Wilkinson, "Palladas and the Foundation," 193–94. See Krautheimer, *Three Christian Capitals*, 60–67.
26. Wilkinson, "Palladas and the Foundation," 194.

shown gazing towards the heavens, and the celebratory imagery of the Roman State.[27] Stephenson remarks that "The disappearance of Sol, therefore, was as gradual as Constantine's conversion, becoming absolute only in his last decade."[28] By at least 325, while praising Plato on many points of doctrine, he can be found criticizing Plato for "introducing a plurality of gods, to each of whom he assigns specific forms."[29] It is thus important to acknowledge that in one sense Barnes was right: Constantine did move from solar monotheism towards Christianity, and towards aniconism and a less friendly posture toward traditional religion. But this requires more nuance: Constantine appears to have progressed from solar monotheism, to Christianized solar monotheism by 312, and to a more exclusive form of this Christianized solar monotheism by 317. By 324, he appears to have advanced in the Christian aspects of his theology to the point where he began to openly despise traditional cultus, though perhaps, I suggest, maintaining that pagan and Christian monotheism were fundamentally still compatible.

It is indeed possible that a solar monotheist like Constantine could have gradually come to understand that even certain Roman sun-deities which he had once venerated, like Apollo, were to be discarded, while certain other incarnations, like Sol Invictus, were to continue to be identified with the Supreme God. Warwick Ball tells us, in fact, that while in the third century Sol, Apollo, and Mithras were sometimes interchangeable, "under Constantine, Sol emerged supreme."[30] Again, in light of the numismatic evidence, this demotion or even obliteration of other traditional sun deities like Apollo in Constantine's theology seems to have occurred around 317. While this move may have been encouraged by the increasing influence of Christianity on his doctrines, we know that Constantine was not the first Roman monotheist to do this. Already in the second century CE, we read of a pagan named Theophilus who once traveled to the oracle of Apollo at Claros to inquire about the Supreme God, and there he asked Apollo, perhaps indelicately: "are you, or another, God?" To this Apollo humbly replied: "Born of himself, untaught, motherless, immovable, not contained in a name, many-named, dwelling in fire—this is God. We angels are but a

---

27. Lenski, *Constantine and the Cities*, 38. It is possible that Constantine's gaze towards the heavens symbolizes his deep connection with the Supreme Divinity.

28. Stephenson, *Constantine*, 173–74. What qualifies as an "absolute" conversion is, of course, entirely debatable.

29. Constantine, *Orat.* 9.

30. Ball, *Rome in the East*, 444.

particle of God."[31] Apollo later confesses that he himself worships "the king of heaven" alongside of human beings, and that he does so "according to tradition."[32] Regarding Apollo's self-identification as both a particle of the one God and as an angel subordinate to God, it is unclear whether we are to think of them as completely separate beings or to imagine them in terms of monotheistic emanationism. Nevertheless, Greek magical papyri from the first three centuries also call Apollo the "first angel" of God, and identify him with the biblical angels Michael and Gabriel.[33] Despite Constantine's increasing preference of Sol over Apollo, we know that the emperor's pagan vision in 310, interpreted by the panegyrist of 311 as a vision of Apollo, continued to be important to Constantine, as evidenced by his consistent self-portrayal as the sun god. He nevertheless appears to have continued to clarify his monotheism throughout his career.

In light of his public censure of Plato for introducing a plurality of gods, it seems right to identify Constantine's monotheism in his last decade as one which held to the existence of only one god. He vigorously argues in his *Oration* (ca. 325) against the traditional deities on the grounds that they engage in war, are subject to the power of fate, and mourn the loss of their own children—all evidence of their powerlessness and "their inability to succor, not strangers merely, but those most dear to them."[34] Speaking of those pagans who would attempt to justify their recent persecution of Christians as acts done only in honor of the gods, Constantine says, "*What gods are these? Or what worthy concept do you have of the divine nature? Do you think the gods are subject to angry passions like you are? Were it so, it would have been better for you to marvel at their bizarre resolve than to obey their harsh command, when they instructed you towards the wicked butchery of innocent men.*"[35] Constantine delivers an additional and outlandish argument against the existence of the traditional gods: he contends that if the gods exist and are immortal, and are continually producing offspring as their devotees say, then no heaven would be large enough to contain the amount of immortal gods that would be produced. Regardless of the force of his arguments, it seems to me that Constantine's monotheism was at this stage not the sort of monotheism which permitted the existence

31. Quoted in Athanassiadi, *Mutations of Hellenism*, 60.
32. Athanassiadi, *Mutations of Hellenism*, 60.
33. *Greek Magical Papyri*, 1.300. See Pachoumi, *Concepts of the Divine*, 103.
34. Constantine, *Orat.* 10; Constantine, *Oration of Constantine*, 567.
35. Constantine, *Orat.* 22.

of even such neutered and insolvent deities as those he assigns to the traditionalists.[36] Indeed, he seems unwilling at this point to accept that the traditional gods might even be subordinate deities beneath the Supreme God, since he faults Plato for simply "introducing a plurality of gods," implying that they posed a challenge to the status of the only true God. Neither do these other divinities seem like real emanations of God, as he boldly affirms "the true God, and his undivided sovereignty."[37] Nevertheless, his comments do remain entirely consistent with a pagan monotheism which confesses a single Supreme God, a unitary entity, recognized by various names. Toom rightly says that the emperor had "gradually moved away from inclusive monotheism to exclusive monotheism with a Christian twist,"[38] but we must take care not to exclude pagan monotheism from this conversation. Again, one form of pagan monotheism could collapse several deities into one. Taking a "some-are-equally-right" approach to religious pluralism, Constantine could disavow the existence of lesser deities while nevertheless maintaining that Hermetic, solar, Jewish, and Christian monotheists were equally correct in regard to monotheism.[39] Regardless of any prior opinions, we should understand that Constantine's monotheism by 325, while certainly now more Christian than it had ever been, maintained an essential compatibility with at least one form of pagan monotheism.

Indeed, evidence of Constantine's tenacious interest in solar monotheism is manifest throughout his career, and it is important to keep this consistency in view: Before he became publicly interested in Christianity, solar imagery abounded in his pagan panegyrics of 310 and 311; in the year 313, the sun god is featured on his golden medallions and the solar quadriga is found on Constantine's shield; in 315, Constantine's arch was completed, was filled with solar images, and identified the emperor with Sol Invictus; Constantine continued to use sun metaphors to refer to God in his letters; in 321, the emperor established Sun-day as the official day of rest and celebration; Constantine's Sol Invictus coins continued to be minted till 325, and in that year at Nicaea, Constantine dressed himself in flame-colored garments mimicking the sun, and proclaimed himself God's agent now being used to lead those ignorant of the divine sun "to the perfect splendor of

---

36. Toom is also of this opinion; see "Constantine's *Summus Deus*," 114, no. 86.
37. Constantine, *Orat.* 23.
38. Toom, "Constantine's *Summus Deus*," 115.
39. Stenmark, "Religious Pluralism," 21–35.

the eternal light";[40] in the year 330, Constantine placed in the most central part of Constantinople a statue of himself wearing the radiate crown in imitation of Sol Invictus; in 336, the year before his death, Eusebius still saw fit to publicly liken the imperial college to the solar quadriga—the image of Constantine driving the chariot of the sun, first enshrined atop his pagan arch in 315, continued to manifest itself more than twenty years later.[41] All of this indicates that certain religious ideas which Constantine had appreciated as a sun-worshiper continued to be important to him throughout his career. Indeed, his unflagging desire to depict himself as the sun god, even in his 330 statue, demonstrates that Constantine's pagan vision of 310, in which he reportedly saw his own face in the visage of the deity, remained as significant to his public messaging and self-identity as any later dream of Jesus.[42] The fact that the imagery of pagan monotheism persisted alongside the Christian imagery and policies he increasingly promoted after 312 is ultimately not evidence of "contradiction" in Constantine's religion, but of a deeply held belief that pagan and Christian monotheism were at an elemental level compatible.

We now know that the pagan sun-worshiper Maternus discussed earlier in this book, who lived during the reign of Constantine (306–37 CE), ultimately converted to Christianity. Maternus thus represents an example of a solar monotheist turning to Christianity around the time of Constantine, and therefore provides a useful analogy.[43] How does his conversion compare to that of the emperor?

We have already discussed his famous astrological treatise *Matheseos*, written around 336,[44] but Maternus, having become a Christian,

40. Lenski, *Constantine and the Cities*, 51.

41. Lenski, *Constantine and the Cities*, 51. As Eusebius opined in 336: "Holding the reins high above them, [Constantine] rides along, traversing all lands alike that the sun gazes upon, himself present everywhere watching over everything" (Eusebius, *Orat.* 3.87).

42. See Pan. VII, 21.5.

43. It was once commonly thought, due to the divergent character of the work, that this Christian book had been written by another man named Maternus. See Schmitz, *History of Latin Literature*, 206. Most scholars now agree that they are one and the same Maternus. See Maternus, *Error of the Pagan Religions*, 172–73. See also the introduction to Jean Rhys Bram's translation of Maternus's *Matheseos*, where it is noted that "doubts as to the single authorship of the *Mathesis* and *De Errore* have been dispelled by the careful study of vocabulary and *clausulae* (rhythmic sentence endings) by Clifford H. Moore" (Bram, *Ancient Astrology*, 1).

44. Mommsen confirmed this dating in his "Firmicus Maternus," 468–72.

wrote another book and dedicated it to Constantine's sons around 346, *De Errore Profanarum Religionum*. In his earlier *Matheseos*, Maternus had prayed to the sun, the Supreme God, and identified him as the inspiring Divine Mind, and in ways strikingly reminiscent of the early Constantinian propaganda. In his later Christian work, however, he openly despises sun-worship, and even portrays the sun himself giving a dramatic speech to his would-be worshipers, discouraging them from venerating him.[45] As has been observed, "[Maternus] remembers well that former prayer of his to the Sun; here he speaks anew of the Sun but with very different language and very different doctrine."[46] The Christian Maternus had come to believe that "solar monotheism, once proclaimed as the official religion of the Roman world by Aurelian in 274 and favored by Neoplatonism, was a serious threat to Christianity."[47] Indeed, the parallels between the two faiths would have made this obvious to Maternus, and he was not alone in his worry. The learned bishop Eusebius of Emesa (ca. 300–ca. 360), a pupil of Eusebius of Caesarea, likewise wrote against Christian participation in the traditions of solar monotheism. In his home of Emesa, solar cult was an integral element of daily life, and the emperor Elagabalus had been the high priest of the sun in that city.[48] The bishop was therefore, like Maternus, "very careful about not giving the sun too much emphasis."[49] For this reason, he was even wary of using the popular analogy of the sun and its rays to describe the emanations of the Christian godhead.[50] Indeed, the nearness between Christianity and pagan solar monotheism was, for Christian leaders like Maternus and Eusebius of Emesa, a cause for concern. Constantine on the other hand saw in these parallels not a problem, but an opportunity for harmony. The contrast between Maternus and Constantine in this regard is revealing. After 312, Constantine continued to embrace and promote solar imagery: his arch, completed in 315, featured not only his close association with Sol Invictus, but displayed a frieze of the Sun himself driving his four-horsed chariot; Constantine's coins prominently featured Sol Invictus, proclaiming him the special companion of the emperor until roughly 325; and Constantine continued to portray himself in this solar imagery, as seen

---

45. Maternus, *De Errore*, 8.1–4.
46. A. Pastorino, quoted in Maternus, *Error of the Pagan Religions*, 173.
47. Maternus, *Error of the Pagan Religions*, 171.
48. Winn, *Eusebius of Emesa*, 43.
49. Winn, *Eusebius of Emesa*, 44.
50. Winn, *Eusebius of Emesa*, 45.

CONSTANTINE THE CHRISTIAN

in his own statue atop his arch, driving the four-horsed solar chariot, and in his Colossus, and in his solar-themed statue and column of 330. Constantine had embraced a Christianity which allowed room for such imagery. Maternus, on the other hand, had converted to a Christianity which saw such imagery as "profane," and as a "crime" against both the Supreme God, and against the sun, God's handiwork. Warning against the traditions of solar monotheism in his Christian book, Maternus puts the following words into the mouth of the sun:

> One who has flattered me a little with winsome talk thereupon makes up the story that I am the driver of a chariot and four. Reject at last such ruinous madness, and being admonished by salutary persuasion, seek the true way of salvation. A foe of God is he who either thought up or dreamed up these ideas, and no simple or ordinary punishment attends the crime of the person who pollutes [holy] secrets by profane notions, makes up such lies about the glorious work of God.[51]

Oddly enough, the two "Most Holy Emperors" who Maternus addresses in this speech are the two sons of Constantine. How might they have felt about such rhetoric, knowing that their own father was guilty of perpetuating the sort of criminal foolishness just described? Regardless, we have in the comparison between Constantine and Maternus a tale of two solar monotheists: Constantine had found it possible to live in both the world of solar monotheism and Christian monotheism; Maternus apparently had not.

Our next question is regarding whether Constantine ever left the pagan world behind. If Constantine's conversion to Christianity really was an extended process, then when was it complete? Or did Constantine never complete his journey towards participation in the body of Christ?

Baptism

Disparaging any quest for the reasons or the psychological process behind Constantine's conversion, Barnes claimed in 2011 that the only thing that really matters is that "Constantine had declared himself a Christian before the Battle of the Milvian Bridge on 28 October 312."[52] Both scholars and the wider public are not, however, as concerned with what Constantine might

---

51. Maternus, *De Errore*, 8.2; Maternus, *Error of the Pagan Religions*, 63.
52. Barnes, *Constantine*, 80.

have declared—rather, they are concerned with what he truly was. It goes without saying that anyone can declare himself a member of any religious group without ever successfully embodying the necessary qualities which authentic participation in that group requires. What, then, might be the minimum criteria which Constantine would need to meet before we could acknowledge him as a genuine convert to Christianity? This is a slippery question. If we are not careful in identifying essential criteria, we risk constructing a Christianity in our own image. Thankfully for our inquiry, it matters very little what we might think qualifies a true Christian, and it matters very much what persons in late antiquity understood.

Inarguably, one essential mark of a Christian convert in the fourth century CE would have been an official and authentic renouncement of former beliefs and ways of life. Religious conversions in general, as Nock rightly understood, require the exchange of a former belief for a new one. It cannot be that one simply tacks new ideas onto a preexisting belief system without some sort of exchange—that may simply be "learning," but it is hardly "conversion." This is actually one of the difficulties which Christian missionaries have sometimes faced when trying to convert Hindus to Christianity: the missionary thinks he has a done a great thing by leading a Hindu to accept Jesus, when all the Hindu has really done is add Jesus to his existing pantheon as yet another guru or emanation of God. This Hindu might even publicly declare himself to be a disciple of Jesus. But would the Christian missionary, upon realizing what has really happened, be content with this result? Would anyone call this a genuine *conversion*?

The "catholic" Christianity to which Constantine attached himself in the fourth century shared similar concerns about authenticity. In fact, it had established a system which guarded against false conversions. If an "inquirer" wished to convert, he would have to first undergo a lengthy *catechesis*, or "instruction by word of mouth," before he could be baptized. After applying for catechesis, church leaders would decide whether or not the applicant was a good candidate for instruction in light of his behavior, and only then, upon approval, would the catechumen receive theological teaching, prayers, and exorcisms. Above all, he would be tested to find out whether or not he had truly renounced his former beliefs and ways of life. The catechumen was examined and was formally asked by the church if he had chosen humility, if he lived "with two minds," or if he was under pressure to convert.[53] Monitors were then appointed to him, who graded

---

53. *Canons of Hippolytus*, 16.

and reported on his behavior. If a catechumen was found to have not repented of his non-Christian ways, he would be kicked out of the program and denied baptism. In other words, he would be denied conversion until he could demonstrate that he was ready to lead a life free from idolatry and wickedness—the life of Christ.

Since Christian baptism was associated with the forgiveness of sins, we know that many potential Christians delayed conversion until they were ready to stop sinning. In the third century, Tertullian, in his *De Penitentia* (203 CE), criticized pagans who had acknowledged the truth of Christ but had stalled their conversions in order to enjoy their lives. By the following century there had also developed in Christian circles a fanatical worry over the consequences of post-baptismal sin.[54] Thus a "tendency to delay one's conversion to Christianity, if possible till the hour of death in order to die [without sin] became extremely prevalent in the fourth century."[55] Constantine is inarguably the most famous example of this tradition, stalling his own baptism until shortly before his death in Nicomedia in 337.

It has regularly been suggested that Constantine delayed his baptism because he knew his role as emperor might involve him in a good deal of less-than-holy activity, and he was right: in the same year that he presided over the Council of Nicaea, he executed his brother-in-law and former co-emperor Licinius on conspiracy charges, and the following year, under mysterious circumstances, he even ordered the murders of his own wife Fausta and favorite son Crispus. And he continued to lead bloody military campaigns against foreign nations in his final years, and was in the process of stirring up what would become a horrific war with the Persians just before he died.[56] Regardless of his reasons, the fact is that

54. Chadwick, "Early Christian Community," 59.
55. Jeremias, *Infant Baptism*, 87.
56. Was the fact of the emperor's necessary role in the military enough to keep Constantine away from official conversion? The twelfth canon of the Nicene Creed seems to promise harsh punishment for Christians who involved themselves with the military: "If persons called by grace, have first renounced the military profession [*eingulum militia deposuerunt*], and then returned to it, as dogs to their vomit; let them, after being hearers for three years, be penitents for ten years, with power in the bishop to modify their sentence according to the evidence of their repentance." As has been pointed out, this may have something to do with the idolatry which attended Roman military service. Kalantzis says that this canon is not reflective of a sharp return to the pacifist stance of the church, and was not a universal prescription but a ruling on a specific case—namely it addressed "those soldiers in the armies of Licinius who first left the army because they were unwilling to offer sacrifices and then sought to return to their former careers"

Constantine forestalled baptism—and thus official conversion. He was not yet ready to give up his life, whatever that entailed, in order to enter Christian catechesis, baptism, and communion.

Alan Kreider reminded us, in a powerful 2013 article, that while Constantine accepted peripheral guidance from Christian counselors like Lactantius, Eusebius reports that Constantine had mostly taught himself about Christianity:

> According to Eusebius, Constantine decided it was safer to be self-taught. He would study by himself in his palace. He would have no teacher, no sponsor who would teach by embodiment as well as conversation; he would "personally apply himself to the divinely inspired writings." He would be a Christian autodidact. He would have priests in his entourage to advise him, and he would foster due rites and fight heresy. But he would not be baptized. So, according to standards of the early church that were still operative, Constantine had not been converted.[57]

These simple facts should give us pause regarding the perennial claims of some scholars that Constantine had already "converted" in the year 312.

Two Conversions

Contrary to many popular portraits, Constantine appears to have ruled, for the whole of his career, not as an officially and exclusively Christian emperor, but as a monotheist interested in Christianity, even a monotheist who sincerely believed in the truth of Christianity. But he was not yet an official member of the body of Christ until his deathbed. What had he been, then, in the many years prior? An unofficial Christian? Lactantius had identified pagan monotheists as precisely that. Indeed, Lactantius taught Constantine that pagan monotheists were already somewhere in the process of becoming Christians. Doubtless the emperor, during his long reign, would have fit into such a category, and in Lactantius's aforementioned requirements for converts Constantine would have been further along the road to conversion than others, having disavowed idols and acknowledged Jesus as God's messenger. But at best Constantine had ruled as an "inquirer"—not yet a catechumen, but as a potential Christian who still required instruction, supervision, and repentance.

(Kalantzis, *Caesar and the Lamb*, 190).

57. Kreider, "Converted but Not Baptized," 43.

Before his baptism, Constantine obviously thought of himself as a worshiper of the Christian deity. He knew he was the true god's right hand and chosen agent, and might have even thought himself a Christian despite the bishop's insistence on baptismal rites. Indeed, what need had he of such rituals? It was obvious to him and to major Christian figures attached to his court that he had already been chosen and well-used by the Christian god apart from those rites. Wouldn't baptism only hamper his ability to rule as an emperor, even his ability to lead the pagan world to the Supreme God? Perhaps he felt it was the deity's will that he remain outside the Christian church until his mission was complete. How else could he fully exercise the sword of empire (which God had clearly granted him), and how else could he truly minister to the heathens if he had been transferred from their realm to the realm of the church? As he said to the Christian leaders at Nicaea, "You are bishops whose jurisdiction is within the church... However I am also a bishop, ordained by God to supervise those who are outside the church."[58] Perhaps it was only when he felt his mission to the pagan world had been finished that he could personally leave that world and be transplanted to another. Leithart and others have counted Constantine, even before his baptism, a "seriously Christian ruler."[59] But Constantine was not yet "serious" enough to suffer catechesis, or to be baptized, or even to receive communion—something reserved for Christians. As Kreider put it, "He could invite the bishops to his palace and receive them at his splendid table. But they could not invite him to their awesome table to receive the Eucharist."[60]

Was Constantine a Christian before his deathbed or not? It may ultimately be helpful to speak of *two* conversions of Constantine: the conversion of faith and the conversion of praxis. Surely, both conversions have always been incumbent on any would-be Christian. As the first disciples of Jesus confirmed, "Faith without works is dead."[61] It is evident that Constantine had sincerely come to believe in the truth of Christ and his God much earlier than 337, but he was not prepared to assume the life of a Christian until his final moments. What sort of Christian refuses the life of a Christian? I argue only a potential Christian.

---

58. Eusebius, *Vit. Const.* 4.24.
59. Leitharit, *Defending Constantine*, 82.
60. Kreider, "Converted but Not Baptized," 45.
61. Jas 2:17, 20.

In 337, now gravely sick, he finally took up the mantle of the catechumen, deciding at last to receive "such preliminary instruction as is required."[62] According to Eusebius, it was only "when he became aware that his life was ending, he perceived that this was the time to purify himself."[63] Eusebius describes what appears to be his (first?) formal "confession" of his sins to God, when "he was [also] first accorded the prayers that go with the laying on of hands."[64] Coming to Nicomedia, according to Eusebius, Constantine finally announces:

> This is the moment I have long hoped for, as I thirsted and yearned to win salvation in God. It is our time too to enjoy the seal that brings immortality, time to enjoy the sealing that gives salvation . . . so it is once and for all decided that I am hereafter numbered among the people of God, and that I meet and join in the prayers with them all together. I shall now set for myself rules of life which befit God.[65]

This is, perhaps, the most important statement of Constantine's for answering the question of when his conversion took place, or, more accurately, when his gradual process of conversion was complete. His speech implies that before this point, he had not yet won salvation, or even the promise of salvation enjoyed by every Christian, and neither had he lived a Christian life or even been able to be counted among the Christians. Indeed, he had only now "decided" to be counted as such. Before this moment, Constantine had been segregated from the body of Christ, performing his self-catechesis and offering prayers to the Supreme God on his own. Again, another question: what sort of Christian is not saved and is unable to be counted among the people of God? Eusebius, in his biography, had worked diligently to produce a portrait of Constantine as not only the first Christian emperor, but as a firmly committed Christian emperor since the year 312. Despite all his sound and color, it is the emperor's own words which reveal that his "once and for all decision" to become a Christian, or to complete his journey of conversion, was made in 337.

As some scholars have rightly noted, the debate must move beyond the question of whether or not Constantine ever became a Christian—I trust that I have sufficiently shown that he gradually did convert, at the

---

62. Eusebius, *Vit. Const.* 4.62.
63. Eusebius, *Vit. Const.* 4.61; Eusebius, *Life of Constantine*, 177.
64. Eusebius, *Vit. Const.* 4.61.
65. Eusebius, *Vit. Const.* 4.62; Eusebius, *Life of Constantine*, 177.

last—and must now focus on precisely what kind of Christian the emperor ultimately became,[66] and on what kind of Christianity he had so vigorously promoted during his reign. Did Constantine ever fully transition himself out of paganism? In a formal and public sense, yes. But whether or not he still maintained that pagan and Christian monotheism were essentially compatible after his baptism may be impossible to know. We are left with a trove of clues, however, that the same theological and historiographical forces which as a pagan had initiated his interest in Christianity continued to be important to Constantine to the very end.

---

66. Drake, *Constantine and the Bishops*, 201; Digeser, "Platonism in the Palace," 55.

11

Death of a Dream

CONSTANTINE, KNOWING HE WAS dying, ordered that his tomb be made ready at the Church of the Holy Apostles in his new city of Constantinople. This grand structure, not yet complete at the time of his death in 337, underwent several renovations and additions before its total destruction at the hands of the Ottomans in 1461. Scholars have thus been left to debate what the original building would have looked like, and what its architecture and its interior furnishings might have signified.

The Emperor's Tomb

According to Eusebius, Constantine had originally announced the building of a church in honor of the twelve apostles of Jesus, and placed within it twelve empty reliquaries for their bones. Reportedly, the remains of several apostles were in fact gathered and deposited at the site. Only later did Constantine reveal that he also intended to be buried among them, and a thirteenth tomb was set up. According to Eusebius, all of this had been designed to communicate that Constantine should be placed among the ranks of the apostles—a *thirteenth Apostle*.[1]

Some have challenged this interpretation, however. J. A. McGuckin has argued that the place of Constantine's tomb, central in a symbolic circle formed by the twelve apostles, signifies far more than Constantine's intention to claim the rank of *isapostolos*—equal-to-the-apostles.[2] Rather, Constantine had identified himself as the new manifestation of the divine *logos*, in other words, as the new Jesus. McGuckin suspects that the emperor's audacity was only "cleverly and successfully deflected by the clergy, through

1. Eusebius, *Vit. Const.* 4.60.
2. McGuckin, "Legacy of the 13th Apostle," 276–78.

the device of transmuting this claim of the emperor into a statement that he was merely of apostolic rank."[3]

I suggest that Constantine's "displacement" of Jesus, an otherwise shocking move, be interpreted in light of his quest for monotheism. We recall that both Lactantius and Constantine had believed that Jesus, the earthly manifestation of the heavenly *logos*, had been on a divine mission to revive a primordial monotheism on the earth. And again, Eusebius had taught that this *logos* was now present in the emperor, and both Constantine and Lactantius were convinced that Constantine had been chosen to take part in the same revelatory mission of Christ in the present age. I therefore suggest that Constantine saw himself as not only taking part in Jesus's mission to establish true religion, but completing it.

Perhaps less than ten months before the emperor's death, Eusebius publicly announced that the blessed partnership between the Supreme God and Constantine, and their grand religious revival, had been a success. In his 336 speech, composed expressly for the pleasure of the emperor, Eusebius "identified polytheism and paganism as the root cause of human enmity and conflict."[4] The entire human race, he says, had become "unable or unwilling to contemplate the Creator" apart from "statues and lifeless images" of "created and earthly objects."[5] This obscuration of the true god was the deceptive work of what Eusebius identifies as "soul-killing demons who fly through the air," and as "demon-deities," who convinced human princes to entreat them with blood.[6] From this primordial mischief resulted "depopulation and captivity," and "adulteries, and the rape of women," and "the woes of Troy, and all of the ancient tragedies so well known by all peoples."[7] The decline-of-monotheism narrative thus continues to manifest here, and the space and attention it demands throughout the bishop's oration reveals quite clearly Constantine's sustained interest in this story, and in its power as a metanarrative which could contextualize and promote his imperial program.

3. McGuckin, "Legacy of the 13th Apostle," 277.

4. Kee, *Constantine*, 75; Eusebius, *Orat.* 16.3. It has been suggested, notably by Drake, that the first ten chapters of this oration alone compose the panegyric delivered on the emperor's jubilee, and the last seven are from the lost oration known as *On the Sepulcher of Christ*; see Drake, *In Praise of Constantine*, 40-45; Kee, *Constantine*, 70-71. The matter is still up for debate.

5. Eusebius, *Orat.* 14.1-2.

6. Eusebius, *Orat.* 7.2-7.

7. Eusebius, *Orat.* 16.2.

In his speech, Eusebius goes on to reveal that God had long ago initiated an extensive plan to resolve this great theological and social tragedy. He says that God had given two benefits to mankind, and these he had delivered "together, and at the same critical moment."[8] The first gift was monotheism (partially restored by the short ministry of Jesus on earth), and the other was the Roman Empire. These were the means by which God, reseeding the world with the germ of monotheism and patiently organizing the human race under the kind of centralized rule required for its growth, would have his revolution. But the earthly campaign of Jesus had been cut short by the Jews. And this too was used by God for the restoration of monotheism: the death of Jesus was, in fact, the key to "the overthrow of the errors of demon worship."[9] Eusebius says that "all nations, which up to that point had been guilty of impious superstition and were under the power of impure and unholy demons," were by the cross set free and "every earth-born and deceptive error" was weakened.[10] God's plan for monotheism on the earth, practically speaking, would nevertheless need to be finished by another. Eusebius says that in the fullness of time, the Supreme Sovereign had "put forth an invincible warrior as his attendant," a title which Constantine had been pleased to entertain through his abundance of piety.[11]

And so God's dream of restoration was finally accomplished by his new agent. Where Christ had begun the work in both the spiritual and mortal planes, now Constantine, through the Savior's power, had both defeated the human emperors who had fought against God and his people, and had at last "driven away from human civilization" the remnant of the deceiving band of evil spirits which "from long ago" had harmed men through their images.[12] For Eusebius, it was now obviously true that during Constantine's reign, God's two gifts to mankind had accomplished their divine purposes:

> [Now] the knowledge of one God was proclaimed to all people, and one universal empire triumphed . . . as children of one God and Father, and having the true religion as their mutual mother, all people welcomed one another in affirmations of peace. Therefore the entire world looked like one orderly and united family . . . in

---

8. Eusebius, *Orat.* 16.4.
9. Eusebius, *Orat.* 15.11.
10. Eusebius, *Orat.* 15.11.
11. Eusebius, *Orat.* 7.2.
12. Eusebius, *Orat.* 17.2–3; 16.9.

short, the ancient oracles and predictions of the prophets were now fulfilled.[13]

Eusebius boldly challenges the people of the empire to "open their eyes" and to receive this truth "not from words but from facts."[14] The ancient prophecies of the Hebrew scriptures, he says, which predicted the universal and peace-filled reign of the Messiah on earth, had come true in Constantine. Eusebius cites as fulfilled those expectations of the Psalmist: "He shall have dominion from sea to sea, and from the river to the ends of the earth" (Ps 72:8); and the vision of Isaiah: "they shall beat their swords into plough-shares, and their spears into sickles: and nation shall not take up sword against nation, neither shall they learn to war anymore" (Isa 2:4b). Those who dared to doubt the obvious and universal peace produced by Constantine must have "slanderous lips."[15] It was the very power of the risen Christ that was visible in the emperor's accomplishments. And it must have been Christ working through the emperor, the bishop insists. Afterall, what deity or hero has ever illuminated mankind to this extent, and with a doctrine like the "bright rays" of the sun, causing every nation on earth to "offer united worship to the one true god?"[16] Despite Christ's hand in it, this grand work, God's own work, was evidently not finally accomplished until centuries after Jesus's ministry, and not by Christ alone, but by the willing hand of Constantine. Alongside his praise of God and Christ, Eusebius has no problem extolling the emperor: "What king or prince is there in any age of the world, or what philosopher or law-maker or prophet is there, in any civilized or barbarian land, who has ever achieved so tremendous a level of excellence, not after death, I tell you, but while still living?"[17] Had Constantine's achievement extended even beyond that of the earthly Jesus, who had seen the wide success of his name only after his death? Perhaps Eusebius means something like that; he says that among all of those who have ever lived since the beginning of time, God gave to Constantine alone "the power to purify the course of human life."[18] But this cannot refer to the purification of sins; I think

13. Eusebius, *Orat.* 16.7.
14. Eusebius, *Orat.* 16.8.
15. Eusebius, *Orat.* 17.12.
16. Eusebius, *Orat.* 17.13.
17. Eusebius, *Orat.* 16.8.
18. "No mortal eye has seen, nor ear heard, nor can the mind in its vesture of flesh understand what things are prepared for those who have been here adorned with the

it is impossible that the Christian Eusebius could have claimed that. This purification of humanity's course must refer to the emperor's redemption of humanity from its polytheistic error, to Constantine's full restoration of monotheism. Indeed, in this passage, what Eusebius says Constantine did with his God-granted power was to set the sign of the Supreme God (the cross? the *labarum*?) against "the idols of error" and the forces of "godless foes" and "demons." From this perspective, Eusebius's Constantine seems at least as great in his life as Jesus was in his death.

Because of his obedience to God to the point of death on the cross, the New Testament says that Jesus had been highly exalted and given heavenly rule.[19] Constantine, says Eusebius, because of his own work on earth, would likewise be given a heavenly rule lasting into eternity. This was not the same reward expected by every Christian, but "a higher recompense."[20] For Eusebius, at least, I think the message was clear: Constantine is no mere "apostle," but a king, and a king forever. Constantine is a heavenly magistrate akin to Christ. But was this a rulership supplanting that of Christ? One displacing, exceeding, and obsoleting Christ, as some have supposed? I do not believe Constantine thought he was Christ himself or that he had in any sense done away with Jesus or the need for Jesus. If that was his public message, then I think no Christian, even one like Eusebius, could have ever lauded such an emperor. Against the analysis of some scholars, I suggest that Constantine, as the new representative of the *logos*, had not intended to usurp the throne of Jesus, but to be known as the finisher of Christ's work. "God was in Christ," the Apostle Paul had said, "reconciling the world to himself."[21] Constantine believed that same God was in him, too, doing something very similar. And he believed this as early as 310, when the pagan panegyrist first told him that he had seen his own likeness in the sun. As the agent of the Supreme God, and not the author but

---

graces of godliness; blessings which await you too, most pious emperor, to whom alone since the world began has the Almighty Sovereign of the universe granted power to purify the course of human life: to whom also he has revealed his own symbol of salvation, whereby he overcame the power of death, and triumphed over every enemy. And this victorious trophy, the scourge of evil spirits, you have arrayed against the errors of idol worship, and hast obtained the victory not only over all your impious and savage foes, but over equally barbarous adversaries, the evil spirits themselves" (Eusebius, *Orat.* 6.21; Constantine. *Oration of Constantine*, 589).

19. Phil 2:8–11; Rev 5:12.
20. Eusebius, *Orat.* 6.10.
21. 2 Cor 5:19a.

certainly the finisher of the Christian faith, it was only fitting that he be buried among the holy apostles, not as one of them, but at their head. This was nevertheless a message which evidently made the church, including Eusebius, uncomfortable. But that was their problem, and theirs to resolve. Constantine's work, as he saw it, was finished. He would be troubled by the sensitivities of Christian bishops no longer.

In 337, knowing his time was short, Constantine headed for the church he had commissioned. He never completed his journey back to Constantinople, however. His failing health forced him to stop in Nicomedia where he had once lived as a member of Diocletian's court. On his deathbed, Constantine was baptized by the Arian bishop Eusebius of Nicomedia.[22] He died soon after, and his remains were laid in a golden sarcophagus. He had ruled for thirty years.

Pagan Monotheism after Constantine

In several ways, the death of Constantine in the fourth century CE reminds us of the passing of Alexander the Great in the fourth century BCE. Like Constantine, Alexander had not only been the greatest general of his age, but he too, after likewise being laid in a golden sarcophagus, had left no single magistrate in charge of his empire. While Alexander left his vast territory to be divided up among his generals, Constantine left the lands he had conquered to his sons. And just as Alexander's men had wasted no time going to war for each other's portions, the sons of Constantine soon went to work slaughtering their competitors.[23] One way these stories

---

22. Later legends developed to the effect that an orthodox bishop, Pope Silvester, had bestowed baptismal rites on the emperor. Such testimonies have proven false, and doubtless were constructed, at least in part, to cover over the fact that Constantine had been baptized by an Arian.

23. Constantius II usually gets the blame for instigating the so-called "massacre of the princes" after his father's death. The situation may have been more complicated, however. Lieu explains that "two years before his death in 337, Constantine had divided the empire among his three sons, Constantine II (b. 316), Constantius II (b. 317), and Constans (b. ca. 320), and his nephews Dalmatius the Younger and Hanniballianus the Younger. Upon Constantine's death, this unwieldy arrangement was upset by the imperial armies who declared that they would have nobody but the sons of Constantine to rule over them ... Egged on by the rumor that Constantine was poisoned by his 'half-brothers,' the soldiers carried out a massacre of the surviving male members of Constantius Chlorus's family together with their male offspring. The army, or a faction of it, clearly feared that Constantine's final arrangement of a five-fold division of the empire was a sure recipe

differ, however, is in the fact that while Alexander's generals operated with the sort of barbarity one would expect from pagan warlords, Constantine's sons ruled, conspired, and murdered as openly Christian emperors. Was it for such contradictions and hypocrisy that their cousin Julian (d. 363 CE), taking up the purple in 355, made his famous break with Christianity? Or did Julian's apostasy have something to do with the personal abuses of his Christian predecessor Constantius II, a strongly Arian emperor, who had massacred all of Julian's relatives? How much of Julian's decision to revive the old traditions was motivated by the political and familial chaos following Constantine's death is difficult to know. Regardless, it was in 355 that Julian, last emperor of the Constantinian dynasty, breathed a final breath into the waning pagan world.

In many ways, Julian's quest for religious revival mirrors that of his uncle Constantine. In this last generation of paganism, the persistence of not only solar monotheism, but Constantine's worship of Sol Invictus as the Divine Mind, can be observed. Having privately been educated by the best Platonists and traditionalists in the empire, in 355 Julian made the stunning announcement that he was a devotee of the old god Sol, whom he called King Helios. Some have detected in Julian's solar religion the influence of the Neoplatonist Iamblichus, who died in 325 CE, and for whom the sun was a special symbol of the One.[24] We must be careful, however, to consider the whole range of solar tradition as the background to Julian's thought,[25] and indeed some have identified Julian as an initiate in the Mithraic cult around the time of his ascension (361 CE).[26] The streams of solar tradition operating

---

for civil war . . . [Constantius II] probably knew of the plot but did nothing to prevent it. Later tradition would place the blame squarely on him . . . This was indeed the view of Julian, who blamed his brother's childlessness on his murder of his paternal relatives, and the view of historians who supported Julian as this provided them with justification of Julian's later rebellion against his imperial cousin" (Lieu and Montserrat, *From Constantine to Julian*, 148). Eventually, the sons of Constantine went to war with one another until only Constantius II was left.

24. See Iamblichus, *Mysteries*, 7.2.252. Iamblichus claimed to have descended from a line of priests from Emesa, doubtless priests of Sol; see Marx-Wolf, *Spiritual Taxonomies and Ritual Authority*, 121–22. We have several letters purporting to be from Julian to Iamblichus in our possession. Potent arguments have been made against the long-standing tradition that these letters of Julian belong to Julian the Roman emperor; for an introduction to these letters, see Elm, "Letter Collection," 60–64.

25. For a discussion of Julian's solar religion, and a warning against an "overly Iamblichan" reading, see Lecerf, "Iamblichus and Julian's 'Third Demiurge,'" 184–86.

26. Smith, *Julian's Gods*, 129–30.

in both Julian and Iamblichus are ultimately difficult to tease apart. From the testimony of Macrobius, we know that Iamblichus saw the sun sometimes as Apollo, sometimes as Attis, and still other times as an all-powerful World Spirit, and in this the influence of Mithraism has also been detected.[27] Garth Fowden has located in Iamblichus a dependence on the Hermetica.[28] Regardless, we may safely identify Julian as a devotee of the sun, and a solar monotheist influenced by Neoplatonic tradition.

Julian, in December of 362, and on the occasion of Aurelian's festival for Sol Invictus, composed a famous hymn to the Sun.[29] "This at least I am permitted to say without sacrilege," he writes, "that from my childhood an extraordinary longing for the rays of the god penetrated deep into my soul."[30] We might interpret "the rays of the god" here to be the many emanations of the Supreme God, the old gods whose traditions he was intent on reviving in Rome. Indeed, for Julian, "there are gods related to Helios and of like substance who sum up the stainless nature of this god, and though in the visible world they are plural, in him they are one."[31] While we might detect the influence of Neoplatonic emanationism, we also detect the elemental theology of Constantine expressed at Nicaea and in his *Oration*, in which the Supreme God emanates deities related to him in substance. Julian continues: "from my earliest years my mind was so completely swayed by the light that illumines the heavens that not only did I desire to gaze intently at the sun . . . I abandoned all else without exception and gave myself up to the beauties of the heavens." The pluriform sun is thus connected with the illumination of mind, as we have already seen in Constantine. Julian furthermore explains: "I regard this god, if we may believe the wise, as the common Father of all mankind." Julian goes on to identify this deity as "the One . . . or, to use Plato's name for him, the Good . . . Helios the most mighty god," and finally identifies him as "Mind" (νοῦς).[32]

---

27. Witt, "Iamblichus as a Forerunner," 54.

28. Fowden, *Egyptian Hermes*, 130.

29. Liebeschuetz, "Speech of Praetextatus," 191, no. 30; cf. Hijmans, "Temples and Priests of Sol," 389.

30. Julian, "Hymn to King Helios Dedicated to Sallust," in Wright, *Works of the Emperor Julian*, 353.

31. Wright, *Works of the Emperor Julian*, 390–91.

32. Julian speaks of "the undefiled activity of Mind pouring light into its own abode." As Wright explains, "Mind, νοῦς, is here identified with Helios; cf. Macrobius, *Saturnalia* 1.19.9: '*Sol mundi Mens est*' (the Sun is the Mind of the universe); Iamblichus, *Exhortation*, 21, 115; Ammainus Marcellinus, *Res Gestae*, 21.1.11" (Wright, *Works of the Emperor*

In addition to reviving the honor of the Roman pantheon, we find in Julian, as in Constantine, a concern for resurrecting an ancient solar monotheism which had lately been obscured. He does not mean to revive merely the rites of Sol Invictus appreciated by the Severans and others, or "the worship of Mithras" and the "games in honor of Helios," which he calls "customs that are somewhat recent." He looks back further, to "the remote past," and to "the Egyptians," whose solar fixations he identifies with his own.[33] Might we have grounds to see Julian and Constantine as less diametrically opposed, at least in this sense, than has been usually allowed? Are they simply two sides of the same coin—one which favors a revival of ancient monotheism led by traditional paganism, and the other a revival led by Christianity?

Julian died battling the Persians in June of 363 CE, and so did his program. Subsequent Christian emperors would swiftly reverse his religious efforts, and history would remember Julian not as a reformer but as an apostate. After Julian's failed revolution, however, we nevertheless continue to encounter the Solar Mind smoldering in the waning pagan world. The pagan aristocrat Praetextatus (ca. 315–84), who held the office of *pontifex solis* and was initiated in the rites of Mithras, argues in a grand speech that all the deities of the world are ultimately manifestations of a single solar deity.[34] Here we find that solar syncretism continued to provide "an underpinning for polytheism in the fourth century, just as the Stoic interpretation of the gods as natural forces had done during the late republic and early empire."[35] As a pagan monotheist, Praetextatus had no problem participating in the cults of several deities, as did many of his colleagues in the Roman Senate.[36]

The Roman Symmachus (340–402 CE) refers explicitly to the Divine Mind (*Mens Divina*) as the Supreme Deity, and, hoping to keep the flame of Julian's revival alight, Symmachus champions this god as the internal unifier of all religions. Because of this great deity, he argues, we can regard whatever each person worships as one and the same. Everyone may have their own religious custom, and this plurality of rites is sanctioned by the Supreme Deity himself, the Divine Mind (*Mens Divina*). In 384,

---

Julian, 363–65).

33. Wright, *Works of the Emperor Julian*, 425.
34. Liebeschuetz, "Speech of Praetextatus," 203.
35. Liebeschuetz, "Speech of Praetextatus," 203.
36. Liebeschuetz, "Speech of Praetextatus," 203–4.

Symmachus famously defended the traditional deities by identifying them as lesser divinities in some sense, assigned to the protection of Rome by the great Mind. As Kahlos points out, these protector-gods correspond to the ethnarch gods and protectors of cities mentioned by Julian in his *Against the Galileans*.[37] Though Symmachus does not explicitly make this point, Khalos understands Symmachus to ultimately mean that "All gods are manifestations of the supreme deity—including the God of the Christians."[38]

A Final Plea for Pluralism

Closing out the fourth century, in the year 390 CE, the pagan Maximus of Madaura wrote a famous letter to Augustine of Hippo (d. 430 CE). Maximus looked diligently for the common theological ground between them, ultimately arguing for a pluriform monotheism, and insisting that this was already the common opinion of most sensible people in the empire:

> That the supreme God is one, without beginning, without offspring, as it were the great and august father of nature, what person is there so mad and totally deprived of sense as to wish to deny. His powers diffused through the world that is his work we invoke under various names, because we are obviously all ignorant of his real name. For the name god is common to all religions. The outcome is that while with our various prayers we each honor as it were his limbs separately, all together we are seen to be worshipping him in his entirety.[39]

In Maximus we detect a monotheistic emanationism: the many deities may appear to be completely distinct, but they remain ontologically connected to an underlying principle. As in the typical analogy of the rays of the sun, for Maximus the various deities are like the outstretched limbs of the one body of the Supreme God.

In this light, there emerges something of a technical overlap between the doctrines of Maximus and Augustine. By this period, the Christian

---

37. Kahlos, *Forbearance and Compulsion*, 97.
38. Kahlos, *Forbearance and Compulsion*, 97.
39. Maximus of Madaura, quoted in Augustine, "Letter 16"; tr. Liebeschuetz, "Speech of Praetextatus," 185–86. Note also the similarity to the god of the Hermetic *Asclepius*: God is "he who cannot be named, or rather he who can be called by every name. For he, indeed, is One and All; so that it needs must be that all things should be called by the same name as his, or he himself called by the names of all."

doctrine of the Trinity had developed to the point that it represented the relationship between the Father, Son, and Spirit in terms of emanationism. While the plurality of entities which compose the Trinity may appear completely distinct, and are distinct in some sense, they are nevertheless individual projections from the one God who remain ontologically linked. Maximus can say that when he separately venerates one of the divine projections, he is worshiping the entirety of the Supreme God. Augustine can say the same as he worships each member of the Trinity.

In his letter, Maximus begs Augustine to see the common ground between their theologies, and to give him a kind and tolerant hearing. His appeal is a deliberately non-technical one, however, and he begs Augustine to momentarily leave behind the philosophical arguments for which he is famous, and to show him plainly the god who the Christians claim belongs exclusively to them. The Supreme God, argues Maximus, belongs to all men. Precisely which form of this god one chooses to worship is only a matter of taste.

It is interesting that Augustine did not readily deny the existence of the beings which his pagan contemporaries referred to as gods, understanding these entities to be merely demons and angels. He did not even care if the pagans called them "gods," so long as everyone understood they were subordinate entities to the Supreme God.[40] For Augustine, "the terms used for describing the divine were irrelevant. What mattered was the underlying theological concept."[41] At a technical level, then, there was no distinction between Christian and pagan monotheism. The penetrating difference was about worship: now that the pagans had recognized the Supreme God, they needed to do away with idolatry. Augustine thought that only the Supreme God, or the three divine members which composed the Christian Trinity, deserved cultic worship.[42] Pagan monotheists like Maximus tried earnestly to convince theologians like Augustine to simply expand the scope of their monotheistic worship to include the traditional deities. This was not too

---

40. Augustine writes that "When the Platonists prefer to call demons (or alternatively angels) gods rather than demons and are prepared to count as gods those who are created by the highest God, about which their originator and teacher Plato has written in the Timaeus, let them express themselves in this way, as they wish, since there is no reason to have a dispute with them about words . . . they are saying the same thing as we are, whatever terminology they use to express themselves" (Augustine, *City of God*, 9.23; Fürst, "Monotheism Between Cult and Politics," 85).

41. Fürst, "Monotheism Between Cult and Politics," 85.

42. Augustine, *City of God*, 9.23; 10.1.

much to ask, Maximus thought. Even if Augustine could not accept that these other figures were real emanations of the One, like Jesus, why could they not at least be venerated as subordinate deities? Why did Christians exclude their pagan neighbors over this matter of preference?

Maximus concludes his letter to the bishop with a mournful sigh: Augustine, he says, is an "excellent man," who has sadly "turned aside from my faith." Despite their differences, he prays that Augustine will "be preserved by the gods, through whom we all, who are mortals on the surface of this earth, with apparent discord but real harmony, revere and worship Him who is the common Father of the gods and of all mortals."[43]

In the fifth century CE, we can hear the last echoes of solar monotheism in the Roman Empire. In Macrobius's *Saturnalia*, we find the Hermetic tradition continuing to play a role in the philosophical admiration of the sun: the Egyptian theologian Hermes, he tells us, referring to him by his Latin name Mercury, had long ago already taught that "the Sun is the Mind of the universe" (*Sol mundi Mens est*).[44] Several more solar hymns contribute to the final refrain: one in the *Dionysiaca*, written by the Greek poet Nonnus (early fifth century CE); the *Hymn to Helios* composed by the Neoplatonist Proclus (412–85 CE); and, finally, a song written for Sol found in the *Marriage of Mercury and Philology* by Martianus Capella around 470–80 CE.

Ultimately, the pagan bid for the revival of pagan monotheism failed. Surprisingly, it failed in the same way in which the Christian bid for biblical monotheism had failed during the great persecutions. Indeed, the early Christian apologists, struggling for survival, had appealed to the common monotheistic ground they believed they shared with the pagans. But the Christian defenders had mostly been rejected, made criminals, and indeed put to death. Lactantius had not suffered this fate, of course: he had been born at the right time, had cultivated his imperial relationships well, and had fostered the right amount of appreciation for pagan achievement. In the generation following Lactantius, however, when the tables of power had flipped on the pagan traditionalists, and when the pagans had themselves tried to use monotheism to justify pluralism, Lactantius's spirit of

---

43. Maximus of Madaura, quoted in Augustine, "Letter 16"; Augustine, "Confessions and Letters of Augustine," 233–34.

44. "*Nam quia mentis potentem Mercurium credimus, appellatumque ita intellegimus* ἀπὸ τοῦ ἑρμηνεύειν, *et sol mundi mens est, summa autem est velocitas mentis, ut ait Homerus:* ὡσεὶ πτερὸν ἠὲ νόημα. *Ideo pennis Mercurius quasi ipsa natura solis ornatur*" (Macrobius, *Saturnalia*, 1.19.9).

appreciation had largely if not completely departed from Christian theology. Rejecting Symmachus's appeal to plural monotheism, the Christian bishop Ambrose in 384 CE would conclude: "We cannot have fellowship with the errors of others."[45] It was in this era, as Theodosius I (d. 395 CE) outlawed all forms of paganism in the Roman empire, that the pagan dream of universal monotheism officially died.[46]

Conclusion

In the final analysis, Constantine, as a pagan, appears to have been attracted to Christianity because he was a monotheist, and because he believed Christianity could help him restore the original religion of mankind. It is misguided to think that in his early reign Constantine had turned from the worship of a pagan god, Sol Invictus, to the Christian God—rather, he thought Sol Invictus *was* the Christian God. Constantine sincerely believed this Supreme Deity had commissioned him to restore a universal monotheism on the earth, and thus its civic benefits for the empire. It was probably the teachings of Lactantius, with his emphasis on both the compatibility of pagan and Christian monotheism and the decline-of-monotheism narrative, which assisted Constantine in coming to these conclusions.

During his reign, Constantine appears to have adopted a "some-are-equally-right" model of religious pluralism. He believed the monotheistic religions of the empire were equally right concerning monotheism, and that in other areas (such as blood sacrifice, or idolatry) only one of them was right. His religious policy was one of concord, in which he urged all Romans to realize the truth of monotheism through the exercise of reason, and to join together in "true religion and simplicity in concord."[47]

It is ultimately not helpful to speak of a purely "political" conversion in an era in which proper religious devotion was always thought to confer political advantages. But neither is it helpful to speak of Constantine's conversion to Christianity without qualification. Indeed, the sequence is

---

45. "*Alieni erroris societatem suscipere non possumus*" (Ambrose, "Letter 17," 1.14).

46. Glimpses of solar monotheism continue, however, to appear detached from the influence enjoyed in pre-Theodosian Rome. Sometime between 412–85, we find a "Hymn to Helios" written by the Neoplatonist Proclus; a hymn to Sol also appears in Martianus Capella's work, ca. 470–80. See Liebeschuetz, "Speech of Praetextatus," 192.

47. Constantine, "Letter to Celsus (315 CE)," preserved in Optatus of Milevis's *Against the Donatists*; Alexander, "Rethinking Constantine's Interaction," 79.

important. The emperor's "conversion experience" cannot be contained to an anxious night in October, *pace* Eusebius, but must be seen as a complex and extended process, which manifested first as a sincere effort to emphasize the common ground shared between Christianity and pagan monotheism, and finally resulted in a decision to become a Christian.

As we have seen, the dream of pagan, universal monotheism did not last long after Constantine. But it is only right to speak of the death of this dream in one sense, and that is in the sense that Constantine had first imagined it. In other ways, the dream has lived on. We cannot ignore the fact that while the worship of the traditional deities of Rome has faded into silence, Christian monotheism has become the most widespread religion on planet earth. That Christianity owes a good deal to Constantine for this triumph is obvious, and at the very least the emperor seems justified in his identification of Christianity as the expression of monotheism which had the elemental power and tenacity to bring the Supreme God to the world. It is true, of course, that most Christians today find their religion utterly incompatible with other monotheisms, and that our religious world is as fragmented and hostile as it ever was. But even in the dominant form of Christian monotheism, echoes of the dream of pagan, universal monotheism have endured, subterraneanly, in the Nicene Creed and in Constantine's inclusion of the word *homoousios*, now thought to be a waymark of orthodoxy around the Christian world. In the end there can be little doubt that ours is a planet forever shaped by the Constantinian quest for true religion. As we engage the problems posed by our modern religious world, we wonder what lessons we can learn from the victories and failures of the emperor's program. Can this history point the way towards answering the challenge of religious diversity in our own time? It remains to be seen. What is clear at this stage is that further scholarly pursuit of Constantine's quest for monotheism, and his "some-are-equally-right" model, will be needed.

Selected Bibliography

Abramowski, Luise. "Dionys von Rom (268) und Dionys von Alexandrien (264/5) in den arianischen Streitigkeiten des 4. Jahrhunderts." In *Zeitschrift für Kirchbengeschichte* 93 (1982) 240–72.

Alexander, David C. "Rethinking Constantine's Interaction with the North African 'Donatist' Schism." In *Rethinking Constantine: History, Theology and Legacy*, edited by Edward L. Smither, 37–90. London: Clarke, 2014.

Armstrong, A. H., and R. A. Markus. *Christian Faith and Greek Philosophy*. London: Darton, Longman, & Todd, 1960.

Ashwin-Siejkowski, Piotr. *Clement of Alexandria: A Project of Christian Perfection*. New York: T. & T. Clark, 2008.

Athanassiadi, Polymnia. *Mutations of Hellenism in Late Antiquity*. New York: Routledge, 2016.

Athanassiadi, Polymnia and Michael Frede, eds. *Pagan Monotheism in Late Antiquity*. Oxford: Oxford University Press, 1999.

Augustine. *Against Julian*. Translated by Matthew A. Schumacher. New York: Fathers of the Church, 1957.

———. *The City of God*. Translated by Marcus Dods. Edinburgh: T. & T. Clark, 1871.

———. "The Confessions and Letters of Augustine." In *Nicene and Post-Nicene Fathers*, edited by Philip Schaff and translated by J. G. Cunningham, 1:233–34. Grand Rapids: Eerdmans, 1983.

Ball, Warwick. *Rome in the East: The Transformation of an Empire*. New York: Routledge, 2002.

Bardill, Jonathan. *Constantine, Divine Emperor of the Christian Golden Age*. Cambridge: Cambridge University Press, 2012.

Barnard, Leslie W. *The Council of Serdica 343 A.D.* Sofia: Synodal, 1983.

Barnes, Timothy D. *Constantine and Eusebius*. London: Harvard University Press, 1981.

———. *Constantine: Dynasty, Religion and Power in the Later Roman Empire*. Hoboken: Wiley-Blackwell, 2011.

———. "Monotheists All." *Phoenix* 55 (2001) 142–62.

Barnstone, Willis, and Marvin Meyer, eds. *The Gnostic Bible: Revised and Expanded Edition*. Boston: Shambala, 2003.

Barr, Stringfellow. *The Mask of Jove: A History of Graeco-Roman Civilization from the Death of Alexander to the Death of Constantine*. Philadelphia: Lippincott, 1966.

SELECTED BIBLIOGRAPHY

Beatrice, Pier Franco. *Anonymi Monophysitae Theosophia: An Attempt at Reconstruction.* Leiden: Brill, 2001.

———. "Eusebius and Marcellus: Conflicting Theological Discourses in the Age of Constantine." *Théologie Historique* 124 (2017) 159–89.

———. "The Word 'Homoousios' from Hellenism to Christianity." *Church History* 71 (2002) 243–72.

Beckwith, Carl. *Hilary of Poitiers on the Trinity: From De Fide to De Trinitae.* Oxford: Oxford University Press, 2008.

Bowersock, Glen. "From Emperor to Bishop: The Self-Conscious Transformation of Political Power in the Fourth Century A.D." *Classical Philology* 81 (1986) 298–307.

Bowlin, John R. "Tolerance among the Fathers." In *Journal of the Society of Christian Ethics* 26 (2006) 3–36.

Bradbury, Scott. "Constantine and the Problem of Anti-Pagan Legislation in the Fourth Century." *Classical Philology* 89 (1994) 120–39.

Bram, Jean Rhys. *Ancient Astrology, Theory and Practice: Matheseos Libri VIII by Firmicus Maternus.* Park Ridge: Noyes Classical Studies, 1975.

Brenk, Frederick E. "Philo and Plutarch on the Nature of God." *Studia Philonica Annual* 26 (2014) 79–92.

Brown, Peter. *The Rise of Christendom.* Oxford: Blackwell, 2003.

Buell, Denise Kimber. *Why This New Race: Ethnic Reasoning in Early Christianity.* New York: Columbia University Press, 2005.

Bunsen, Christian C. J. *Hippolytus and His Age.* Vol. 1 of *Christianity and Mankind: Their Beginnings and Prospects.* London: Longman, Brown, Green, & Longmans, 1854.

Burckhardt, Jacob. *The Age of Constantine the Great.* Reprint, Los Angeles: University of California Press, 1940.

Carcopino, Jérôme. *Aspects mystiques de la Rome païenne.* Paris: L'Artisan du Livre, 1942.

Carroll, James. *Constantine's Sword: The Church and the Jews.* New York: Houghton Mifflin, 2002.

Chadwick, Henry. "The Early Christian Community." In *The Oxford Illustrated History of Christianity*, edited by John McManners, 21–61. Reprint, Oxford: Oxford University Press, 2001.

Chandler, Kegan A. *The God of Jesus in Light of Christian Dogma.* McDonough, GA: Restoration Fellowship, 2016.

Chapman, John. "Paul of Samosata." In *The Catholic Encyclopedia*, 11:589–90. New York: Appleton, 1911.

Cohen, Shaye J. D. *The Beginnings of Jewishness: Boundaries, Varieties, Uncertainties.* Los Angeles: University of California, 1999.

Coleman, Bush. *Constantine the Great and Christianity: Three Phases: The Historical, the Legendary, and the Spurious.* New York: Columbia University Press, 1914.

Constantine. *Oration of Constantine.* Translated by Ernest Cushing Richardson. In *Nicene and Post-Nicene Fathers*, edited by Philip Schaff and Henry Wace, 1:561–80. Oxford: Parker, 1890.

Copenhaver, Brian. *Hermetica.* Cambridge: Cambridge University Press, 1995.

Corcoran, Simon. "From Unholy Madness to Right-Mindedness: Or How to Legislate for Religious Conformity from Decius to Justinian." In *Conversion in Late Antiquity: Christianity, Islam, and Beyond*, edited by Arietta Papaconstantinou et al., 79. New York: Routledge, 2015.

SELECTED BIBLIOGRAPHY

Corduan, Winfried. *In the Beginning God: A Fresh Look at the Case for Original Monotheism*. Nashville: B&H Academic, 2013.

Cumont, Franz. *Oriental Religions in Roman Paganism*. New York: Dover, 1956.

Curta, Florin. "First Dedication to Sol Invictus in Rome (AD 158)." In *Great Events in Religion*, edited by Florin Curta et al., 1:182–84. Denver: ABC-CLIO, 2017.

Demarsin, Koen. "Paganism in Late Antiquity: Thematic Studies." In *The Archaeology of Late Antique Paganism*, edited by Luke Lavan et al., 1–40. Leiden: Brill, 2011.

Digeser, Elizabeth DePalma. "Lactantius and Constantine's Letter to Arles: Dating the Divine Institutes." *Journal of Early Christian Studies* 2 (1994) 33–52.

———. "Lactantius, Porphyry, and the Debate over Religious Toleration." In *The Journal of Roman Studies* 88 (1998) 129–46.

———. *The Making of a Christian Empire: Lactantius and Rome*. London: Cornell University Press, 2000.

———. "Platonism in the Palace: The Character of Constantine's Theology." In *The Life and Legacy of Constantine: Traditions Through the Ages*, edited by M. Shane Bjornlie, 49–61. New York: Routledge, 2017.

Dijkstra, Jitse H. F. Review of *New Epigrams of Palladas: A Fragmentary Papyrus Codex* by Kevin W. Wilkinson. *Phoenix* 3 (2014) 370–73.

Dillon, John N. *The Justice of Constantine: Law, Communication, and Control*. Ann Arbor: University of Michigan Press, 2012.

Dmitriev, Sviatoslav. "Traditions and Innovations in the Reign of Aurelian." *The Classical Quarterly* 54 (2004) 568–78.

Domach, Zachary. "Conversion of Constantine the Great (ca. AD 312–337)." In *Great Events in Religion*, edited by Florin Curta et al., 1:209–14. Denver: ABC-CLIO, 2017.

Drake, Harold. *Constantine and the Bishops: The Politics of Intolerance*. London: John Hopkins University Press, 2000.

———. "Constantine and Religious Extremism." In *Constantine: Religious Faith and Imperial Policy*, edited by Edward Siecienski, 11–26. New York: Routledge, 2017.

———. *In Praise of Constantine: A Historical Study and New Translation of Eusebius' Tricennial Orations*. University of California Classical Studies 15. Berkeley: University of California Press, 1976.

———. "Suggestions of Date in Constantine's Oration to the Saints." *The American Journal of Philology* 106 (1985) 335–49.

———. "When Was the 'De Laudibus Constantini' Delivered?" *Historia* 24 (1975) 345–56.

Drijvers, Jan Willem. *Helena Augusta: The Mother of Constantine the Great and the Legend of Her Finding of the True Cross*. Leiden: Brill, 1992.

Durant, Will. *Caesar and Christ: A History of Roman Civilization and of Christianity from their beginnings to A.D. 325*. New York: Simon & Schuster, 1980.

Dutta, Krishna, and Andrew Robinson, eds. *Rabindranath Tagore: An Anthology*. New York: St. Martin's, 1997.

Dyck, Andrew. *A Commentary on Cicero, De Legibus*. Ann Arbor: University of Michigan Press, 2004.

Augustine. *Augustine: The City of God Against the Pagans*. Translated by R. W. Dyson. Cambridge Texts in the History of Political Thought. Cambridge: Cambridge University Press, 1998.

Ebeling, Florian. *The Secret History of Hermes Trismegistus*. Ithaca: Cornell University Press, 2007.

Edwards, Mark. "Alexander of Alexandria and the Homoousion." *Vigiliae Christianae* 66 (2012) 482–502.

———. "The First Council of Nicaea." In *Cambridge History of Christianity, Vol. 1: Origins to Constantine*, edited by Margaret M. Mitchell et al., 531–67. Cambridge: Cambridge University Press, 2006.

———. "Pagan and Christian Monotheism in the Age of Constantine." In *Approaching Late Antiquity: The Transformation from Early to Late Empire*, edited by Simon Swain et al., 211–34. Oxford: Oxford University Press, 2004.

Edwards, Mark J. "Origen." https://plato.stanford.edu/archives/sum2018/entries/origen/.

Elliott, T. G. "Eusebian Frauds in the Vita Constantini." *Phoenix* 45 (1991) 162–71.

Elm, Susanna. "The Letter Collection of the Emperor Julian." In *Late Antique Letter Collections: A Critical Introduction and Reference* Guide, edited by Cristiana Sogno et al., 54–68. Oakland: University of California Press, 2017.

Elsner, Jas. "Perspectives in Art." In *The Cambridge Companion to the Age of Constantine*, edited by Noel Lenski, 255–310. Cambridge: Cambridge University Press, 2007.

Erickson, Millard J. *God in Three Persons*. Grand Rapids: Baker, 1995.

Erlewine, Robert. *Monotheism and Tolerance: Recovering a Religion of Reason*. Bloomington: University Press, 2010.

Errington, R. Malcom. "Constantine and the Pagans." *Greek, Roman and Byzantine Studies* 29 (1988) 309–18.

Eysturlid, Lee W. "The Long-Term Decline of the Roman Military." In *Enduring Controversies in Military History: Critical Analyses and Context*, edited by Spencer C. Tucker, 62–64. Santa Barbara: ABC-CLIO, 2017.

Eusebius. *Life of Constantine*. Translated by Averil Cameron and Stuart G. Hall. Clarendon Ancient History Series. Oxford: Oxford University Press, 1999.

Evans-Pritchard, E. E. *Theories of Primitive Religion*. Oxford: Oxford University Press, 1987.

Ezigbo, Victor I. *Introducing Christian Theologies, Vol. 1*. Voices from Global Christian Communities. Eugene: Cascade, 2013.

Faulkner, Neil. *Rome: Empire of the Eagles, 753 BC–AD 476*. New York: Pearson Education, 2008.

Fowden, Garth. *The Egyptian Hermes: A Historical Approach to the Late Pagan Mind*. Reprint, Princeton: Princeton University Press, 1993.

Fox, Robin Lane. *Pagans and Christians*. New York: Knopf, 1987.

Fraschetti, Augusto. *La conversion: dalla Roma pagana alla Roma cristiana*. Bari: Laterza, 1999.

Frede, Michael. "The Case for Pagan Monotheism in Graeco-Roman Antiquity." In *One God: Pagan Monotheism in the Roman Empire*, edited by Stephen Mitchell and Peter Van Nuffelen, 53–81. Cambridge: Cambridge University Press, 2010.

———. "Monotheism and Pagan Philosophy in Later Antiquity." In *Pagan Monotheism in Late Antiquity*, edited by Polymnia Athanassiadi and Michael Frede, 41–68. Oxford: Oxford University Press, 1999.

Fredriksen, Paula. Review of *Lord Jesus Christ: Devotion to Jesus in Earliest Christianity* by Larry Hurtado. *Journal of Early Christian Studies* 4 (2004) 537–41.

Freeman, Charles. *The Closing of the Western Mind: The Rise of Faith and the Fall of Reason*. New York: Vintage, 2002.

Frend, W. H. C. *The Donatist Church: A Movement of Protest in Roman North Africa*. Oxford: Oxford University Press, 1952.

SELECTED BIBLIOGRAPHY

Frothingham, A. L. "Diocletian and Mithra in the Roman Forum." *American Journal of Archaeology* 1 (1914) 146–55.

Fürst, Alfons. "Monotheism between Cult and Politics: The Themes of the Ancient Debate Between Pagan and Christian Monotheism." In *One God: Pagan Monotheism in the Roman Empire*, edited by Stephen Mitchell and Peter Van Nuffelen, 82–99. Cambridge: Cambridge University Press, 2010.

Gerberding, Richard, and Jo Ann H. Moran Cruz. *Medieval Worlds*. New York: Houghton Mifflin, 2004.

Grant, Robert M. *Augustus to Constantine: The Thrust of the Christian Movement into the Roman World*. London: Harper & Row, 1970.

Green, Bradley G. *The Gospel and the Mind: Recovering and Shaping the Intellectual Life*. Wheaton: Crossway, 2010.

Grillmeier, Aloys. *From the Apostolic Age to Chalcedon (451)*. Vol. 1 of *Christ in Christian Tradition*. Translated by John S. Bowden. Atlanta: John Knox, 1975.

Halsberghe, Gaston H. *The Cult of Sol Invictus*. Leiden: Brill, 1972.

Hanson, R. P. C. *The Search for the Christian Doctrine of God*. Reprint, New York: T. & T. Clark, 2005.

Harding, Sarah. *Paul's Eschatological Anthropology: The Dynamics of Human Transformation*. Minneapolis: Fortress, 2015.

Harries, Jill. *Imperial Rome AD 284 to 363: The New Empire*. Edinburgh: Edinburgh University Press, 2012.

Heck, Eberhard. *Die dualistischen Zusätze und die Kaiseranreden bei Lactantius*. Heidelberg: Winter, 1972.

Heil, Uta. *Athanasius von Alexandrien. De Sententia Dionysii*. Berlin: de Gruyter, 1999.

Heiser, Michael S. "Monotheism, Polytheism, Monolattry, or Henotheism? Toward an Assessment of Divine Plurality in the Hebrew Bible." In *Bulletin for Biblical Research* 18 (2008) 1–30.

Hick, John. "Religious Pluralism." In *A Companion to the Philosophy of Religion*, edited by Philip L. Quinn et al., 607–14. Blackwell Companions to Philosophy 8. Oxford: Blackwell, 1997.

Hijmans, S. E. "Temples and Priests of Sol in the City of Rome." *Mouseion* 10 (2010) 381–427.

Homo, L. *De la Rome païenne á la Rome chrétienne*. Paris: Laffont, 1950.

Hood, Ralph W., Jr., et al. *The Psychology of Religion, Fourth Edition: An Empirical Approach*. New York: Guildford, 2009.

Horrell, David G. "Race, Nation, People: Ethnoracial Identity Construction in 1 Pet. 2.9." In *Becoming Christian: Essays on 1 Peter and the Making of Christian Identify*, 133–63. New York: T. & T. Clark, 2013.

Hurtado, Larry W. "The Earliest Evidence of an Emerging Christian Material and Visual Culture: The Codex, the Nomina Sacra and the Staurogram." In *Text and Artifact in the Religions of Mediterranean Antiquity: Essays in Honour of Peter Richardson*, edited by Stephen G. Wilson et al., 271–88. Waterloo: Wilfrid Laurier University Press, 2000.

Iricinschi, Eduard. "Good Hebrew, Bad Hebrew: Christians as *Triton Genos* in Eusebius's Apologetic Writings." In *Reconsidering Eusebius: Collected Papers on Literary, Historical, and Theological Issues*, edited by Sabrina Inowlocki et al., 69–86. Leiden: Brill, 2011.

James, William. *The Varieties of Religious Experience*. New York: New American Library, 1958.
Jeremias, Joachim. *Infant Baptism in the First Four Centuries*. Eugene: Wipf & Stock, 2004.
Johnson, Luke Timothy. *Among the Gentiles: Greco-Roman Religion and Christianity*. New Haven: Yale University Press, 2010.
Justin Martyr. *The Dialogue with Trypho*. Translated by Arthur Lukyn Williams. London: SPCK, 1930.
Kahlos, Maijastina. *Forbearance and Compulsion: The Rhetoric of Religious Tolerance and Intolerance in Late Antiquity*. London: Duckworth, 2009.
Kalantzis, George. *Caesar and the Lamb: Early Christian Attitudes on War and Military Service*. Eugene: Cascade, 2012.
Kaufman, Peter Iver. *Redeeming Politics*. Princeton: Princeton University Press, 1990.
Kee, Alistair. *Constantine Versus Christ: The Triumph of Ideology*. Eugene: Wipf & Stock, 2016.
Keresztes, Paul. *Constantine: A Great Christian Monarch and Apostle*. Amsterdam: Gieben, 1981.
Keri, Szabolcs, and Christina Sleiman. "Religious Conversion to Christianity in Muslim Refugees in Europe." In *Archive for the Psychology of Religion* 39 (2017) 283–94.
Kirsch, Jonathan. *God Against the Gods: The History of the War Between Monotheism and Polytheism*. New York: Penguin, 2004.
Koch, Dietrich-Alex. "The God-fearers between Facts and Fiction: Two Theosebeis-inscriptions from Aphrodisias and Their Bearing for the New Testament." *Studia Theologica* 60 (2006) 62–90.
Krautheimer, Richard. *Three Christian Capitals: Topography and Politics*. Oakland: University of California Press, 1983.
Kreider, Alan. "Converted but Not Baptized: Peter Leithart's Constantine Project." In *Constantine Revisited: Leithart, Yoder, and the Constantinian Debate*, edited by John D. Roth, 25–67. Eugene: Pickwick, 2013.
Lactantius. *Divine Institutes*. Translated by Anthony Bowen and Peter Garnsey. Liverpool: Liverpool University Press, 2003.
———. *The Divine Institutes: Books I–VII*. Translated by Mary Francis McDonald. Reprint, Washington, DC: Catholic University of America Press, 2008.
———. *The Works of Lactantius, Vol. I*. Translated by William Fletcher. Edinburgh: T. & T. Clark, 1871.
Lanckau, Jörg. "Hypsistos: Cultural Translation of Jewish Monotheism in the Hellenistic Period." *Asiatische Studien* 65 (2011) 861–82.
Lecerf, Adrien. "Iamblichus and Julian's 'Third Demiurge': A Proposition." In *Iamblichus and the Foundations of Late Platonism*, edited by in Eugene V. Afonasin et al., 172–202. Leiden: Brill, 2012.
Ledegang, Fred. "Eusebius' View on Constantine and his Policy." In *Violence in Ancient Christianity: Victims and Perpetrators*, edited by Albert Geljon et al., 336–37. Leiden: Brill, 2014.
Lee, A. D. *Pagans and Christians in Late Antiquity: A Sourcebook*. Reprint, New York: Routledge, 2016.
Lefebure, Leo D. "The Reign of God and Constantine's Disputed Legacy: Religious Freedom, Sacred Empire, and the American Experience." In *Religion, Authority and the State: From Constantine to the Contemporary World*, edited by Leo D. Lefebure, 123–44. New York: Palgrave Macmillan, 2016.

Leithart, Peter J. *Defending Constantine: The Twilight of an Empire and the Dawn of Christendom.* Downers Grove: Intervarsity, 2010.

Lenski, Noel. *Constantine and the Cities: Imperial Authority and Civic Politics.* Philadelphia: University of Pennsylvania Press, 2016.

Leon, H. J. *The Jews of Ancient Rome.* Peabody: Hendrickson, 1995.

Liebeschuetz, Wolf. "The Speech of Praetextatus." In *Pagan Monotheism in Late Antiquity*, edited by in Polymnia Athanassiadi and Michael Frede, 185–205. Oxford: Clarendon, 1999.

Lieu, Judith M. *Image and Reality: The Jews in the World of the Christians in the Second Century.* Edinburgh: T. & T. Clark, 1996.

———. *Neither Jew nor Greek?: Constructing Early Christianity.* New York: Bloomsbury, 2015.

Lieu, Samuel N. C., and Dominic Montserrat. *From Constantine to Julian: Pagan and Byzantine Views.* New York: Routledge, 1996.

Ljubomirovic, Irena. "Latin Panegyrics used for Imperial Propaganda as Exemplified by Constantine the Great." *Teme* 39 (2015) 1419–34.

Logan, Alistair H. B. "Marcellus of Ancyra (Pseudo-Anthimus)." *Journal of Theological Studies* 51 (2000) 81–112.

Lohse, Bernhard. *A Short History of Christian Doctrine.* Reprint, Philadelphia: Fortress, 1985.

Louth, Andrew. "The Date of Eusebius' Historia Ecclesiastica." *Journal of Theological Studies* 41 (1990) 111–23.

MacDonald, Nathan. *Deuteronomy and the Meaning of "Monotheism."* Tübingen: Mohr Siebeck, 2003.

MacMullen, Ramsay. *Christianizing the Roman Empire A.D. 100-400.* New Haven: Yale University Press, 1984.

———. *Paganism in the Roman Empire.* New Haven: Yale University Press, 1981.

Magie, David. *Historia Augusta, Volume II.* London: Harvard University Press, 1924.

Mahé, J. P. *The Way of Hermes.* Reprint, Rochester: Inner Traditions, 2000.

Marlowe, Elizabeth. "Framing the Sun: The Arch of Constantine and the Roman Cityscape." *Art Bulletin* 88 (2006) 223–42.

Martin, David. *On Secularization: Towards a Revised General Theory.* Burlington: Ashgate, 2005.

Marx-Wolf, Heidi. *Spiritual Taxonomies and Ritual Authority: Platonists, Priests, and Gnostics in the Third Century C.E.* Philadelphia: University of Pennsylvania Press, 2016.

Maternus. *The Error of the Pagan Religions.* Translated by Clarence A. Forbes. New York: Newman, 1970.

McCormick, Michael. *Eternal Victory: Triumphal Rulership in Late Antiquity, Byzantium and the Early Medieval West.* Cambridge: Cambridge University Press, 1990.

McGuckin, J. A. "The Legacy of the 13th Apostle: Origins of the East Christian Conceptions of Church and State Relation." *St. Validimir's Theological Quarterly* 37 (2003) 251–88.

McKenzie, John L. "Aspects of Old Testament Thought." In *The New Jerome Biblical Commentary*, edited by Raymond E. Brown et al., 23–24. New Jersey: Prentice Hall, 1990.

Mead, G. R. S. *Thrice Greatest Hermes: Studies in Hellenistic Theosophy and Gnosis.* Reprint, Boston: Weiser, 2001.

Menzies, Allan, ed. *The Gospel of Peter, Apocalypses and Romances, Commentaries of Origen*. Vol. 9 of *The Ante-Nicene Fathers*. New York: Scribner's, 1912.

Mitchell, Roger Haydon. *Church, Gospel, and Empire: How the Politics of Sovereignty Impregnated the West*. Eugene: Wipf & Stock, 2011.

Mitchell, Stephen. "The Cult of Theos Hypsistos Between Pagans, Jews, and Christians." In *Pagan Monotheism in Late Antiquity*, edited by Polymnia Athanassiadi and Michael Frede, 81–148. Oxford: Oxford University Press, 1999.

———. "Further Thoughts on the Cult of Theos Hypsistos." In *One God: Pagan Monotheism in the Roman Empire*, edited by Stephen Mitchell and Peter Van Nuffelen, 167–208. Cambridge: Cambridge University Press, 2010.

Mitchell, Stephen, and Peter Van Nuffelen, eds. *One God: Pagan Monotheism in the Roman Empire*. Cambridge: Cambridge University Press, 2010.

Mommsen, Theodore. "Firmicus Maternus" *Hermes* 29 (1894) 618–19.

Moralee, Jason. *Rome's Holy Mountain: The Capitoline Hill in Late Antiquity*. Oxford: Oxford University Press, 2018.

Nash, John F. "Hermeticism: Rise and Fall of an Esoteric System: Part II." *The Esoteric Quarterly* (2009) 33–42.

Nicholson, Oliver. "Constantine's Vision of the Cross" In *Vigiliae Christianae* 54 (2000) 309–23.

Nixon, C. E. V., and Barbara Saylor Rodgers. *In Praise of Later Roman Emperors: The Panegyrici Latini*. Reprint, Berkeley: University of California Press, 2015.

Nock, A. D. *Conversion: The Old and the New in Religion from Alexander the Great to Augustine of Hippo*. Oxford: Oxford University Press, 1933.

North, John. "Pagan Ritual and Monotheism." In *One God: Pagan Monotheism in the Roman Empire*, edited by Stephen Mitchell and Peter Van Nuffelen, 34–52. Cambridge: Cambridge University Press, 2010.

Novak, Ralph Martin, Jr. *Christianity and the Roman Empire: Background Texts*. Harrisburg: Trinity, 2001.

Odahl, Charles. *Constantine and the Christian Empire*. Reprint, New York: Routledge, 2010.

Orlin, Eric M. *Temples, Religion, and Politics in the Roman Republic*. Leiden: Brill, 2002.

Pachoumi, Eleni. *The Concepts of the Divine in the Greek Magical Papyri*. Tübingen: Mohr Siebeck, 2017.

Parkes, H. W. *Oracles of Apollo in Asia Minor*. London: Croom Helm, 1985.

Parvis, Sara. *Marcellus of Ancyra and the Lost Years of the Arian Controversy 325–345*. Oxford: Oxford University Press, 2006.

Peppard, Michael. *Son of God in the Roman World: Divine Sonship in Its Social and Political Context*. Oxford: Oxford University Press, 2012.

Plutarch. *Plutarch's Lives, Vol. I*. Translated by Bernadotte Perrin. London: Heinemann, 1914.

Pohlsander, Hans A. *The Emperor Constantine*. New York: Routledge, 2004.

———. "Philip the Arab and Christianity." *Historia* 29 (1980) 463–73.

Potter, David. *Constantine the Emperor*. Oxford: Oxford University Press, 2013.

Prestige, G. L. *God in Patristic Thought*. Reprint, Eugene: Wipf & Stock, 2008.

Quispel, Gilles. "The Asclepius." In *Gnosis and Hermeticism from Antiquity to Modern Times*, edited by Roelof van den Broek et al., 69–78. New York: State University of New York Press, 1998.

———. "Hermes Trismegistus and the Origins of Gnosticism." *Vigiliae Christianae* 46 (1992) 1–19.

Rankin, David. "Arianism." In *The Early Christian World*, edited by Philip Francis Esler, 2:1102–27. New York: Routledge, 2000.

Redford, Donald B. "The Monotheism of Akhenaten." In *Aspects of Monotheism: How God is One*, edited by Hershel Shanks and Jack Meinhardt, 11–26. Washington, DC: Biblical Archaeological Society, 1997.

Roberts, Alexander, and James Donaldson, eds. *Fathers of the Second Century*. Vol. 2 of *The Ante-Nicene Fathers: Translations of the Writings of the Fathers down to A.D. 325*. Grand Rapids: Eerdmans, 1951.

———. *Justin Martyr and Athenagoras*. Vol. 2 of *Ante-Nicene Christian Library: Translations of the Writings of the Fathers, Down to AD 325*. Edinburgh: T. & T. Clark, 1868.

Roberts, Mark. "The Origins of Christmas and Epiphany, and the Position of the Feasts in the Christian Calendar." Master's thesis, Durham University, 1996.

Rosen, Steven. *Essential Hinduism*. Westport: Greenwood, 2006.

Roubekas, Nickolas P. *An Ancient Theory of Religion: Euhemerism from Antiquity to the Present*. New York: Routledge, 2017.

———. "What is Euhemerism? A Brief History of Research and Some Persisting Questions." *Bulletin for the Study of Religion* 43 (2014) 30–37.

Rubenstein, Richard E. *When Jesus Became God: The Epic Fight Over Christ's Divinity in the Last Days of Rome*. New York: Harcourt Brace, 1999.

Salem, Mohamed Omar, and John Foskett. "Religion and Religious Experiences." In *Spirituality and Psychiatry*, edited by Chris Cook et al., 233–53. London: Royal College of Psychiatrists, 2009.

Schmitz, Leonhard. *A History of Latin Literature*. London: Collins, 1877.

Schott, Jeremy M. *Christianity, Empire, and the Making of Religion in Late Antiquity*. Philadelphia: University of Pennsylvania Press, 2008.

Schweig, Graham M. "Krishna, the Intimate Deity." In *The Hare Krishna Movement: The Postcharismatic Fate of a Religious Transplant*, edited by Edwin Bryant and Maria Ekstrand, 13–30. New York: Columbia University Press, 2004.

Scott, Roger. "Narrating the Reign of Constantine in Byzantine Chronicles." In *Byzantine Culture in Translation*, edited by Amelia Brown and Bronwen Neil, 8–32. Leiden: Brill, 2017.

Setaioli, Aldo. "Physics III: Theology." In *Brill's Companion to Seneca: Philosopher and Dramatist*, edited by Andreas Heil and Gregor Damschen, 379–401. Leiden: Brill, 2014.

Smith, Rowland B. E. *Julian's Gods: Religion and Philosophy in the Thought and Action of Julian*. New York: Routledge, 1995.

Sommer, Michael. "The Challenge of Aniconism: Elagabalus and Roman Historiography." *Mediterraneo Antico* 11 (2008) 583–88.

Stead, Christopher. *Divine Substance*. Oxford Scholarly Classics. Oxford: Clarendon, 1977.

Steiner, Richard C. "On the Rise and Fall of Canaanite Religion at Baalbek: A Tale of Five Toponyms." *Journal of Biblical Literature* 128 (2009) 507–25.

Stenmark, Mikael. "Religious Pluralism and the Some-Are-Equally-Right View." *European Journal for Philosophy of Religion* 1 (2009) 21–35.

Stephenson, Paul. *Constantine: Roman Emperor, Christian Victor*. New York: Overlook, 2010.

Stout, Anna, and Simon Dein. "Religious Conversion and Self Transformation: An Experiential Study among Born Again Christians." *World Cultural Psychiatry Research Review* 8 (2013) 29–44.

Strickland, M. P. *Psychology of Religious Experience*. New York: Abingdon, 1924.

Syme, Ronald. *Emperors and Biography: Studies in the Historia Augusta*. Oxford: Clarendon, 1971.

Terry, Milton S., trans. *The Sibylline Oracles*. New York: Eaton & Mains, 1899.

Thiessen, Matthew. *Paul and the Gentile Problem*. Oxford: Oxford University Press, 2016.

Thompson, Glen L. "From Sinner to Saint? Seeking a Consistent Constantine." In *Rethinking Constantine: History, Theology and Legacy*, edited by in Edward L. Smither, 5–24. Eugene: Wipf & Stock, 2014.

Timaeus of Locri. *On the Nature of the World and the Soul*. Translated by Thomas H. Tobin. Chico: Scholars, 1985.

Toom, Tarmo. "Constantine's *Summus Deus* and the Nicene *Unus Deus*: Imperial Agenda and Ecclesiastical Conviction." *Vox Patrum* 34 (2014) 103–22.

Tóth, István. Review of *The Cult of Sol Invictus* by Gaston H. Halsberghe. *Acta Archaeologica* 26 (1974) 447–50.

Tuggy, Dale. "On Counting Gods." *TheoLogica* 1 (2017) 188–213.

———. "Tertullian the Unitarian." *European Journal for Philosophy of Religion* 8 (2016) 179–99.

———. "Theories of Religious Diversity." https://www.iep.utm.edu/reli-div/.

———. *What is the Trinity? Thinking About the Father Son, and Holy Spirit*. New York: Tuggy, 2017.

Tzamalikos, Panayiotis. *Anaxagoras, Origen, and Neoplatonism: The Legacy of Anaxagoras to Classical and Late Antiquity*. Berlin: de Gruyter, 2016.

Van Dam, Raymond. *Remember Constantine at the Milvian Bridge*. Cambridge: Cambridge University Press, 2011.

Van den Broek, Roelof. "Gnosticism and Hermetism in Antiquity: Two Roads to Salvation." In *Gnosis and Hermeticism: From Antiquity to Modern Times*, edited by Roelen van den Broek and Wouter J. Hanegraff, 1–20. New York: State University of New York Press, 1998.

Van Kooten, George H. "Pagan and Jewish Monotheism according to Varro, Plutarch and St Paul: The Aniconic, Monotheistic Beginnings of Rome's Pagan Cult—Romans 1.19–25 in a Roman Context." In *Dead Sea Scrolls and Other Early Jewish Studies in Honor of Florentino Garcia Martinez*, edited by Anthony Hilhorst et al., 633–51. Supplements to the Journal for the Study of Judaism 122. Leiden: Brill, 2007.

Van Nuffelen, Peter. "Pagan Monotheism as a Religious Phenomenon." In *One God: Pagan Monotheism in the Roman Empire*, edited by Stephen Mitchell and Peter Van Nuffelen, 16–33. Cambridge: Cambridge University Press, 2010.

Varner, Eric R. *Mutilation and Transformation: Danatio Memoriae and Roman Imperial Portraiture*. Leiden: Brill, 2004.

Veyne, Paul. *When Our World Became Christian: 312–394*. Cambridge: Polity, 2010.

Wallraff, Martin. "Constantine's Devotion to the Sun after 324." *Studia Patristica* 34 (2001) 256–69.

Watson, Alaric. *Aurelian and the Third Century*. New York: Routledge, 2003.

Weedman, Mark. *The Trinitarian Theology of Hilary of Poitiers*. Leiden: Brill, 2007.

Weiss, Peter. "Die Vision Constantins." *Colloquium aus Anlass des* 80 (1993) 143–69.

SELECTED BIBLIOGRAPHY

———. "The Vision of Constantine." Translated by A R. Birley. *Journal of Roman Archaeology* 16 (2003) 237–59.

White, Cynthia. *The Emergence of Christianity: Classical Traditions in Contemporary Perspective*. Minneapolis: Fortress, 2011.

Whittaker, John. "Ammonius on the Delphic E." *Classical Quarterly* 19 (1969) 185–92.

Wilkinson, Kevin W. "Palladas and the Age of Constantine." *The Journal of Roman Studies* 99 (2009) 36–60.

———. "Palladas and the Foundation of Constantinople." *The Journal of Roman Studies* 100 (2010) 179–94.

Williams, Rowan. *Arius: Heresy and Tradition*. Reprint, Grand Rapids: Eerdmans, 2001.

Wilson, B. R. *Religion in Secular Society*. London: Watts, 1966.

Winn, Robert E. *Eusebius of Emesa: Church and Theology in the Mid-Fourth Century*. Washington, DC: Catholic University of America Press, 2011.

Witt, R. E. "Iamblichus as a Forerunner of Julian." In *De Jamblique a Proclus*, edited by Heinrich Dörre, 35–68. Genève: Fondation Hardt, 1975.

———. *Isis in the Ancient World*. London: John Hopkins University Press, 1971.

Wright, Wilmer Cave. *The Works of the Emperor Julian*. Vol. 1. New York: Macmillan, 1913.

Yates, Frances. *Giordana Bruno and the Hermetic Tradition*. London: Routledge, 1964.

Index

Abraham, 19, 27n22
agent of god, 37, 38, 38n14, 40, 4, 54, 56, 58–63, 81, 144, 151, 156, 158
Akhenaten, 22–23, 22n1
Alexander Severus, 26–27, 28, 32, 41, 42
Alexander the Great, 159–60
Alexander of Alexandria, 5n18, 96–97, 99, 104–5
Amandus, 24
Ambrose, 5n18, 166
Amun-Ra, 22
angels, 13, 15, 17, 35, 35n1, 44, 51, 142–3, 164, 164n40
aniconism, 46–48, 84, 96n52, 126, 134, 142
Antioch, Council of, 103, 104–5
Apollo, 24, 24n7, 30, 32, 41, 74–75, 85, 142–43, 161
Apollo, subordination to God, 142–43
Arch of Constantine, xi, 62–63, 64, 72, 73, 77–78, 78n63, 79, 81, 92, 128, 144–45, 146–47
Arius, 96, 99, 99n1–2, 104–6, 105n32, 117n78, 118n85, 119–20
Arles, Council of, 94, 96
ascent, mystical, 68
Asclepius, 52–53, 53n40, 66, 68, 76, 80, 108, 127–28, 138, 163n39
Athanasius, 5n18, 98n56, 99, 103, 106–7, 118n85
atheism, 13, 14n11, 35, 35n1
Augustine, 8–10, 17n21, 46n2, 47, 53n40, 65, 163–65, 163n39, 164n40

Augustine, rejection of pluralism, 164–165
Augustine, sympathy for Hermes, 53n40
Aurelian, 29, 30–34, 30n38–39, 35, 36n5, 42, 85, 128, 146, 161
authentic humanity, 50–51n26

Baal, 32–33, 32n48
Baalbek, 33n48
Babylas of Antioch, 28
Babylon, 39, 54, 108
Bardill, Jonathan, 6, 73, 78–79
Barnes, Timothy, 4–6, 4n14, 7, 10–11, 16n18, 39n19, 40, 60, 75, 78, 117, 129–30, 133, 134, 142, 147
Basilica of Maxentius, 62, 123
Beatrice, Pier Franco, xii, 5–6, 5n18, 60, 100–02, 107–10, 119, 120n92
Brenk, Frederick, 16, 47
Burckhardt, Jacob, 1n2, 2, 6, 30n39, 83–84

Capitoline Hill, 70n28, 126–27, 127n11
catechesis, 148, 150–52
Chi-Rho, 72–73
Christ as the Sun, 29
Christian bishops, authority, 86
Christian bishops, judicial rulings, 91–92
Christian conversion, formal process, 148–150
Christian inquirer, 148, 150
Christian rejection of pluralism, 165–66, 167
Christian, population, 23, 83

181

INDEX

Christians, as a new race, 88–90
Christians, military service, 149n56
Christians, persecution of, 27–28, 35n1, 37–38, 38n15, 40, 42, 43, 49, 55–56, 83–84, 87–88, 89, 93n43, 129, 129n20, 143, 165
Cicero, 47, 65, 65n5, 66, 69–70, 87, 92
Clement of Alexandria, 49, 70n31, 89n21
coalition of monotheists, 44, 51, 72, 82, 124
Colossus of Constantine, 62, 62n22, 147
communion of mind, 67, 77, 79
communion, Christian, 150–51
concord, policy of, 124–25
Concordia, 70
Constans, 133, 147
Constantine, age, 40
Constantine, as apostle, 3n7, 154, 158
Constantine, as bishop, 151
Constantine, as religious example, 97–98
Constantine, coins, x, 7, 44–45, 61–62, 73, 76, 81, 141, 144, 146
Constantine, connection to God, 76, 79, 142n27
Constantine, construction projects, 62, 62n20, 73, 128, 140–41, 154
Constantine, edicts, 42, 87, 93, 93n43, 95, 97, 129, 129n20, 130
Constantine, face, 62, 62n21–23, 74, 145
Constantine, fulfillment of biblical prophecy, 157
Constantine, military action against Christians, 95
Constantine, on Capitoline Hill, 126–127
Constantine, on Christology, 111–18
Constantine, pragmatism, 42, 84
Constantine, tolerance, 130–31
Constantine's tomb, 154, 159
Constantine, visions, 1, 8, 9–11, 39, 41n28, 72–76, 75n49, 76, 137, 139, 143, 145
Constantinople, dedication, 141
Constantius Chlorus, 38–39, 39n19, 128, 159n23
Constantius II, 133, 147, 159–60
conversion, contemporary paradigm, 9–10, 9n39, 137–39

conversion, old paradigm, 9–10, 9n39, 137
Crispus, 3, 3n8

Dalmatius the Younger, 159n23
Danubia, 73
Decius, 29
decline-of-monotheism narrative, 46–57, 58, 84, 90, 94, 125, 126, 127, 155, 166
demons, 13, 14, 15, 35, 35n1, 49, 51, 51n26, 53n40, 155–56, 164, 164n40
Digeser, Elizabeth, xii, 5–6, 5n15–18, 10, 39n18, 42, 44, 50, 54, 60, 108, 124, 128, 134, 138–39
Dio Chrysostom, 32
Diocletian, 30n39, 34, 36–38, 36n4, 38n14, 38–42, 39n19, 43, 50, 50n22, 53–54, 61–62, 61n19, 86–87, 108, 127, 129, 131, 159
Diocletian, propaganda, 36–38, 61
Diodorus, 48–49
Dionysus, 32
Dionysus of Alexandria, 103
dominus et deus, 37
Donatist controversy, 55, 92–97, 99, 121, 135
Drake, Harold, 5, 5n15, 6, 12, 42, 45, 64, 75, 81n79, 86, 86n13, 118, 131, 131n31, 155n4

Edict of Milan, 93, 93n43, 129n20, 130
Edwards, Mark, 5n18, 15–16, 16n18, 59–60, 83
Egyptian religion, 17, 22–23, 22n1, 33n48, 50, 52, 53n40, 54, 108–10, 162, 165
Elagabalus, 25–27, 25n12, 32–33, 128, 146
Elagabalus, stone of Sol Invictus, 25–26
emanationism, 18, 24, 30, 33, 35, 68n25, 70n31, 101–2, 105, 112, 116, 143, 144, 146, 161, 163–64, 165
Emesa, 146, 160n24, 25–26, 30
Ennius, 48–49
eternal generation, 99, 103, 113, 117

INDEX

Euhemerism, 48–49, 48n15, 50, 52n32, 57n57, 58, 72
Euhemerus, 48
Eusebius of Caesarea, ix, 1, 3n6, 4, 5n18, 9, 10, 27–28, 38–39, 42n31, 49, 52n32, 58, 60, 61n17, 63, 72, 75–76, 74n48, 85n5, 89, 89n28, 100, 102, 106–7, 112–121, 117n79–80, 129–33, 129n20, 141, 145–46, 145n41, 150, 152, 154–59, 167
Eusebius of Emesa, 146
Eusebius of Nicomedia, 119, 159
exorcism, 148

falsae religiones, 51, 51n26, 55
Fausta, 3, 3n8, 149
forum, Roman, 62, 62n22, 123, 141

Galerius, 37–38, 38n15, 53, 93n43
Genesis, book of, 49–50
gladiatorial games, 28, 140
gnosis, 67, 138
Gnosticism, Gnostics, 5, 23, 66, 67n22, 71, 85, 100–07, 107n41–42, 115n72, 118–20, 120n91, 121
golden age, 36, 46–48, 48n12, 51, 53n40, 56, 59, 84, 91, 91n36, 96, 129, 144
Gordian III, 28
gradual conversion, 9–11, 137–40, 142, 152, 167
greek philosophers, monotheism, 15–17, 16n18, 44, 66, 67n22

Hannibal, 69
Hannibalianus, 159n23
haruspices, 140
Heiser, Michael, 12–14
Helena, 3n7–8, 40
Heliopolis, 33n48, 110n54
Helios, 24, 30, 32, 85, 141, 160–62, 161n32, 165, 166n46
Hercules, 31, 37–38, 61
Hermes, 52–53
Hermes Trismegistus, 52–53, 52n32, 53n40, 66, 68–69, 77, 79–80, 109, 120n91, 138, 165
Hermetic cult in Gaul, 71

Hermetica, dating, 66n16, 66–67
Hermeticism, x, 5–6, 5n18, 7, 10, 17, 44, 52, 52n32, 53n40, 60, 61, 64, 66–69, 67n16–22, 69n26, 71–72, 76–80, 81, 84–85, 96, 101, 104, 107–10, 118, 120–21, 126–29, 134, 138–39, 138n8, 161, 163, 165
Hermeticists, as creators of gods, 126
Herodotus, 48
Hinduism, Vaishnavite, 19–20, 19n26
Hinduism, 19–20, 16n26, 31, 83, 148
Hinduism, conversion, 148
history of religion, 44, 46–57
homoousios, 100–113, 112n65, 116, 118–20, 121n93, 167
homoousios, gnostic use, 100–105, 107, 108n49, 120
homoousios, materialistic connotations, 105, 120
homoousios, differing interpretations, 106, 106n36, 118–19
human sacrifice, 53–54

Iamblichus, 160–61, 160n24–25, 161n32
idolatry, 46, 164, 166, 53, 60, 82, 125–26, 135, 138, 149, 149n56
imperial court, 39, 39n19, 40, 43–44, 71, 86, 91, 108, 151, 159
impersonal god, 13, 15–16, 44
intelligent design, 47n11
intolerance, policy of, 124–25
isapostolos, 7n7
Islam, Muslims, 19, 20–21, 83

Jerusalem, 3n8
Jesus, ix, 8, 27, 34, 37n10, 42, 59, 72, 78, 85, 85n5, 88–90, 91, 96, 99, 99n2, 104, 111, 115n72, 148, 150, 151, 154–58, 165
Jews, 19, 19n25, 20, 21, 25, 26, 34, 37n7, 46–47, 85, 85n5, 88–89, 89n21, 156
Julia Mamea, 27
Julian the Apostate, 30n39, 128n18, 160–63, 160n23–25, 161n32
Julian, as solar reformer, 162

183

INDEX

Jupiter, 32, 37–38, 40, 47, 50, 50n22, 51, 56, 61, 61n19, 65, 71, 76, 76n56, 95, 126, 126n11, 127–28
justice, 47, 51, 55, 56, 58–59, 58n4, 87, 91–92, 91n36
Justin Martyr, 14n12, 28n30, 35n1, 68n23, 86, 90, 99, 117n82

Kee, Alistair, 4n10, 9, 73, 89n28
Keresztes, Paul, 3–4, 4n10
Krishna, 19, 31

labarum, heavenly sign, 72–73, 158
Lactantius, x, xii, 4–5, 7, 37, 39–40, 41, 41n28, 43–45, 48, 49–57, 57n57, 58–60, 67n19, 69–73, 69n26, 70n31, 82, 84, 87, 87n13, 89–92, 90n34, 96, 99n3, 108–9, 110, 113, 121, 125, 127, 131, 135, 138–40, 150, 155, 165–66
Leithart, Peter, 1n2, 4n9, 6–7, 129, 140, 151
Libanius, 132–33
Licinius, 3n8, 78n63, 93, 93n43, 129, 129n20, 130, 149, 149n56
Licinius, monotheism, 129n20
lightning strikes, 43, 140
logos, 41n28, 65, 68, 89–90, 89n28, 101, 107–8, 110, 112, 113, 115, 117n80–82, 139, 154–55, 158

MacMullen, Ramsay, 31–32
Macrobius, 165
Mahe, Jean-Pierre, 66
Manichaeism, 104–5
Marcellus of Ancyra, 106, 120–21, 120n91–2, 121n93
Marlowe, Elizabeth, 61–63, 78
Mars, 31, 44
Martianus Capella, 165
Maternus, as solar monotheist, 70–71, 76, 81, 81n43
Maternus, conversion to Christianity, 145–47
Maxentius, xi, 3, 62, 62n20–22, 72–73, 123, 126, 129
Maximian, 3n8, 37, 38, 38n11, 61

Maximinus Daza, 38n15, 93n43
Maximus of Madaura, 163–64
Maximus of Tyre, 32
Memphis, 39, 54, 108
mia hypostasis, 121n93
Milvian Bridge, 6, 45, 72, 75, 123, 127, 147
Mithraism, 29, 29n32, 30, 30n39, 36, 36n4, 85, 142, 160–62
monoousios, 103
monotheism, Hindu, 19–20, 19n26, 31, 148
monotheism, reasonableness of, 48, 125
monotheism, pluriform, polymorphous, 17–20, 24, 31–32, 35, 41–42, 68, 79, 161, 163
monotheism, solar, 18–34, 42, 63–64, 68, 70–72, 76–77, 80–81, 142, 146–47, 160, 162, 165, 166n46
monotheistic emanationism, 18, 68n25, 143, 163
monotheistic rule, 41–42
monotheistic state, 44, 87, 125, 135, 140

names of God, 17–18, 20, 30, 53, 63, 68–69, 69n26, 79, 144, 163, 163n39
Nero, 62
Nicaea, Council of, 35, 99–122, 127, 144, 149, 151, 161
Nicomedia, 43, 108, 149, 152, 159
Nock, A.D., 8, 137, 148
Nonnus, 165

Odahl, Charles, 6, 81, 99n3, 140
Origen, 27–28, 70n31, 99n2, 102–3, 103n23, 105, 117n80
Origen, subordinationism, 102–3, 103n23
Origen, use of *homoousios*, 102–3
original monotheism, *urmonotheismus*, 46, 46n1, 48, 50, 55, 59
Ovid, 47

Palatine Hill, 25
Palladas, 4, 134–35
Paul, 3, 8–9, 47–48, 47n10, 48n12, 49, 51, 53n40, 58, 139, 158

INDEX

Paul of Samosata, 104–5, 107n41
Persians, war with, 149, 162
Philaster, 71
Philip the Arab, 27–28
Philo, 16, 47
Plato, 15, 24n6, 44n39, 52n32, 68n23, 69, 92, 108–10, 111, 120n91, 121, 142–44, 164n40
Plato, plurality of gods, 142, 143, 144
Platonism, 13, 15, 16, 18, 20, 23–24, 30, 33, 34, 66, 70, 109, 120n91, 128, 134, 139, 146, 160–61, 164n40, 165, 166n46
Platonism, Middle, 23, 66, 66n11
Platonism, Neoplatonism, 30, 33, 34, 70, 123, 128, 134, 139, 146, 160–61, 165, 166n46
Plotinus, 15–16, 15n17, 70n31, 103–4
Plotinus, controversy with gnostics, 103–4
Plutarch, 16, 32, 47
Poimandres, 66, 66n12
political power, ix, 1–3, 42, 83–84
pontifex maximus, 28, 40, 116
pontifices solis, 30n38, 162
Porphyry, 33–34, 37, 43, 104, 128
Posidonius, 66, 66n12
post-baptismal sin, 149–50
Praetextatus, 162
privatization, 3n5
Proclus, 165

Quispel, Gilles, 67

radiate crown, 62, 62n21, 141, 145
religio mentis, 67
religious diversity, x, 19–20, 20n31, 167
Romulus, 62n22, 123
Rufinus, 102

sacrifice, ban on, 125, 129–34
sacrifice, pagan rejection of, 128
Saturn, 50, 51, 91
Secular Games, 28, 127n11
Seneca, 44n39, 65, 66
Severa, 28
Severan dynasty, 24, 29, 36n5, 162

Silvester, Pope, 159n22
Sol Invictus, xi, 17–18, 24–26, 24n8, 25n14, 29, 29n32, 30–31, 30n39, 30–33, 35, 36, 36n5, 39, 40, 45, 61–63, 68, 76–81, 84–85, 86n7, 128, 141–42, 144, 145–46, 160, 161–62, 166
Sol Invictus, temples, 25, 30, 32, 33n48, 86n7, 128
solar halo, 74–75, 74n48
solar quadriga, xi, 24, 29, 63, 92, 144, 145–47
some-are-equally-right model, 20–21, 144, 166, 167
Son of God, 23, 23n5, 38, 60, 100, 101, 110, 112n65, 117
Spes and Fides, 70
staurogram, 72–73
Stenmark, Mikael, 20–21, 144n39
Stoicism, 24n7, 47n11, 52n32, 64–67, 65n3, 70, 76n56, 162
subordinationism, 13, 17, 18, 99, 102, 108n44, 113, 116–17, 117n80, 118, 143, 144, 164–65
Summus Deus, 129n20, 140
Sunday, 29, 144
Symmachus, 162–63, 166
Synagogue of Severus, 27n22
Syrian religion, 24–25, 25n14, 33, 128
Syringes, 109, 110n54

Tertullian, 52n32, 89, 105n32, 114, 114n68, 149
Tetrarchy, 36, 36n5, 37, 41, 41n28, 87, 123
Theodosian Code, 130
Theodosius I, 132–33, 166
Theos Hypsistos, 16, 16n20
third century crisis, 34, 53
Thoth, 52, 139
Timaeus of Locri, 66, 66n11
totius mundi regna, 41–42
Trier, 44, 108
Trinity, 101, 164
Troy, fall of, 50
Tuggy, Dale, 13–14, 16n18, 20n31, 20n32, 21, 106, 114n68

Two Dionysii controversy, 103
Tyche, 141

union with God, oneness, 67–68, 70n31, 77, 79
unitarianism, 99, 121

Valentinianism, 102, 104, 105, 120n91, 121
Varro, 46–48, 46n2, 58, 126
Venus, temple, 70, 70n28
Vespasian, 62
Victoria, 70

Virgil, 47, 69, 90, 90n34

Wallraff, Martin, 78
Watson, Alaric, 31
Weiss, Peter, 74–75
Wilkinson, Kevin, 4, 134, 141
wreaths, heavenly, 74, 74n48

Xenophanes, 48

Yahweh, 12–13, 44, 95

Zeus, 13, 24, 24n7, 65, 68, 78n63

www.ingramcontent.com/pod-product-compliance
Lightning Source LLC
Chambersburg PA
CBHW062042220426
43662CB00010B/1610